A Light
Shines
in Harlem

A Light Shines in Harlem

New York's First Charter School and the Movement It Led

MARY C. BOUNDS

Foreword by Dr. Wyatt Tee Walker

Lawrence Hill Books

Chicago

Copyright © 2014 by Mary C. Bounds

All rights reserved

First edition

Published by Lawrence Hill Books

An imprint of Chicago Review Press, Incorporated

814 North Franklin Street

Chicago, Illinois 60610

ISBN 978-1-61373-749-1

Library of Congress Cataloging-in-Publication Data

Is available from the Library of Congress.

Interior design: PerfecType, Nashville, TN

Printed in the United States of America

5 4 3 2 1

"For it is here, where we stand, that we should try to make shine the light of the hidden divine life."

—MARTIN BUBER, *THE WAY OF MAN*

"The Sisulu-Walker Charter School of Harlem
It is the best and the first of them all.
Since 1999, the school continues to strive,
For achievement, honor and service are our motto."

—SONG WRITTEN BY STUDENTS OF THE SISULU-WALKER
CHARTER SCHOOL OF HARLEM

Dedicated to my husband, Peter Applebome,
and to my children, Ben and Emma, whose own journeys
from preschool to college and beyond
showed me just how important education is
in the lives of children.

CONTENTS

FOREWORD

In 1959, while still a young minister in Virginia, I organized and led the first local Prayer Pilgrimage for Public Schools, an event that protested Virginia state officials' attempts to block public school integration. Forty years after my foray into human rights and the struggle for justice, in 1999, as a senior minister in Harlem, I joined with others as part of another nonviolent revolution and march for justice, forming the first charter public school in the state of New York. This book is a history of that pioneering school and its formation, and of the movement for better public schools for all of America's children.

The United States is a child of revolution—political, social, and cultural—all for perfecting the reality of our experiment to create a democracy that is DE FACTO rather than only DE JURE! All of these revolutions were achieved through sacrifice and the coming together of diverse people who were like-minded in their dedication to solve an identifiable crisis that faced the nation. The march for better public schools, as symbolized by the charter school movement, is one more such revolution, and it is just beginning. The future of millions of children depends on the success of its reforms. Now, with so many industrialized nations ahead of the United States in education quality, the international standing of our nation depends on it as well.

The American Revolution and Civil War cost us nearly a million lives. Fortunately, the revolution for better public education can be achieved nonviolently! Participation in this movement for better schools will be diverse and nonexclusionary. This book might serve as our playbook for such an effort.

In his recent book *David and Goliath*, the writer Malcolm Gladwell described my work and others' work in the Birmingham civil rights campaign of 1963 as a David versus Goliath story. The effort to create great new charter schools now is another such story, requiring community leaders and educators to overcome many obstacles and much entrenched opposition.

That which commends the charter school movement to such a daunting task is the diversity of the personnel it has attracted to its ranks: former teachers, clergy, social change activists, lawyers, philanthropists, community organizers, and parents of school-age children. In this book, you will hear of my colleagues such as Marshall Mitchell, a skillful and accomplished former congressional chief of staff; Minnie Goka, a retired assistant school principal, and about other public school personnel who have viewed the problems from inside the broken system; Steven Klinsky, a Harvard-trained lawyer and philanthropist who has had much experience creating after-school learning centers, as well as vast Wall Street skills; Ruben Diaz Sr., a Latino clergyman and community activist; Floyd Flake, former congressperson and community leader; Judith Price, a businesswoman with extensive management skills and experience; dedicated school trustees, teachers, and school leaders such as Michelle Haynes, who grew up in Harlem public schools herself; and the parents of children in failing school districts. You will hear of the work of President Bill Clinton and Governor George Pataki in the successful passage of charter school laws across America and in New York, cementing the fragile beginning. All the participants together form a coalition that is non–gender specific, racially diverse, professional and nonprofessional, bound together by a common interest in education for every child. All are seeking to repair a system that is broken, which now produces students who are unemployable, and which may be beyond repair.

What made me join the charter school movement?

The movement for justice, of which I was a frontline participant, taught me the importance of quality education. The congregation in Harlem that I ministered for thirty-seven years chiefly served the children of District Five of the public school system of New York City; a district which had long been judged nonperforming and unable to produce students who were proficient in reading, math, and the sciences.

As I worked on other justice issues (housing, employment), I was frustrated that I had no tools to better the school system that served the families of my congregation. Was not the matter of quality education a justice issue also? I became convinced that quality education was the undeniable complement of the struggle that I had given my life to.

That's what led me to dive into the charter school movement. I have no regrets whatsoever. All of the experience I gained in the human rights struggle was applicable to this new frontier of human rights. In my most reflective moments, I believe this is where Dr. King would be if he were still alive!

In the charter school movement, I am continuing the work of Dr. King that has far-reaching meaning. Every American child is deserving of a quality public school education. It is education that will guarantee that segregation and second-class citizenship will never return!

Dr. Wyatt Tee Walker
Author, theologian, cultural historian,
former chief of staff to Dr. Martin Luther King Jr.

ACKNOWLEDGMENTS

More than seven years ago, when Victory Education Partners commissioned me to write a history of New York's first charter school, I thought that I would be writing the simple story of one school. I quickly discovered, though, that to tell it was also to tell a much larger and more complex story about the charter movement and education reform as a whole, as well as to illuminate how people unify across wide backgrounds to achieve a social mission. That story has evolved over the years into this book. At all times, I have intended to let the voices of the children, parents, educators, political leaders, and reformers come through, while also writing only the facts that I myself believe to be true as a journalist of more than thirty years. My goal is to tell both the inside story and an accurate story, and I hope this book succeeds at both.

It's impossible for me to thank everyone who gave their time, effort, and support for this project, but I'll mention some of them:

On the education side, my thanks go to the students, staff, and teachers at the Sisulu-Walker Charter School of Harlem, especially educator extraordinaire Michelle Haynes and three students whose stories brought life to the book—Mylaecha Aska, Traiquan Payne, and Tori Saldivia. Other educators' help was also invaluable—the Center for Educational Innovation's Sy Fliegel and Harvey Newman, longtime educator Peg Harrington, Mary Ranero-Cordero, and Harvard professor Paul Peterson.

Paul Augello helped on financial and data questions, and Deborah Cox, who assisted with research and organized the book's photos, always with grace and efficiency, can't be thanked enough.

Several state leaders were generous with their time and recollections. In the course of researching this book, I interviewed former New York governor George Pataki; Edward Cox and Randy Daniels, the then cochairmen of the Charter Schools Committee of the State University of New York (SUNY) Board of Trustees; Scott Steffey, who formerly headed up SUNY's Charter Schools Institute; former state assemblymen Steven Sanders and John Faso; and Peter Murphy, the former policy director of the New York Charter Schools Association. Each, from their own perspective, shed light on a pivotal time in the state's charter school history.

Dr. Wyatt Tee Walker, a hero of the civil rights movement, spoke with me extensively both by phone and in person in Virginia, where he now lives. My thanks go out to him for unselfishly sharing his knowledge and wisdom with me, and to his wife, Theresa Ann, for her gracious support of this book. I thank, too, Dr. and Mrs. Walker's son, Wyatt T. Walker Jr., who, in lengthy interviews with me, generously provided many of the book's rich details about Dr. Walker, the civil rights movement, and Harlem, as well as several of the book's most important photographs.

As the story broadened over time, Dr. Walker, Steve Klinsky, Michelle Haynes, Marshall Mitchell, Peg Harrington, James Stovall, and others involved in the school had extensive involvement with this book. They reviewed and commented on multiple versions of the book and large sections of the history chapters over the years, as did Sisulu's board chair, Martez Moore, and its board member and former chairman, William Allen. I thank them all for it.

My thanks go out, too, to my book editors at Lawrence Hill Books, Yuval Taylor and Michelle Schoob Williams, for their insightful questions and skillful editing, which greatly improved the quality and rigor of the reporting with each draft. And to Bruce Wexler, who recognized early on that the Sisulu-Walker story was worth telling and was instrumental in launching the book, thank you for your editorial guidance that gave shape to what was once just a vague idea.

As my writing career stretched across four states, many of my colleagues helped shape my career, and friends made the journey a joyful one. It's impossible to name all of those friends, but I'll mention some from each stop along the way: the B-53s (aka the Island Girls), Nina and Craig Flournoy, Lucy and Chris Sullivan, Nora and Bill Tung, and Melinda and Jeff Blauvelt.

I owe a huge debt of gratitude to everyone in my family, including the Applebomes, my daughter-in-law, Bethany, and especially to my parents, Martha and the late Dean Bounds, and my brothers, Dean and Walter Bounds, for a lifetime of love and support and many happy memories from our days on Southland Park Drive and beyond. Lastly, I thank my husband, Peter Applebome, who was my sounding board throughout this project, and my children, Ben and Emma. They wholeheartedly supported my efforts, even when it meant I was preoccupied with it for long periods of time. To them, and everyone else who helped me out, this book also belongs.

INTRODUCTION

They had begun their education as the first kindergarteners in the first public charter school to open its doors in New York State. Now, six years later, they were assembled together one last time to celebrate their graduation as fifth graders from the Sisulu-Walker Charter School of Harlem.

These seventy-two children stood as living symbols of the charter school movement—perhaps the most important public education reform movement in America today—and of the 2.5 million children now enrolled in charter schools nationwide.

Some of Sisulu-Walker's students had names you would find in most any of the nation's classrooms, others had names as lyrical and proud as the streets of their neighborhood: Mylaecha Aska, Tori Saldivia, Traiquan Payne. But as they came together on June 22, 2005, the girls in pristine white dresses, the boys decorous in their dark suits, they carried with them as many stories of hope, risk, and triumph as any group of pioneers striving to build something new and better.

Six years earlier, their parents and teachers had made an enormous leap of faith. They had entrusted their children and their educations to a new type of public school—a charter school—that most had never heard of. Back then, Sisulu-Walker was a promise only: a school without a history or a track record, without a staff, without a proven curriculum, and without a permanent school building; it would receive less public funding per child than the nearby traditional public schools. Its students had been selected through an open lottery process, with no consideration for intellectual aptitude or behavior, and 87 percent of them came from families whose incomes were low enough to qualify for federal free or reduced-price lunches.

Most of the children lived in central Harlem's School District Five, which had been labeled an educational "dead zone" in a Public Education Association report published just months before the school began. In a neighborhood where many traditional public schools had failed for decades, there was every reason to expect that this new charter school would fail as well.

But now, as graduating fifth graders, these children, along with their families and their teachers, had succeeded. A full 90 percent of the class had scored on or above grade level on the New York City reading test, almost twice as high as students in the comparable schools in the neighborhood where most of Sisulu's fifth graders lived. In math, 77 percent of the class had scored in those highest two categories compared to about 30 percent of students in their neighborhood, and about 50 percent in the city's public schools overall. Not surprisingly, many of Sisulu-Walker's fifth graders were now headed to some of the city's most selective middle schools.

Sisulu-Walker, which opened its doors on September 8, 1999, was the first charter school to begin operations in New York State, and was soon followed by two others. Sisulu would be the only one of this pioneering class of 1999 to survive. But by 2014 there were more than 250 charter schools in the state and about 6,500 charter schools nationwide, often in at-risk neighborhoods, like Harlem, where traditional public schools had been mostly broken for generations. Some of the charter schools established in those intervening years were no better than the traditional public schools around them and would also fall by the wayside. But others were succeeding in new and innovative ways, following the trail that Sisulu-Walker had helped clear, raising expectations for all schools, and creating methods and approaches to help all schools. And because of charter schools, which are tuition-free and open to all applicants equally, for the first time even the poorest inner-city families had the freedom and power to choose *their own* schools and *their own* paths in a way that was once only available to the wealthier and more socially privileged.

■ ■ ■ ■ ■

A charter school is a public school operated according to a contract, or charter, which a government regulatory body issues. The charter school's leaders then manage it independently of the traditional board of education bureaucracy. The charter education reform movement emerged in the 1990s as a way to give parents, teachers, community leaders, and school districts more autonomy to create and run schools so long as they could accountably produce the improved educational results they promised. Currently, charter schools have been established in forty-two states and the District of Columbia. They have been championed by a diverse range of educators, civil rights leaders, and political leaders of both parties, including Presidents Clinton, both Bushes, and Obama.

This book seeks to tell the history of one notable charter school and its first class of children as a way of telling the broader story of all of these schools. It is a look at the hundreds of small decisions and big risks that go into creating and leading a school, not the generalities of textbooks and education manifestoes. The book then approaches this same topic of education reform through a broader public policy lens, surveying current academic research about the effectiveness of charter schools today, such as that of Stanford University professor Caroline Hoxby, and including interviews with Harvard University professor Paul Peterson and others.

At every level of analysis, this book seeks to come back to the two fundamental real-world questions that matter most to every parent and teacher. What makes a charter public school, or *any* school, succeed or fail? How can these lessons be applied to all other public and private schools to also make them better? Coming to understand the struggles, strengths, weaknesses, and triumphs of Sisulu-Walker—both on its own and as a part of the broader charter school movement—may shed light on the right path forward for many schools.

As you read this story, you will meet educators, presidents, Wall Street stars, inner-city activists, Ivy League academics, and real-world parents and kids, all working together to build something new.

But first, to truly understand the need for charter schools and for Sisulu-Walker, you need to understand the education conditions that existed before they began.

You need to begin on an October day in 1968 when a grief-stricken Harlem minister heard the voice of a dear, departed friend.

A Civil Right

The voice said nothing about education. It didn't mention schools. It gave solace, not direction.

But perhaps the true history of the Sisulu-Walker Charter School and the mission it symbolizes began on a sorrowful day in Harlem in October 1968, the day that Rev. Dr. Wyatt Tee Walker heard in his thoughts the voice of his departed friend and ally, Rev. Dr. Martin Luther King Jr., who had been gunned down in Memphis just six months before.

Walker knew King's voice almost as well as his own. They had met in 1952 when both were young men studying for the ministry: Walker at Virginia Union University in Richmond, and King at Crozer Theological Seminary near Chester, Pennsylvania. They had been inseparable allies during the darkest and most joyful hours of the civil rights era when Walker served as King's indispensable strategist and chief of staff and as the first full-time executive director of the Southern Christian Leadership Conference. As King's chief of staff, Walker was in the forefront of the civil rights movement, often working behind the scenes as an advance man and slipping surreptitiously into unfamiliar towns to get the lay of the land. As the key strategist for some of the movement's most memorable moments, he had been King's "field general" for the 1963 Birmingham civil rights campaign, which paved the way for the sweeping civil rights laws that passed during the 1960s. He organized Project C (for "confrontation") in Birmingham to face down Sheriff Eugene "Bull" Connor and end segregation in one of the South's toughest cities. Walker had also been in the Gaston Motel the night it was bombed and had assembled the scraps of King's nearly illegible handwriting smuggled from jail to help compile, form, translate, and name King's now famous "Letter from Birmingham Jail."

Walker worked with King to organize the 1963 March on Washington, where King gave his immortal "I Have a Dream" speech. Then, a year later, Walker accompanied King to Oslo to receive the Nobel Peace Prize. They were so close that Walker's four children, using an affectionate expression, thought of King as their "play-play" uncle and called him Uncle Martin.

After his years with King in the South, where Walker was eventually arrested seventeen times for his civil rights work, Walker moved north to Harlem to pursue a new ministry. And when Walker and King's civil rights work led them to share another small Birmingham jail cell together for five days in 1967, the two planned a grand and joyous ceremony in which King would come to New York and personally install Walker as pastor of the Canaan Baptist Church of Christ on West 116th Street in Harlem.

The next year, on March 24, 1968, in a festive service replete with emotion and pageantry, churchgoers packed the pews and spilled out into the aisles in a multicultural array that transcended political, ethnic, and religious boundaries. On this special day, at Walker's installation, King preached an eloquent, powerful sermon, full of passion and heart.

Earlier in the service, King had stepped away from the pulpit and strolled over to the open doorway of an office at the back of the sanctuary, where a teenager was studiously taping the ceremony with a bulky reel-to-reel recorder. King exchanged the usual pleasantries with the teenager, Walker's son, Wyatt T. Walker Jr. But as King was about to return to the pulpit, he said something that now seems prophetic, as if he somehow knew where his fate was heading. "Your father means so much to me," Walker Jr., recalls King saying. "I want you to take good care of him." The sermon King gave that day was the last he would preach in New York City. Eleven days later, he was shot dead in Memphis.

Harlem and Dr. Walker were still stunned six months later, as the spiritually wounded Walker wandered aimlessly along 125th Street. This street was at the heart of Harlem, and at another time, the pastor's spirits might have been uplifted by the street life and by the music that often played there. But Harlem was still in mourning, and instead of music, the air was filled with the sounds of King's speeches, blaring out from stereo speakers propped up by shopkeepers to spread the word to the streets outside.

Walker couldn't help but hear his friend's familiar voice, but he couldn't quite focus on it either. In fact, the man who walked along Harlem's streets that day was so distraught that he could barely function. A prominent, powerful pastor, he had lost his preaching voice. King's passionate words reverberated as if from the grave, but they did little at first to soothe his pain. They only rekindled the raw anger Walker felt and hardened his resolve to never have anything to do with white people again.

And then something very odd happened. Along with the familiar voice booming out of the speakers, Walker heard a small, quiet, intimate version of the same voice in his head. It was, Walker recalls, King's voice speaking—not to the world, but just to him—in a quiet but unmistakable whisper: "What you ought to do is thank the Lord that I was with you as long as I was."

That was it. No more. At last, Walker's grief lost its crippling edge; his bitterness ceased being a stone wall in front of him. "I couldn't get over my grief until that moment," he later recalled. Once the moment passed, he knew it was time to return to the living, to the work, so momentous in the 1960s, that was really just beginning.

It was hardly a straight line from that day to Walker's involvement with the first charter school to open in New York, as his life took many turns from there. When almost everyone else had all but given up on Harlem, Walker spearheaded efforts to reclaim it, and he worked tirelessly for human rights beyond Harlem's borders as well. Eventually, he would confer with presidents, author fifty-five books, and travel to one hundred countries, including South Africa, where he allied with antiapartheid leaders Nelson Mandela and Walter Sisulu (Si-SOO-loo), for whom the school would one day be named. But through it all Walker never forgot the importance of high-quality public education, and the reform of public education never stopped being a central part of his own views on civil and human rights.

Reflecting back, Walker is certain of three things. First, education had opened doors, offered opportunity, and unlocked potential in his own life. Second, all too often the door today opens on rusty, creaky hinges to a dysfunctional, unequal system in need of major improvement, and a huge part of changing life in Harlem and places like it had to begin with the schools. And third, King would have been right there fighting alongside him because education is very much a human rights issue today in the way that voting rights and integration were civil rights issues in the 1960s.

"I'm a disciple of Martin Luther King. I think I know as much as anybody of what he would support," Walker says when interviewed at his home in Chester, Virginia. And, Walker believes, if King had lived to see traditional public schools failing generations of students, he would have supported charter schools as a way of combating the "discrimination against low-income people trying to get their children a quality education."

Looking back, Walker minces no words: "The public schools were not doing their jobs." And given that most inner-city families can't afford private schools, "children in the inner city don't have the same access to education as kids in private schools or more affluent suburbs." Walker explains, "It's a human rights issue. It's part and parcel of the struggle— to make quality of education accessible to people of modest means.

"Education for *all* of America's children," he says, "is the civil rights issue of the twenty-first century."

In retrospect, it's easy to see why education mattered so much to Walker, King, and others and how that journey from a Birmingham jail led quite naturally to education reform in Harlem.

The grandson of a slave, Walker was one of eleven children in a family where education was revered. His mother was a nurse, and his father, an erudite man who read Hebrew and Greek each day, was a Baptist pastor. Money was scarce, but books were everywhere. Even at a young age, Walker had an insatiable curiosity, a relentless wanderlust. When he was a child, he would ask his mother if he could go uptown and watch the evening trains come in. He looked in awe as the town's businesspeople, carrying their newspapers and briefcases, stepped off the train. "I remember wondering as a kid if I would ever go anywhere," he would recall some seventy years later. But with his ferocious intensity and a love of learning instilled by his parents, he did.

When Walker graduated from high school in 1946, though, he told his classmates he didn't want to go to college. "I had no ambition to go to college because I figured I couldn't afford it. I was too poor," he would later say. But to Walker's surprise his family found a way to send him to Virginia Union University in Richmond, where his father had been in the first graduating class. As he boarded the train, his mother pressed one hundred dollars in his hand. He wouldn't learn until after his mother died several years later where that money had come from: his parents had scraped it together by mortgaging their life insurance.

Walker was a stellar student. At first, he wanted to be a doctor, and he graduated magna cum laude in 1950 with undergraduate degrees in physics and chemistry. He then decided to become a pastor and entered seminary at Virginia Union where he finished summa cum laude and earned a master of divinity degree. Later, he would earn a doctorate with distinction in African American studies with a specialization in music from the Rochester Theological Center in upstate New York.

In 1952, at an interseminary meeting, Walker met a witty, engaging student from Crozer Theological Seminary who would forever change his life. Even then, King knew how important education was. Walker recalls King's very first words to him: "You're the brilliant science student who went into the ministry." Indeed, Walker replied, he was.

Walker went on to pastor one of the country's oldest African American churches, the historic Gillfield Baptist Church in Petersburg, Virginia. While there, he and his wife, Theresa Ann, whom he had married in 1950, were actively involved in the nascent civil rights struggle that was beginning to sweep the country. Looking back, it's impossible not to realize that securing equal educational opportunities for all was one of the driving forces behind much of what would later be accomplished.

At about that time, in 1954, the US Supreme Court struck down racial segregation in the nation's public schools in its landmark *Brown v. Board of Education* decision. No longer would "separate but equal" schools be legal. Later, after state officials closed down some of Virginia's schools rather than integrate them, Walker organized protests. Like everything he had done up to that point, Walker's civil rights work in Virginia was planned with tactical precision, and his approach caught the eye of the seminary student Walker had met a few years earlier—Dr. King. King liked to bring educated, highly trained people into his inner circle, Walker recalled, and he asked Walker to bring his impeccable organizational skills to the national arena.

"Both of us valued education," Walker would later say. "It was one of the means by which the civil rights movement went ahead. It was education that helped us devise what we did."

But by 1968, Harlem, like many of America's inner cities, faced monumental challenges of a different sort than segregation. Jobs were few, and unemployment soared. Crime was rampant, and drug dealers openly sold heroin and whatever else anyone wanted. The notion of decent *and* affordable housing was an oxymoron, as many landlords walked away from their once stately buildings, leaving them vacant or practically giving them away. Others refused to make repairs, leaving tenants to live in squalor.

So, after picking himself back up after that fateful October day in Harlem, Walker and his congregants tackled those problems job by job, block by block, building by building.

For the next thirty years, Walker tended to the spiritual and material needs of his Harlem congregation and to the religious, civil rights, and human rights needs of Harlem and the world at large. He was instrumental in leading much-needed real estate development in the blocks of abandoned buildings around him. Today, the Wyatt Tee Walker Senior Housing building on Frederick Douglass Boulevard bears his name. He was also a driving force behind construction of the nineteen-story state office building on 125th Street. He fought to close drug dens, even at great personal risk, and he raised his own church, Canaan Baptist Church of Christ, to prominence. In 1993, because of Walker's work and stature, *Ebony* magazine included him in its list of the fifteen greatest black preachers.

But there was a huge piece of the puzzle that didn't seem to be getting much better—Harlem's public schools. Increasingly, Walker heard stories from his congregants about how inner-city schools were failing their children. Graduation rates and academic scores were dismal. Many teachers were apathetic. Classrooms were overcrowded. Books, and even the most basic school supplies, were in short supply. Children were frequently being branded "unteachable," and they and their families were all too often abandoned as lost causes. As a result, academic achievement lagged terribly, with the exception of just a few bright spots. Walker thought of opening his own private church school, but the economics were unworkable for both the church and for the local parents, who could not afford to pay tuition. Walker felt there had to be a public solution, and he never stopped searching for it.

"The schools had to get better," Walker said. And, he explained powerfully, "I saw that as an extension of my work in the South."

■ ■ ■ ■ ■

New York's public school system had not always been so troubled. For years, it had been a gateway to opportunity for its children, highly respected and a source of public pride. But by the 1960s, social upheaval had ravaged the nation's inner cities, unleashing a devastating cocktail of unemployment, crime, and drugs. Jobs vanished, and middle-class families fled, destabilizing huge swaths of once vibrant communities. Not surprisingly, the poorest neighborhoods, like Harlem, were hit especially hard, and these broad social problems began showing up at the schoolhouse door.

Matters worsened as the adults responsible for children's education began battling each other. On one side stood community activists who argued that they knew their neighborhood schools better than anyone else and should have more say in how they were run. On the other side remained the traditional educational establishment, which wanted to keep control of the city's schools under one central board of education. Finally, by 1970, management of New York City's schools had been decentralized into thirty-two smaller districts, each with its own elected board and superintendent. Community activists had won, in their estimation; but as events played out this would eventually prove to be a hollow victory.

In some districts, school decentralization worked. In others, where political patronage and conflict reigned, it didn't. But across the city, the years of acrimony and paralyzing teacher strikes had wounded the system. By the mid-1970s, New York City had also fallen into financial and fiscal crisis, and its already bare-bones school budgets were slashed even further. Waves of educators were laid off. Others were demoralized, and they quit, retired, or—worse yet—stayed on the payroll but stopped trying. A few years later, when there was money to hire again, many of the city's best teachers had fled to the suburbs or had launched other careers. For decades, test scores remained stagnant or declined.

In 1983, a national study made it painfully clear that the educational problems in New York City and other troubled public systems were a national disgrace. The landmark report, "A Nation at Risk," painted a disturbing portrait of an American public educational system in crisis. "If an unfriendly foreign power had attempted to impose on America the mediocre educational performance that exists today," the report stated, "we might well have viewed it as an act of war."

In December 1998 (just months before New York's first charter schools opened) a report from the nonprofit Public Education Association gave further hard evidence to verify what Walker and everyone else on the front lines of public education already knew.

The report, "State of the City Schools '98," was featured prominently in the headlines of the city's major newspapers. It used the city's own test scores and other data to prove the overall weaknesses of New York City's school system, particularly highlighting the extreme weaknesses in fourteen of the city's thirty-two school districts, which the Association described as an educational "dead zone," according to a December 23, 1998, *New York Post* article.

Just 45 percent of the city's public school students, as a whole, were graduating from high school in four years, the report said, and when stricter graduation standards were proposed to begin in a few years, only 18 percent were expected to receive a high school diploma.

In the fourteen lowest-achieving districts—chiefly the poorest African American and Latino neighborhoods of New York, including central Harlem—matters were even worse. Just 38 percent of the third graders in those districts could read at or above grade level compared to about 57 percent for the city's other school districts. About three hundred thousand students were stuck in poorly performing schools, according to the *Post* article, including about ninety thousand kids in schools classified as being under registration review. Academic performance was so poor at the schools under review that state education officials threatened to shut them down if they didn't improve.

Students who don't earn high school diplomas face bleak futures, the report stated, according to the *New York Post*: "Dropouts don't go to college, have difficulty getting and keeping jobs, have an average income barely above the poverty line and are more likely to wind up on welfare or in prison."

The racial and income disparity among the zones and behind the results were obvious. "In reality," the report stated, "the city operates two quite different public school systems."

So, by 1998, the public school system was failing miserably for many of the city's students. Many good teachers, educators, parents, and students continued to do heroic work every day, but in the long run something about the system itself seemed to overwhelm and cancel out many of their individual efforts.

Kathleen Sherry, a Harlem elementary school teacher in the 1970s, symbolized the steadfastness of thousands of other well-intentioned teachers. When her school ran out of basic school supplies, she and her colleagues bought their own. One evening on her way home from school, she was accosted by a teenager trying to rob her. She fought off her attacker with her pocketbook, realizing only later that his knife had torn through her wool coat, drawing traces of blood. Yet she was back at school teaching the next morning because the children in her classroom were eager to learn. "That was the really great part of it," she recalled. By the late 1990s, though, she had left teaching to raise her own children outside the city, just like so many other skilled teachers.

Another public educator, Seymour Fliegel, created a "Miracle in East Harlem" in School District Four, the predominantly Hispanic neighborhood where academic achievement was once ranked absolute last among the city's school districts. In partnership with talented and idealistic colleagues like Harvey Newman and school directors Colman Genn, John Falco, and Deborah Meier, Fliegel established thirty-one new alternative public schools in East Harlem, raising the district's reading scores more than threefold in eight years. District Four moved up to the middle of the city's thirty-two districts, surpassing some of the city's middle-class communities. When Fliegel began, only 7 percent of the students at East Harlem's Benjamin Franklin High School were graduating. By 1986, four years later, all 150 of its students were graduating, and all 150 of them were going to college.

Fliegel's accomplishments were highlighted in his well-received book, *Miracle in East Harlem*. However, after Fliegel and his team retired, the flaws in the system reasserted themselves and their good work was mostly undone. By the end of the 1990s, only about one-third of the students in District Four's third through seventh grades could read at grade level, and the East Harlem district was once again an educational dead zone.

Another leading New York City educator, Dr. Margaret "Peg" Harrington, pioneered the small-schools model, converting the mammoth and floundering twenty-two-hundred-student Andrew Jackson High School into four separate and highly successful thematic Campus Magnet High Schools, each with its own principal. So impressive was her work that teachers and educators came from around the country to study the small-schools model so they could apply the concept elsewhere.

Like Fliegel, Harrington was recognized for her groundbreaking work. She won numerous awards, including nineteen educator-of-the-year or similar accolades. She became a superintendent of high schools in Queens and was eventually promoted to chief executive of school programs and support services for all of the city's K–12 grades, giving her responsibility for managing about one-third of the $10 billion, 1.1 million-student system. Yet, despite everything, bureaucratic inertia made it impossible for her to implement her best ideas on a larger scale. By the late 1990s, she was preparing to retire from her high-ranking position at the Board of Education headquarters downtown and leave the political infighting behind her.

Students, too, were facing their own trials and tests of inner strength, showing heroism in their own ways. One of them was a young woman named Michelle Haynes, who grew up in the 1980s attending the public elementary and middle schools of Harlem's District Five, the same central Harlem neighborhood where Kathleen Sherry had taught. Michelle grew up in a home overflowing with books. Her mother, Madeline Haynes, who was a Head Start teacher in Harlem and later a first-grade teacher at a private school in Harlem, read to Michelle and her two siblings when they were children and took them to libraries at every opportunity. If ever Michelle's mother heard that a neighborhood school was doing something better or had more resources, she moved Michelle there.

Michelle went to three different elementary schools in central Harlem. At the second one, fistfights were frequent, and Michelle, when she needed to defend herself, got into a few fights herself. But Michelle was an able student, and by fifth grade she was placed into a gifted and talented program in another elementary school. About all that really meant, though, was that her classroom had a few more books than Michelle's other schools and offered the free reading time that she so cherished.

By the time Michelle entered high school in 1991, things were "interesting," she recalls. Students milled around in the hallways. If students wanted to, they played cards in the lunchroom instead of going to class. There were no extracurricular activities other than sports and band. Michelle was no longer in a gifted and talented program, simply because there wasn't one. As the quality of her schools fell, so did Michelle's own motivation. "To say I was an average student would be stretching it," she remembers. "I just got through the day." Sadly, by the time Michelle entered college in 1995, it seemed her intellectual curiosity had been snuffed out, and she appeared destined to become part of the cycle of educational dysfunction that had stretched unbroken for decades.

Fortunately, however, in college, she once again found an internal spark of idealism and motivation. By 1999, she had decided to become, of all things, a teacher.

As the stories of Walker, Fliegel, Newman, Sherry, Harrington, and Haynes show, there was no lack of good people inside or outside the failing traditional system. Rather, there was an absence of innovative ways within the system for their talents and efforts to bear fruit. Clearly, reformers thought, a new type of structure was needed to give children, parents, and educators a way to break out of the system, create new schools, and create fresh hope. Even one self-sustaining and survivable example of school success would prove that the children weren't at fault and that the problems could be solved, raising expectations for all other public schools.

The question was: what approach could enable the reform that Walker and others considered the key human rights issue of our time? What method, person, or structure could empower reformers to achieve their dreams for educational excellence after so many decades of systematic failure? Some educational leaders and thinkers thought the answer was to allow a new type of public school—the public charter school—to blossom across the nation.

In Washington, DC, a dynamic, education-minded US president was working to do just that.

2

Laying the Groundwork

It was February 4, 1997, and President Bill Clinton was about to deliver his annual State of the Union message. Finally, after years of behind-the-scenes efforts to break the mold in American public school reform, he was bringing a novel idea to center stage.

A brilliant orator who was known for changing his speeches right up to the last minute, Clinton had uncharacteristically finished this one by late afternoon. The president had spent years thinking about education. He had viewed it as a signature issue during his tenure as governor of Arkansas. Tonight, he knew exactly what he wanted to say.

Clinton's staffers had already eliminated any potential distractions, or so they thought, the *New York Times* reported, when they moved the State of the Union address by a day so that it wouldn't conflict with the Miss USA pageant. But an hour before Clinton was to take the podium at the Capitol, something happened that they had not expected.

There was a verdict in the O. J. Simpson civil trial.

Suddenly, the nation's news commentators were in a tizzy, and their coverage veered away from speculation about what the president was about to say. Now they wondered if the celebrity athlete, who in a criminal trial had been acquitted of murdering his former wife and her friend, would be found liable in a civil trial. And, if the verdict was announced, would the president of the most powerful country in the world be relegated to one side of a split screen, with a scandalized former pro football player on the other?

The nation was caught between dueling stories: one of sex and blood that had mesmerized the country, the other concerning the momentous issue of education and progress that many thought should have taken center stage long before. It was, as NBC News anchorman Tom Brokaw put it mildly, "an unlikely confluence of events," and no one, not even the media big guns, knew exactly what to do.

It was impossible not to see the irony. As much as any other trial in a generation, O. J. Simpson's earlier criminal trial had revealed a disturbing fissure among Americans that broke down all too often along racial and cultural lines. Tonight, though, the president would urge his countrymen to put their differences aside and take fundamental steps forward to heal those fissures for the generations to come.

Clinton remained confident, and to everybody's relief, the O. J. Simpson verdict was delayed. So despite the evening's distractions, all eyes finally focused on the president.

As he delivered his address, President Clinton presented a vision of what he hoped to accomplish in his last term in office: access to quality healthcare, cutting-edge technology, and economic opportunity for everyone. But mostly he talked about education. Clinton, whose father had died in an automobile accident three months before he was born, had willed himself to become a star student. He had attended Georgetown University on a scholarship and become a Rhodes scholar. And on this night, as he turned to a subject that was close to his own heart, he was at his passionate best. "Now, looking ahead," Clinton promised, "the greatest step of all, the high threshold of the future we must now cross—and my number one priority for the next four years—is to ensure that all Americans have the best education in the world."

A year earlier, in his January 23, 1996, State of the Union speech, Clinton had made a general call for school choice and charter schools, saying, "I challenge every state to give all parents the right to choose which public school their children will attend and to let teachers form new schools with a charter they can keep only if they do a good job."

Now, in this hour-long speech, he unveiled the specifics of his "call to action" to create an America where every eight-year-old can read, every twelve-year-old can log on to the Internet, and every eighteen-year-old can go to college. He pressed the nation to rebuild its deteriorating schoolhouses, connect every school to the Internet, and set high educational standards. Midway through his ten-point plan, he said something that many on the front lines of education had been waiting to hear for years: "Every state should give parents the power to choose the right public school for their children," Clinton said. "Their right to choose will foster competition and innovation that can make public schools better."

The president went on to describe a brash, new kind of public school, and he issued a bold challenge: he urged the nation to open three thousand of these novel schools by the next century—nearly seven times as many as existed at that pivotal moment.

The schools Clinton was talking about were charter schools. Like traditional public schools, charter schools are tax-funded, tuition-free, open to all public school children, and overseen by the state. But unlike traditional public schools, charter schools can be created and operated by educational and community groups outside of the traditional education bureaucracy, and families decide for themselves whether they want to enroll their children in the charter schools.

Some charter schools are also freer from the bureaucratic board of education–style rules that govern other public schools, a key factor that, charter school supporters maintain, allows innovative, entrepreneurial educational projects to thrive. At the same time, and in exchange for this increased flexibility, charter schools promise to achieve a high level of specific and measurable educational success and can be shut down by their authorizers if they fall short. For this reason, supporters of the charter movement argue that bad charter schools will soon die out because either they won't attract students or their charters will be revoked. At the same time, proponents believe, the good ones will survive and flourish, creating higher levels of success and creating a path forward for traditional public schools to emulate.

By the time Clinton wound up his speech, he had been interrupted by applause seventy times. Everyone, it seemed, was poised to seize the moment. One of the nation's greatest sources of strength during the Cold War had been its bipartisan foreign policy, where "politics stopped at the water's edge," the president said. Now, he urged, education is a "critical national security issue for our future," one that cries out for "a new non-partisan commitment."

Moments later, news that O. J. Simpson had been found liable in his civil trial flashed across the screen. The long-awaited verdict arrived—but not before Clinton had appealed to the nation's better side, at least as far as education was concerned. "Politics," the president pronounced, "must stop at the schoolhouse door."

When Clinton spoke that night, most Americans had probably never heard of charter schools. But the notion of charter schools had been percolating on the front lines of education reform for years, and at every step of the way, the idea had been embraced by a stunningly diverse coalition: there were conservatives who fervently believed in the power of free markets and wanted to apply those same principles to the educational arena; teachers who wanted to try out new ways of teaching, or return to the basics; private companies that sought to make educational improvement their business; and plain ol' philanthropic types who simply wanted a more educated nation and good schools for everyone. Most important, this group of allies included frustrated families and advocates, many of them low-income, inner-city parents, whose children were trapped like prisoners in broken schools and who wanted to find another way.

In time, this unlikely band of allies would become more visible. Charter schools would eventually be supported by Democrats, such as President Clinton, President Barack Obama, Secretary of State Hillary Clinton, and Secretary of Education Arne Duncan, as well as by Republicans, such as President George H. W. Bush, President George W. Bush, Senator John McCain, and Governor Mitt Romney. Even in New York City, where opinions often clash, charters would come to be supported by a diverse group of people, including Rev. Al Sharpton, New York City mayor Michael Bloomberg, multimillionaire entrepreneurs, grassroots community organizers, and idealistic educators. In 2005 the New York City teachers' union would open a charter school of its own.

As far as anybody can tell, though, the first person to use the word *charter* to describe these upstart schools was a harmonica-playing, former typing teacher and junior high school principal named Ray Budde. As early as the 1970s, Budde, by then a professor at the University of Massachusetts Amherst, was talking about his unorthodox ideas for education reform, but, like lots of other unproven educational ideas, it was far from certain that the concept would ever go anywhere. Wouldn't it be better, he suggested, if educators were awarded charters to create their own schools where they could explore new educational approaches? What if, in exchange for more autonomy, they were held accountable for delivering the academic achievement they promised? Budde's vision, which he wrote about in a 1988 report, was indeed way ahead of its time.

Hundreds of miles away in Minnesota eager education reformers were taking note. They invited battle-tested educator Seymour Fliegel, among others, to speak to them. Fliegel's alternative schools in East Harlem weren't technically charter schools because they reported to the traditional New York City Board of Education. However, the schools functioned a lot like charters and were forerunners of the charter school vision. In 1991, Minnesota passed the nation's first charter school law, and other states soon followed.

(Minnesota state senator Ember Reichgott Junge later told Fliegel that she was inspired to write Minnesota's charter school law after learning about the success of the East Harlem project and hearing Fliegel speak about it. In her book *Zero Chance of Passage: The Pioneering Charter School Story*, Reichgott Junge later wrote: "Fliegel's presentation inspired me. What he said sounded like a charter school to me.")

Other states followed Minnesota's lead. Surprisingly, however, there was one high-profile state that still didn't have a charter school law by the late 1990s: New York State.

In 1998, this would change, and the story of how New York State's charter law came to pass is a window into the rough-and-tumble politics of charter law reform nationwide. In New York, some members of the traditional education establishment resisted the charter concept as unwelcome competition and waged fierce opposition against it behind the scenes. At the same time, the state's reform movement was composed of a mind-bogglingly diverse bipartisan coalition led by Republican governor George Pataki, who was heading up the battle for charter schools at about the same time that President Clinton, a diehard Democrat, was extolling them nationally.

Pataki, an Ivy League–educated lawyer, was a longtime supporter of public school choice. The grandson of a Hungarian immigrant, Pataki had grown up on his family's farm in New York's Hudson River Valley. Like President Clinton, he attended a prestigious university on an academic scholarship, earning his undergraduate degree from Yale University, and later a law degree from Columbia University. As it had been for Clinton, Fliegel, Walker, and so many others, education was the cornerstone of his success.

Even in the early days of his 1994 campaign for governor, Pataki's belief in school choice was both heartfelt and pragmatic. He made that clear one day as he met with some twenty high-powered potential supporters, including former secretary of state Henry Kissinger and Edward F. Cox, a son-in-law of the late President Richard Nixon and then a senior partner at the law firm of Patterson Belknap Webb & Tyler. This was the sort of well-heeled crowd in which most everyone could probably afford to send their children to private schools, and probably did; and as expected the subject of school choice came up. "We all have a choice about where we send our children to school," Pataki said. "Why shouldn't a poor parent in the inner city have a choice, too?"

Later that year, Pataki pulled off a stunning victory, defeating incumbent Democratic governor Mario Cuomo. Maybe, just maybe, he thought, he could get a charter school law passed as well. In an interview for this book, Pataki explained the pragmatic part of his vision. "I have always believed in the importance of creating competition and encouraging parental involvement within the public school system," he said. "If you take a look at the higher education system in America, students are treated as consumers. They have a choice based on private versus public, religion and lots of other factors, and it works. But when K–12 public education fails, all too often parents have limited or no other choices for their children, and often they're inner-city parents. Creating competition in K–12 level schools would give parents choices and get them more involved in their children's education."

Then came the heartfelt part: "If we force a child to go to a public school that we know has been failing to properly educate students year after year, that's not educating them properly," Pataki said, "and what we're doing is simply wrong."

"It was lonely" early on, the governor said, when he first began pushing for a charter school law.

Over the course of 1997 and 1998, concerns about charter laws arose from a wide range of leaders in the traditional education establishment and the state's political establishment, on both the Republican and Democratic sides of the aisle. Some suburban Republican legislators, whose districts already had good schools, did not want to upset the status quo. Many local superintendents and school board members echoed those and other points.

New York City schools chancellor Rudy Crew would also later speak out publicly against the proposed law in the days leading up to a crucial vote on that law. A *New York Times* article quoted him as saying, referring to the proposed law, "I do think it's fundamentally flawed." He cited accountability issues and concerns that funding for the charter schools would come from the traditional public schools' budgets and that groups other than the state's Board of Regents or local school boards could approve charters for new schools. "To now fragment the system by this desire to have everybody and their brother able to charter a school just doesn't make sense."

The publicly expressed position of the teachers' unions about the charter school idea was sometimes more nuanced, but they also became increasingly concerned with how the law would be written, especially as it applied to some key areas, such as teacher quality and teachers' rights.

In 1996, for example, the 2.2 million-member National Education Association (the nation's largest teachers' union) announced its support for charter schools, saying it would help start five new charter schools in five states—Arizona, California, Colorado, Georgia, and Hawaii. The NEA had agreed to spend $1.5 million over five years assisting those charter schools with their staff training, budgets, and community outreach.

"Frankly, we believe that, if done right, charters offer new and excit-ing possibilities," Keith Geiger, the NEA's then-president was quoted as saying in *Education Week*. "Charter schools have the capacity to remove the bureaucratic handcuffs and offer NEA members opportunities to remake schools to respond to diverse learning needs."

As part of the program, the NEA would also hire researchers to assess those schools and would consider helping additional charter schools. The NEA's intention, Geiger explained in the *Education Daily*, was "to use charter schools as vehicles for learning to serve the greater cause of qual-ity public education by applying what is transferrable to the greater num-ber of learners who reside within our public schools."

But, in what some saw as significant, in those states where there was collective bargaining, the charter schools' teachers would receive the same protections and equal benefits as traditional public education teachers, according to an *Education Week* report. "We're trying to walk a fine line between encouraging flexibility and losing all the rights of employees," Geiger said in that same article.

In an interview with the *New York Times* in early 1997, Sandra Feld-man, president of the United Federation of Teachers at the time, said this about the proposed charter schools for New York. "I am not enthusias-tic. . . . We are prepared to be helpful and cooperative in setting them up. But they are not a solution, by any means, to providing a quality educa-tion to one million schoolchildren in New York City." In particular, she cited concerns about how any New York charter law would preserve state certification standards for teachers and whether or not charter schools would be bound under the existing union contracts already in existence for each district.

The concerns of many charter opponents would later be thoughtfully expressed by Marc F. Bernstein, then superintendent of the Bellmore-Merrick Central High School District of North Merrick, New York. In the August 1999 issue of *School Administrator* magazine, he laid out the case against charter schools in an essay entitled "Why I'm Wary of Char-ter Schools."

In his article, Bernstein began by citing arguments he believed char-ter proponents often made for charter schools. These included that charter schools would "permit and encourage a more creative approach to teaching and learning," "establish models of educational reform for other schools in the same community," be "more reflective of parent and community priorities through the alternative programs that cater to special interests and needs," "operate in a more cost-effective manner," and be "more responsive" than other public schools because parents, educators, and members of the community would serve on their boards.

But, he maintained, charter schools' ability to achieve such benefits had not been proven by academic studies at that time, and these benefits hadn't "accrued" to most charter students. Then he wrote at greater length about three overarching concerns he had.

First, he wrote, funding for charter schools comes out of the budget of the traditional public school districts, reducing that budget. Second, he maintained that charter schools are typically "more homogeneous" than traditional public schools, which will have "a Balkanizing effect when young children are most open to dealing with differences among people." And finally, he believed that "the constitutional separation between school and religion will be compromised by people of goodwill (and others) who see opportunities to provide alternate education to children in need."

As a superintendent in New York for thirteen years, Bernstein had concerns about traditional public districts sharing a portion of their previous budgets with charters when students choose to leave that traditional district's schools for a public charter school.

Challenging charter school proponents' claims that "the money is merely following the student," he wrote: "This simplistic argument totally ignores the economic concept of marginal cost. It costs less to educate the 24th student in the class than the initial 5, 10, 15 or 20." Then, quoting from a letter of his published in the *New York Times* earlier in the year, he argued that a traditional public elementary school with one thousand students would lose about a half million dollars if ten students in each grade enrolled in a charter school. "No teacher, custodian or secretary salaries can be eliminated as a result of the reduction in the number of students," he had written in that letter. "However, the public school would have $500,000 less available to educate its remaining students."

The education reformers and many parents of children in perpetually failing public schools, however, saw matters very differently. To them, taxpayer dollars for education were meant to serve the schoolchildren, not to serve the adults or keep inferior schools afloat. If public charter schools could produce superior results at the same or lower cost per student, then the money *should* follow the student. The traditional system should improve its own cost and performance, they believed, not work to prevent better competitors from rising, or force children to stay trapped in a failing traditional system.

By then, education reformers, including some, like Seymour Fliegel, who had once worked in the traditional public system, were convinced that charter schools could work. From working in East Harlem, Fliegel had seen firsthand that public school choice could be a powerful tool for transforming schools. He also knew, from watching Minnesota implement the nation's first charter law, that charter schools could work, and he was inspired to support the charter movement. "I saw the success we had in East Harlem, and I saw charter schools as an extension of the small schools movement there," said Fliegel, whose East Harlem program was thought to be one of the first, if not the first, successful school choice programs in the nation. "I also knew by then that Minnesota had some good charter schools," he explained. "Why wouldn't that work for everyone?"

Along with his colleagues at the Center for Educational Innovation and other education reformers, he began pushing for a charter law in New York, and eventually, he would help write it.

But perhaps most important, parents and community leaders in the neighborhoods most hurt by failing public schools became active in the debate. The need for better public schools in Harlem, the South Bronx, and elsewhere was painfully obvious to the residents in those neighborhoods and was only reemphasized by the publication of the Public Education Association's report and similar data. The drive for reform kept growing, not just in the White House, the governor's mansion, and think tanks, but on the streets of the communities themselves.

The roster of charter supporters began to read like a who's who of high-profile, inner-city ministers whose congregants wanted better public schools. They included Rev. Ruben Diaz Sr., a Pentecostal minister in the Bronx and president of the New York Hispanic Clergy Organization; Rev. Floyd Flake, a former US congressman and pastor of the large Greater Allen African Methodist Episcopal Cathedral in Queens; and to no one's surprise, Harlem's very own Dr. Wyatt Tee Walker.

Walker had been inspired to support the charter movement after reading about the concept and watching firsthand as his community's schools all too often failed its children. Later, in a speech in Manhattan, he would eloquently express why he was fighting to bring this new form of public education to New York. Speaking at New York City's Norman Thomas High School as the debate raged, he began his talk (entitled "Why We Need Charter Schools") with these words:

> Let me say at the outset that I remain a strong and aggressive advocate of public schools. It is grounded in the philosophy of our American experiment that every child has the right to free public education that is designed to prepare him or her to become productive and worthwhile citizens of the nation. That is a right that must not be abridged under any circumstances. However, it must be said in the same breath that the *product* of our existing public educational system here in New York City, particularly, and in many places across the state, generally, is unsatisfactory. Too many graduates of our public school system are ill-equipped to survive in a marketplace driven by information technology and/or are ill-prepared to compete for admission into institutions of higher learning. They cannot surmount the obstacles to college entrance requirements. The disastrous results are the flooding of our communities with young people who are unemployable. They are ill-suited to productive and meaningful employment and thus are consequently demoralized, without sufficient self-esteem and inevitably become a negative statistic of one sort or another in our communities. These are our children who have come from the loins of our lives, and if we do not seek viable alternatives to the present dilemma of our public school crisis, we will bear the responsibility of our children's bewilderment with an

education that is valueless, induces little self-esteem and hardly any skills applicable to the present job market.

This is why we so desperately need an alternative to the present construct of public schools here in New York City and across the land.

By 1998, the ministers had become vocal and organized. They led a widely publicized rally at City Hall Park that drew hundreds of supporters and other clergy. Standing before a banner demanding "CHARTER SCHOOLS NOW!," they spoke out in favor of the schools.

A little noted—but ultimately highly effective—neighborhood effort called Parents for School Choice supported their efforts and caught almost everyone by surprise. The group's field operations were headed up by Flake's politically savvy former chief of staff, an outgoing twenty-nine-year-old Howard University graduate and Union Theological seminarian, Marshall Mitchell. Supporters from Parents for School Choice swept across New York City's inner-city neighborhoods and unleashed hundreds of students and volunteers to neighborhood street corners, where they collected signatures supporting charter schools. They sent postcards to state legislators, overwhelming local politicians—some who almost never received correspondence—with thousands of cards signed by their real-life, grassroots constituents. By the time Parents for School Choice's work was finished, Mitchell recalled, the group had compiled a sophisticated computerized database of 125,000 supporters who had signed the postcards.

"We were able to cobble together a disparate group of people with far-flung ideologies—disgruntled black and Hispanic parents, conservative think-tank types, and good government folks who just wanted good schools," Mitchell explained. "It was just amazing."

As 1998 wound down, Pataki, too, was emboldened. He had just been decisively reelected and was ready to forge ahead. If he had to expend some political capital to give New York a charter school law, he would. So he did what all good politicians do when they need to: he got creative.

State legislators desperately wanted a pay raise, and state law prohibits them from voting on a raise for themselves. But because a new assembly had just been elected in November and was not yet seated, the sitting legislature had one brief window—until the end of December—to pass a pay raise bill. Pataki, who had ten days to either sign or veto the legislature's pay raise bill, seized the moment. His message to the legislators couldn't have been clearer: pass an acceptable charter school law, or I will veto your pay raises.

The standoff went down to the wire, as New York City's schools chancellor Rudy Crew and others spoke out publicly against the proposed law.

But at 1:30 AM on December 18, 1998, the state senate passed a charter school law, and the state assembly followed in the wee hours of the morning. Most left for the holidays happy. The legislators got their $20,000 a year pay raise, and New York would become the thirty-fourth state to usher in charter schools. "We always said that the legislators' spouses were our best lobbyists," Mitchell said, only half jokingly. "We gave a Christmas gift to the students, and we gave one to the legislators."

In the end, there was cause for celebration among charter proponents. The creation of charter schools was "the single greatest improvement in education in state history," Governor Pataki proclaimed in a statement reported in the *New York Times*.

But, even though passing the charter law was a significant legislative achievement, it left many real-world challenges unresolved. Compared to other states, New York's charter law was considered to be well crafted and strong in many respects, and it would come to be ranked among the nation's strongest. But the law also had weaknesses, particularly in the key areas of funding and facilities, which had the potential to prove fatal to the charter schools themselves.

As the years went on, state charter laws would be ranked by the National Alliance for Public Charter Schools (NAPCS) based on twenty components it considered essential to a strong charter school law:

1. Establishing no set number, or cap limiting the growth of charter schools in the state

2. Making allowances for the state to authorize different types of charter schools, including "new start-ups, public school conversions and virtual schools"

3. Having more than one organization that is allowed to authorize charter schools

4. Requiring an "Authorizer and Overall Program Accountability System"

5. Providing sufficient funding for those authorizers, who must also be accountable for how that money is spent

6. Ensuring transparency regarding how organizations can apply to open charters, how those charter applications are evaluated, and how decisions about them are made

7. Requiring that contracts between charter schools and authorizers include, among other areas, expectations for academic performance

8. Ensuring thorough charter school monitoring that includes systems to verify data

9. Clearly defining procedures for renewing, not renewing, or revoking schools' charters

10. Providing opportunities for educational service providers to operate charter schools

11. Establishing structures that allow for public charter schools and their boards to have financial and legal autonomy

12. Instituting transparent rules determining how students enroll in charters and how the lotteries to select them are held

13. Exempting charter schools from many, but not all, state and district regulations and laws

14. Exempting charter schools from automatic collective bargaining

15. Allowing charter school boards to operate more than one school

16. Providing opportunities for students to participate in the same types of extracurricular activities and interscholastic programs as students in traditional public schools

17. Clearly defining special education requirements

18. Ensuring the same levels of operational and categorical funding as that received by traditional public schools

19. Ensuring equitable access to funding for buildings

20. Providing opportunities for employees to receive retirement benefits from the state system

The 1998 New York law was strong on many of these technical and governance measures, and by 2014 the state's law would rank seventh strongest among the laws of forty-two states and DC, according to the

NAPCS rankings. For example, the New York law generally had clear and transparent processes in place and, unlike in some states, created multiple authorizers. The law allowed school districts to convert an unlimited number of existing public schools into charter schools. And it authorized two different bodies to approve fifty new charter schools each. One body was the Board of Regents. The other was the Board of Trustees of the State University of New York (SUNY), where charter advocates felt they would have a fair hearing because most of the SUNY trustees had been appointed by pro-charter Governor Pataki.

New York's charter schools would be required to follow many of the same rules as traditional public schools. They would have to provide, for example, the same special education programs that are required of traditional schools, and would be held to the same regulations affecting health and safety, civil rights, and student assessment.

But, in keeping with the spirit of the charter law, New York's charter schools would also be exempted from some of the rules and regulations that the state's traditional public schools were required to follow. They could choose their own curriculum (as approved by the charter school authorizers), and 30 percent of their staff (not to exceed five teachers) did not need to be formally certified. That meant a charter school could hire a computer expert like Microsoft's Bill Gates or a local computer sciences expert to teach computer science, even though neither holds a formal teaching degree.

In addition, charter schools that began with more than 250 students would automatically begin as part of the same union and collective bargaining units as their local traditional districts—unless the SUNY trustees used one of their ten potential waivers of this rule. A new charter school that began with fewer than 250 students wouldn't automatically start with its school district's preexisting union contract, although the charter school teachers would be free to form their own unions as they chose. If the teachers did not choose to unionize, wage scales would be worked out between the school and the teachers who chose to work there, and their pay could be more or less than that at nearby traditional schools. Those rules generally seemed like proper compromises to both charter advocates and skeptics.

Many of the state's lawmakers were justifiably proud of their achievement. However, challenges and difficulties remained, so much so that a potential charter school founder could feel almost as if they had been embedded in the law to slow down or stop the creation of successful new charter schools, especially pioneering ones.

Of course, the first challenge for a charter school founder would be the fundamental difficulty of the educational task itself, independent of the technical aspects of the law. The New York law specified that, while charter schools were intended to increase learning opportunities for all children, they should especially emphasize expanding those opportunities for students considered to be at risk of academic failure. This meant that smaller and wealthier suburban districts would be less likely to feel competition from charter schools, and that the charter schools would be concentrated in the exact neighborhoods, like Harlem, where public schools often (or almost always) failed. The emphasis on putting charter schools in at-risk neighborhoods raised the moral importance of the charter movement, but it increased the movement's risk of failure.

Next, unlike private schools or even many selective public and magnet schools, charter schools wouldn't be allowed to pick and choose their students. Instead, charters had to take everybody who applied, no matter how advanced, disruptive, or poorly prepared they were. If there were more applicants than spaces, a charter school was required to choose all of its students through an open lottery. And once those students were enrolled, the charter schools would be required to follow expulsion rules that were analogous to those at other traditional neighborhood schools.

The greatest challenge was that charter schools would get no sustained state money for school buildings. Instead, they would have to build or rent their own buildings, a potentially Herculean task, especially for prospective charter operators in New York City, where real estate costs are among the most expensive in the country. That weakness—one that's shared by most states—still existed as of 2014 when the NAPCS gave the New York law a score of just 1 on a scale of 0 to 4 (with four being strong in that category), as it related to "equitable access to capital funding and facilities."

A traditional public school generally receives use of its school building rent free, and the capital budget to build school buildings is separate and in addition to the average funding per student in the annual operating budget. Charter schools in New York, however, were not given a piece of any capital budget. They were required to pay for their facilities out of the operating budget amount that, established by a complicated formula, already began at less than the home district average.

Taking the lack of facilities funding and other smaller factors into account, charter schools would receive only about 70 percent of what their home districts spent per student, according to the New York Charter Schools Association (NYCSA).

At the same time, less affluent home districts like Harlem already received far less public money per child than wealthier districts like Scarsdale because taxpayers in each home district set their own school budgets. For example, the 1995–96 summary data that was available as the charter law was being passed showed average spending per student of $13,453 in Scarsdale, $17,722 in Great Neck, and $21,796 in Amagansett in the Hamptons compared to a much lower $8,213 in New York City that same year and $9,508 in Buffalo. In short, the charter schools would have to generally survive on a 70 percent piece of an already smaller pie, even as they fought the hardest educational battles.

And when it came to operational funding, the NAPCS, in 2014, would also rate New York's law with a low score of 1 for "equitable operational funding and equal access to all state and federal categorical funding." (Many of the other states would also receive a 1 or 0 rating in both categories in the NAPCS ratings.)

Home districts would provide some free services and resources to charter schools, like busing, textbooks, and some health services, but on the face of it and according to 1995–96 figures that were available at the time, a charter district operator in a town that spent $8,213 per student would have received just $5,435 per charter student, and no building. Even with inflation over time, the $5,435 amount would still be only $6,023 by the 1999–2000 school year, and still a fraction of the 1995–96 spending levels at the wealthier districts. These harsh realities led charter proponents to feel the equitable funding they were supposed to receive by law wasn't equitable at all.

"The formula in New York City has always been a mystery," said Sy Fliegel. "Few people, including most school superintendents, fully understand it. Most educators and administrators don't know how the numbers are arrived at. They just accept it."

Over the years that followed passage of the law, funding in almost all of the budgets of traditional district schools in New York would grow substantially, and the charter school funding per student would grow as well at the same fractional proportion. Some schools would also later get free space in traditional school buildings and an influx of philanthropic money. But even though charter schools would be required to meet or exceed academic achievement in their traditional districts within several years, they would receive much less public funding. In short, they had to do more with less.

There were other potential hurdles as well. The law left it to the local school districts to transfer public tax funds over to the charter schools in their district, based on the number of district children who chose to go to the charter schools. Entrenched traditional districts, though, might not like sharing funds with schools they considered competitors, and the law failed to build in any penalties or interest charges to be levied against the districts if they didn't pay.

And although New York's law allowed an unlimited number of existing public schools to convert to charter schools, the total number of new charter schools that the SUNY trustees and Board of Regents could open was capped at one hundred schools.

New York's law also required that only an organization formally approved by the US Internal Revenue Service as a 501(c)(3) not-for-profit corporation could apply to control a school. A financially strong, high-quality private sector services organization that was not an IRS-approved 501(c)(3), such as consulting firm McKinsey & Company, could not apply for a charter itself, nor, for example, could the *New York Times* organize a charter high school for journalism or the New York Giants run a charter school with a sports theme. Some in the traditional education sector harbored a deep-seated distrust of "for profits," although "for-profit" textbook companies, newspapers, family farmers, book-stores, filmmakers, musicians, doctors, lawyers, authors, and others had long served the public interest with good results. While this provision eliminated a potential source of competition for traditional educators, some felt it could weaken the economic and management strength of the charter movement, especially early on.

Issues might also arise with the trustees of 501(c)(3) organizations who could be self-appointed and self-sustaining and were not required to have term limits. No one could say for sure, especially while the charter movement was still young, how such boards could find the economic and managerial resources to create schools, nor could they predict what would happen if a board fell into dysfunction after the charter was approved.

Meanwhile, authorizers would closely oversee charter schools, and if a charter school failed to achieve its promised test score results in just a few years, it could be shut down.

Some of the key difficulties facing any new charter school in New York were well summarized in a memorandum found in President Clinton's presidential papers. Written by education expert Julie Mikuta to a senior Clinton advisor a year before New York's charter law was adopted, the memo presented an overview of the "major obstacles" charter school creators faced. As the movement marched forward, Mikuta's words would prove to be exceptionally prescient, both in New York and nationwide.

Mikuta drew upon a report published by the Hudson Institute, "Charter Schools in Action," and a Department of Education study, "A Study of Charter Schools: First Year Report." In her November 3, 1997, memorandum, she outlined a number of critical start-up issues for charter schools:

"Political and bureaucratic opposition." Political push back from school districts and school boards, along with resistance from unions and bargaining agreements and other factors, posed "difficult" or "very difficult" challenges for 46 percent of the charter schools when they were being created, according to the Department of Education study. This statistic only covered schools that opened, however, and the opposition may in fact be even more onerous if one factors in the schools that were unable to overcome it, the Hudson Institute report found. Barriers include low funding and inferior charter laws. Charter schools often had to "run a fearsome political gauntlet," Mikuta reported.

"Facility woes." Those problems often "top the list" of charter schools' most difficult challenges, and typically involve the need to find school locations, obtain permits, undertake renovations, and find the funds to pay for facilities. The facility area, Mikuta suggested, "could be a need that the federal government addresses."

"A late, rushed frantic start." Many charter schools, particularly those that had just a few months between when their charters were granted and when school opened, didn't have enough time to plan. Meanwhile, those schools that spent a year planning often needed start-up money "to stay alive" during that planning year.

"Lack of business acumen and managerial competence." Mikuta then posed a question that reflected on a belief many charter proponents held: that charter school success requires management skills as well as education skills. "Is there any way that the federal government can encourage persons with expertise in these areas to help out charter schools?" Mikuta asked.

So the challenges for New York's charter operators loomed large, particularly for whoever opened the *first* charter school. The finance and facility roadblocks would be severe. And not only that, New Yorkers were legendary for their ability to fight politically, in the media and in the courts, with no holds barred. If the movement's opponents could delay, shut down, or embarrass the state's inaugural charter schools, they might, some charter supporters believed, be able to stop the entire movement before it gained momentum.

Anyone bold enough to open the first charter schools could come under withering attack. There could be legal challenges, regulatory hurdles, media attacks, and, some charter proponents feared, possibly even attempts by opponents to inflate or create scandal, much like in a bare-knuckles political campaign.

New York's inaugural charter schools would also be up against their own time crunch. In the interest of getting the law up and running quickly, the SUNY board decided that, if the trustees thought any qualified applicants were ready to successfully open up—and if those applicants agreed to go through the expedited process—the board would award the first charters in June 1999 (just months after the law was passed) and allow the schools to open in September 1999. Typically a team of educators needs a year or more to develop a new school's design. But anyone seeking to open New York's first charter schools would have only about three months to draft and submit the charter application. If selected, the school would have about twelve weeks over the summer to hire a principal and full staff of teachers, recruit hundreds of students, buy all of its supplies, create the school's operational systems, and open its door—to intense media scrutiny—in September.

Now that New York had its charter school law, who would accept the challenge of going first? And who—if anyone—would succeed at the task?

Dr. Wyatt Tee Walker and his church in Harlem would be one part of the answer. To everyone's surprise, though, the other key part would begin in a place far from New York City, raised up through one brother's kindness toward another.

3

A Brother's Legacy

In the 1960s, as the seeds of education reform were being planted within Wyatt Tee Walker's Harlem, they were being sowed in another and very different place as well. In Southfield, Michigan, a middle-class suburb on the northern edge of Detroit, a twelve-year-old boy was helping his five-year-old brother learn to read.

The older boy, Gary Klinsky, who had been born in 1949, was a handsome child with broad, flat features, curly brown hair, and soulful brown eyes. Although he looked the picture of perfect health, it was a small miracle that he was alive at all.

As a newborn, Gary had been diagnosed with Niemann-Pick disease, a rare enzyme deficiency caused by two recessive genes carried by his parents, who were of Eastern European Jewish descent. Doctors had told his parents, Connie and Bill, who were barely twenty-one themselves, that Gary would die by the age of two.

But the family refused to give up, and moved for months to Boston, where Gary received treatment from a beloved physician, Dr. Sidney Farber, for whom the Dana-Farber Cancer Institute is now named. Gary's spleen was surgically removed, and he underwent painful bone marrow treatments. But Connie and Bill refused to let the very real possibility that the deadly genetic disease would reoccur dissuade them from having more children. Despite a one-in-four chance of genetic disaster each time and trusting in fate, they chose to go to term twice more, and the couple's next two sons, Richard and Steven, were disease-free. Even more miraculously, Gary defied the medical predictions and grew to be, by all outward appearances, a normal, healthy boy.

As a young child confined to bed, Gary began to create and direct performances with his toys on his bedcovers, which developed into a talent for puppetry and, later, directing theater. As the three boys grew, Gary, who was four years older than Richard and seven years older than Steven, enlisted his younger brothers as his actors in the shows he produced. And beyond theater, Gary took an almost parental pride in his younger brothers' development, including their educations.

After Steve walked home from kindergarten and first grade at the local E. J. Lederle public elementary school, Gary would meet him and organize his own "school after school." This was no casual affair. Gary used store-bought workbooks and lesson plans, and he organized reading circles. His other brother, Richard, participated or assisted in the after-school sessions as well. Their mother, Connie, had earned her own teaching degree from the University of Michigan's School of Education, and their father, Bill, the first member of his family to attend college, had gone on to earn a law degree. Education and a belief in its power permeated the household.

Not surprisingly, as Steve grew, he became a strong student, known for always having a book in his hand, and his progress continued to accelerate as the years passed. After high school, he attended the University of Michigan, completing the four-year bachelor of arts program in about two years from September 1974 to December 1976. He earned high honors in economics and political philosophy and revived and edited the university's humor magazine. In September 1977—when he was about the age of a college senior—he started at Harvard Business School as one of the youngest members of the class and was simultaneously accepted into Harvard Law School. By 1981, four years later, he had completed both his two-year MBA program and three-year JD program and had founded and led the JD/MBA Association for fellow students. Academically, he showed a particular talent for macroeconomics at the business school and for constitutional law at the law school. He was invited by Watergate prosecutor and constitutional law professor Archibald Cox to be a teaching assistant, and he worked as a summer assistant to another constitutional law professor, Laurence Tribe, one of the country's best-known Supreme Court practitioners. Throughout these years, as Steve grew up and attended school, Gary looked healthy, but his internal metabolic chemistry and white blood cell count were far from normal. While Steve was in his first year of graduate school, Gary contracted hepatitis and, due to the genetic weakness in his system, couldn't fight it off. One medical complication led to another, and Steve returned home to Michigan from Harvard for the summer after his first year to be with his family and with Gary as he struggled. In August of that summer of 1978, Gary died at the age of twenty-nine.

The family mourned, and Steve returned to graduate school to decide what to do with his own life, quietly hoping to find a way to honor Gary's memory someday.

Steve's family had owned a business for many years, Albert's, which had begun as a single moderately priced woman's clothing store in Detroit. Steve's grandfather, Albert, and grandmother, Bertha, had managed the store together for thirty years; Steve's father and uncle then built it into a chain of stores as shopping centers rolled out across the landscape in the 1960s and 1970s. The family sold the business to a bigger company soon after Gary died, though, and Steve had no wish to return to it. He considered a career in constitutional law, and then a whole new field—growth-oriented private equity investing—emerged and caught his eye.

In private equity, the investors are not like stockbrokers, trading stock. Rather, they are like businessmen who acquire *entire companies* and then, as their majority owners, are responsible for overseeing and building those companies. They work on behalf of groups like pension plans or college endowments that provide the investment capital in return for approximately 80 percent of the gains. And they generally buy several companies each year in a wide range of fields, working in private partnerships designed for this purpose.

Steve liked the intellectual challenge of getting to know and build businesses in many industries. He also thought private equity could be a path to reunite with his father, brother, uncle, and cousins to create a new family business someday.

When he graduated in 1981, the idea of private equity as a profession was still very new, and he became one of the early leaders in the field. After leaving school, Steve joined Goldman, Sachs and Co., where he soon cofounded their original private equity group. Then, in late 1984, Steve was recruited to join Forstmann Little & Co., which was one of the best-known private equity specialist firms. Forstmann Little's business principles fit well with Steve's own personality because the firm's founders opposed corporate raiders, excessive debt, and junk bonds, and they took a great deal of pride in adding value to the companies they bought. The companies that Forstmann Little successfully acquired and improved in the 1980s and 1990s included the makers of Dr Pepper soda, Topps baseball cards, Moen faucets, Minwax wood stains, Gulfstream jets, Department 56 giftware, Yankee candles, Ziff Davis computer magazines, and others.

By the early 1990s, Steve—still in his mid-thirties—had become the most senior partner of Forstmann Little outside of the Forstmann brothers, and the firm was the second-largest private equity fund in the world by assets and was just entering its most successful years.

He proved to have a natural affinity for his line of work. He had been broadly educated and was a good problem solver with a creative and strategic mind. At six foot three inches tall, he looked the part. By personality, he dealt with everyone in an equally respectful and low-key Midwestern manner that was the opposite of the Wall Street stereotype. Coming from a family business background himself, he tried to grow businesses and protect them.

General Instrument (GI) Corp. provided just one example of Steve's growth-oriented business-building approach. He led the analysis that convinced his partners to acquire the company for $1.6 billion in 1990, and he helped oversee it for nine years.

When Steve first found GI, it manufactured cable-television set-top boxes and satellite television equipment, and many people warned that American consumer electronics companies like GI would soon be overtaken by foreign competitors. Within just a few years of the acquisition, however, Klinsky and his partners had greatly increased GI's research budget, reorganized and changed its senior management, built a new board, focused its strategy, and expanded the business globally. The increased research and the growth-focused strategy led to a range of major new product breakthroughs for General Instrument during Forstmann Little's ownership, including all-digital high-definition television (HDTV) technology, digital set-top boxes, small dish satellite receivers, digital video on demand, early versions of cable modems, broadband fiber-optic networks, and one-thousand-channel cable television systems. In 1992, Steve stood under the US Capitol dome, alongside GI's top research scientists, as Congress witnessed the world's first-ever demonstration of an over-the-air, all-digital high-definition television broadcast, made possible by GI's new technology breakthroughs. By the time the 1990s ended, General Instrument had gained over $10 billion of market value and had played a key role in that decade's renaissance of American technology companies.

As the years went on, the success of Forstmann Little and its companies placed the low-key Klinsky into a level of corporate glamour he never would have chosen for himself. The firm's senior partner, Ted Forstmann, loved corporate jets and served as chairman of Gulfstream Aerospace, the corporate jet manufacturer that Forstmann Little owned. Soon the five-partner firm of Forstmann Little had its own private aircraft hangar at the Morristown, New Jersey, airport with its own corporate jets, plus a twin-engine two-pilot Sikorsky helicopter, just to make the trip back and forth from Manhattan to Morristown easier.

The firm's offices at Fifth Avenue and Fifty-Ninth Street featured some of the best views of Central Park in the city. Forstmann Little's bipartisan advisory board grew to include former secretaries of state Henry Kissinger, Colin Powell, and George Shultz; Senators Sam Nunn and Bob Dole; former Democratic Party chairman Robert Strauss; Newt Gingrich; and others. Each September, Ted Forstmann organized a Forstmann Little partners' retreat in Aspen, where top political and business leaders joined them, and which *Time* magazine described, along with Davos, as one of the world's most high-powered corporate camps. Guests ranged from journalist Bob Woodward to presidential confidant Vernon Jordan and the English embryologist Ian Wilmut (who had just cloned Dolly the sheep), and among the entertainers were Jay Leno, Willie Nelson, and James Taylor.

In contrast to his glamorous life with Forstmann Little, however, Steve's own private life remained unchanged. He lived in a two-bedroom rental apartment on Second Avenue and ate mostly at the corner diner because the light there was good to read by. He worked out at a boxing gym in the mornings, and on summer nights, played backgammon on Broadway with the street hustlers until he learned to beat them. He went to bookstores, movies, and occasional plays, and sometimes wrote about public policy for a small journal.

His life took a major turn on a misty night in December 1988. Klinsky had just watched a melancholy movie and was thinking about life and death—and his brother Gary—when he looked out his cab window and saw a beautiful woman crying in the rain. Acting uncharacteristically on instinct, he stopped the cab, got out, and approached her.

He would marry the woman, Maureen Sherry, in 1995. They would have four wonderful children together, and Maureen would bring Steve into her extended family. Klinsky—descended from Polish Talmudic scholars on his mother's side and Silver Star-winning soldiers on his dad's—now added church every Sunday and Irish ceilidh dances in Rockland County to his already eclectic world of boxers, Wall Street chieftains, world leaders, digital research technologists, and street hustlers.

As Klinsky's life became more fulfilling and as he grew more successful, his desire to honor the legacy of his brother, his family, and his long-held ethical and philosophical ideals grew stronger. He felt unclear, though, about what to do. Where, when, and how should he begin?

One night, on a business trip to London, by chance, he picked up philosopher Martin Buber's thin book, *The Way of Man,* at an airport bookstore. Buber's thoughts and metaphors resonated so strongly with Klinsky as he read on the flight that he began copying entire paragraphs into his notebook. It was as though Buber was saying clearly what Klinsky had felt inchoately for years.

The central message of Buber's book, which can be read either as theology or simply as a path to good secular ethics and a meaningful life, is that a "divine spark" lives in everything and every being and that the spiritual purpose of human life is to bring out that spark by joyfully hallowing the everyday world we live in, "here where one stands."

In his interpretation of the story and drawing from other theological sources, Klinsky later explained "the central folk tale or metaphor" this way:

> God put all of his divine light in a jar, and then the jar broke into billions and billions of pieces. The slivers of light were spread into every part of our everyday world, into everything, and every event and every person. Over time, the light gets covered with the crust of dirt and grime and the shell of day-to-day existence.
>
> The purpose of a person's life—part of our job description as human beings, really—is to break through these shells and let the light shine through. If you're the king of a country, you do it countrywide. If you're a farmer with one acre of land, you do it on your one acre of land. Everyone's "way" may be different, but the goal is the same. This is our job, and it's a *joyful a*pproach that's very focused on this world.

The same metaphor of light and soul had been used centuries before in mystical medieval religious texts, such as the Zohar, but Klinsky did not approach the idea in this literal or cultish way, and he did not think Buber did either. Rather, he saw Buber's ideas as part of a broader non-denominational, humanist approach to ethics, which used religious-themed metaphors to focus on respect for others. Klinsky, as a former political philosophy student, noted and took comfort from the fact that Dr. Martin Luther King Jr. had cited Buber by name (alongside Saint Augustine and theologian Paul Tillich) as an ideological influence in his famous "Letter from Birmingham Jail."

In Klinsky's view, Buber was simply teaching the importance of respect for every person and for each individual's essential spirit; the philosopher was making a call to bring out that spirit in others, rather than debase others by treating them as objects.

As he read the philosopher's book, Klinsky realized that Buber's way was the way that his brother, Gary, and his family had always lived and treated him and others. It was the common thread in the lives of the people Klinsky most admired—from the poorest immigrants trying to make better lives for their children, to the greatest figures in history trying to protect their countries—and it was also the characteristic mostly missing in those he had usually tried to avoid. Klinsky knew he was far from perfect. He felt his own flaws very deeply. He was just a businessman, not a spiritual hero like King or Buber. Still, he felt that he wouldn't be doing his job as a human being, or living a well-rounded and meaningful life, if he didn't try to do something socially positive with at least a part of his life as well.

As Klinsky thought about Gary's divine spark and what path to take forward, his ideas kept coming back again and again to education. Gary's after-school sessions may well have changed the course of Steve's entire life, and Klinsky thought that the work of a teacher with a student was the essence of bringing the light out in another person. Klinsky could never cure Niemann-Pick disease, he thought, but maybe he could start an academic program that would help other public school children after school, just like Gary had helped him. He would start it "here" where he stood, in New York City, in whichever part of New York City it was most needed, and he would start it "now."

Steve began to think about and explore the question, and soon he found his way to the Brooklyn Bureau of Community Service (BCS), a 150-year-old organization that was one of New York City's oldest and largest not-for-profit social service agencies. The BCS staff had an intimate knowledge of local neighborhoods, schools, leaders, strengths, and challenges. But when Klinsky approached them with his idea of establishing a new program, they seemed somewhat surprised at first. The concepts of social entrepreneurship and venture philanthropy were still new in 1993, just as private equity had been a new idea in 1981, and digital electronics and HDTV had been new ideas in 1990. Social service agencies were accustomed to dealing with large, passive funders, like government agencies, not hands-on social entrepreneurs like Klinsky. Still, the bureau shared Steve's goals, and before long they had assigned a team to help him scout out sites.

On the first day of their search, the bureau's staff took Klinsky to a beautiful new school that was being built in a relatively affluent section of Brooklyn. Klinsky took one look at it and said, "Oh, no. This is nicer than where I went to school." "Oh, well," the staff members said, "if you want to go to a place that really needs help, let us take you out to East New York where we've been doing violence-prevention work." Their search ended there—at the elementary school they visited on their next outing, PS 149 on Sutter Avenue. Its neighborhood had a host of problems, including some of the highest crime rates and poverty levels in the country, as well as some of the lowest academic scores, but the grand old school was housed in a century-old, five-story building with empty classrooms that were perfect for after-school activities. Most important, it had a warmhearted principal who was just as enthusiastic as Klinsky about the benefits of an academic-oriented after-school program. Right then, the deal was sealed.

Now that he had a site, Klinsky naively thought he could simply write a check, and that it would be put to good use. He asked the local school district administrators to propose an after-school program that would be academic, fun, innovative, cost-effective, and replicable. He was met with blank stares. One staffer suggested that they could string a tennis net across the parking lot. No, Klinsky repeated, he'd like to see something academic, fun, innovative, cost-effective, and replicable. By then, it was clear to Klinsky that, if he wanted the kind of program he was envisioning, he would need to design and develop it himself.

As he had always done in his private equity career, Klinsky took one of his deep dives and began analyzing other academic programs across the city. For months, he visited some of New York City's best programs, including inner-city gems like the East Harlem Tutorial Program and Boys & Girls Harbor. He was impressed. But just as Buber had written, Klinsky concluded that there was no single right or wrong way to do what he wanted to do. Instead, he realized, the real magic happened in the direct interaction between a great teacher and a willing student. And Klinsky had his own ideas for how to enable that.

Klinsky thought they could never implement, on a large scale, some of the outstanding programs he had seen, because those programs depended on one charismatic leader and a specific (and expensive) stand-alone building. He realized that if he could find a way to house the after-school program right in the public school buildings themselves and hire public school teachers from the traditional school day to stay after school, then he could build a model that could be replicated to help kids in lots of neighborhoods.

Over the next few months, Klinsky devised a simple, common-sense design for the centers, which he would later name in honor of his brother, and the Brooklyn Bureau agreed to implement that vision. Teachers and kids in New York's most disadvantaged elementary schools would stay after school together every school day in fun academic clubhouses with one adult for every ten kids. Costs would be kept low by establishing the clubhouses right in the traditional public school building, rent-free. The curriculum would be based on thematic learning that would make academics feel like play. A group studying the rain forest, for example, might read a book about the rain forest, turn its class into a rain forest with art, visit the New York Botanical Garden, build a terrarium, and graph rainfall mathematically. The extra three hours of learning time each day would equate to a 50 percent increase in daily learning time, equal to three and a half extra years of life-changing academic time for a child who attended all grades from kindergarten through sixth grade. The children would remain safely within the same school building from morning drop-off until end-of-the-day pickup, which was especially important for children of working parents, and the academic and social benefits of the after-school program would be tied back into the regular school day itself.

The Gary Klinsky Children's Center (GKCC) opened in 1993, at first funded entirely by Klinsky, serving sixty children at the single PS 149 site in East New York. The program eventually expanded to multiple sites, serving more than seven hundred children every day (including all day throughout the summer and on most holidays). The GKCC program has remained in continuous operation for twenty years and has become one of the city's most successful public-private partnerships. As of 2014, the program has served thousands of children and raised approximately $20 million in philanthropic funding from multiple public and private donors.

After Steve and Maureen were married, she, too, took an active role in supporting the centers. Both Steve and Maureen visited frequently and gained fresh insights from their experiences and visits.

The major observation that struck Klinsky from his time in East New York was how different the children and teachers at PS149 were from their neighborhood's reputation for low test scores and social and academic failure. East New York in 1993 was in the midst of the crack cocaine wars; it was one of the nation's most violent and murder-ridden neighborhoods and was described by the *New York Post* that year as a "killing field" with one murder every sixty-eight hours and later as a "death precinct." For their safety, the GKCC children at PS 149 stayed inside their brick school behind a locked, solid-steel industrial door, protected by a guard in uniform. Even so, whenever Klinsky arrived, he was always impressed by how happy, well-behaved, and engaged in learning the kids were, even though the regular school day had ended hours before. He was also struck by the sincere dedication of the staff members and their eagerness to teach. Both the students and teachers came from the regular public school day system, but, for whatever reasons, it seemed that the traditional day system didn't allow their talents to flourish. It all hit home for Steve late one afternoon when he ran into one of the center's most enthusiastic teachers. "You must love your job during the day to want to stay after," Klinsky told her. "No," she responded. "I hate it during the day. I stay after school so I can be creative and do the kind of teaching that I really love." It made Klinsky think: if an innovative after-school program could make a difference, imagine how effective allowing innovation within the regular school day would be.

As 1998 ended, Steve and Maureen had a two-year-old son, Cavan, and a second child on the way, and Steve made another major career decision. After almost twenty years of consistent career success working for firms started by other people, he broke away and started a growth-oriented private equity firm of his own. His new firm's goal was to be the best anywhere at "building great businesses," and to create a team-based culture, combining financial, strategic, and hands-on operating skills in a way that his own children could really be proud of.

But a second, more unexpected, idea had caught his passions as well: since he was leaving Forstmann Little to start his own firm, he would control his own work time and be free to take on a major new social project.

He had watched New York's political leaders push the state's charter school law through at the conclusion of 1998, and he saw the great power in it. To him, the tens of thousands of students in New York's educationally underperforming zones weren't just faceless facts and figures. They were like the kids he knew at the Gary Klinsky Children's Centers. The charter school law, he figured, could bring innovation to the regular school day, just as he and his allies had done with after-school hours. If he became a pioneer in this movement, he could build a socially important enterprise, take another step down Gary's path and Martin Buber's way, and perhaps add more meaning to his own life.

Klinsky knew that whoever tried to create New York State's very first charter school would face intense difficulties—financial, practical, and political. But that gave the goal even more importance and meaning to him. Klinsky was not a trained professional educator, and he very intentionally never claimed to be one. Rather, he figured he was used to tough challenges and fights from his years in academia and business, and he thought if he could combine his own strengths and experience with those of the best educators, grass-roots community leaders, and private-sector specialists, together they might be able to tackle the education reform mission and give it a chance to survive and succeed.

By nature, Klinsky was always happiest when he was fully engaged in an important project. Now he would have three—building his family, building his business, and building schools that could help launch the school reform movement. He felt energized and determined to succeed. But he was also aware that, once he left the glamorous and highly successful world of Forstmann Little, the door would be closed behind him, and he could not turn back. He secretly reflected on the fact that he would be like a player in the board game Chutes and Ladders; he would need to plunge far, far down the chute toward failure and then climb the ladder all over again. He had been lucky and successful before. But what if he failed this time?

The stakes were high, and he needed a road map and a team.

So far, all he had were his good intentions and a blank legal pad.

4

Building a Team

Wall Street was giddy in early 1999. The initial Internet boom was roaring, and multibillion-dollar fortunes were being made almost overnight. But as Steve Klinsky's Wall Street compatriots were huddled in power breakfasts all over the city planning a path to online glory, he was at a meeting of a different sort, dreaming about a new and better type of inner-city public school.

In January 1999, just days after New York's charter law passed, Klinsky had formally announced to his partners that he would be wrapping up his sixteen years at Forstmann Little and leaving the firm by June. At the same time, he was beginning his analytical work on charter schools, and as he searched for outside advice on his charter school quest, he placed his very first call to two longtime friends—Sy Fliegel and Harvey Newman.

By then, Fliegel and Newman had retired from the traditional New York City school system and their East Harlem miracle had been substantially undone by the education bureaucracy that followed them. Fliegel and Newman hadn't walked away from their life's mission, though, and they now helped lead the Center for Educational Innovation (CEI), a New York City–based not-for-profit organization that worked to create successful public schools and educational programs. Klinsky had been a trustee of CEI for some years, supporting Fliegel and Newman's efforts to improve traditional public schools. Fliegel and Newman, in turn, knew all about the Gary Klinsky Children's Centers and respected Klinsky's years of innovative and philanthropic work there.

The three gathered one day in the private wood-paneled dining room at Forstmann Little's Fifth Avenue offices, sitting beneath a wall lined with original Frederic Remington paintings. Klinsky had his ever-present legal pad and pen ready, and over a bowl of cereal he asked his question: Could Fliegel and Newman tell him everything they knew about the state's new charter law?

As it turned out, they knew a lot. CEI had been active behind the scenes in getting the charter law passed, and although the CEI staff didn't want to set up a charter school of their own, they were happy to provide intellectual resources and experience to anyone who did. Meanwhile, Fliegel had appointed Newman as CEI's point man to help the new charter school movement.

The two explained that the state's Board of Regents and SUNY's trustees could approve up to fifty charters apiece, and that the SUNY trustees would probably be more supportive initially because most of them had been appointed by the governor.

There would be a very compressed time period to prepare the first set of charter applications, and once the applications were submitted, the authorizers at SUNY would approve only a few of the very best. By law, every charter school would be a 501(c)(3) not-for-profit organization, run by a board of trustees. Funding would be lower than at traditional public schools, and the neighborhoods the schools served would be challenging. Authorizers would closely oversee the charter schools, and the schools would be shut down within several years if their test scores weren't equal to or better than their district's schools—something they agreed to in their charters.

Fliegel and Newman pulled no punches as they described the difficulties. They then gave Klinsky a copy of the state's new charter law itself, which ran on for pages, and a charter school application form, which ran even longer. They explained that the application had sixty-six (often multipart) questions that would require the applicant to provide a detailed blueprint for every aspect of the school's design.

To apply, Klinsky would need to come up with detailed written answers on a whole range of topics, a project usually taken on by a full team of educators with a year or more to prepare. The questions and topics included: What is the mission of the school? How does the school serve at-risk populations? Does the local community really want this new school? Can you prove that? What exactly is the curriculum? How does the curriculum satisfy all state performance standards? How will special education students be served? How will discipline issues be handled? What educational achievements will the school promise to the authorizers? What tests and measures will be used to verify those achievements? How will food service be provided? How will social work and health services be provided? Where will the school be located, and what is the building's layout? Has the building been obtained (even though the charter hasn't yet been granted)? Who will the school's board members be? What are their backgrounds and what is the code of ethics that will apply to them and the school's officers and employees? What are the school's bylaws? Who will the school's principal and teachers be? Are they properly certified? What are the school employees' compensation and retirement benefits packages? Is the school properly insured? How will the school comply with the admissions lottery law and open meeting law requirements? Are the school's fire control systems in place? What is its financial budget? Does the budget balance? Who will cover cash shortfalls, if there are any? How will the school expand if it succeeds? How will the school's assets be liquidated if it does not succeed?

And there were many more questions besides.

The state's charter schools were intended to expand learning opportunities for all children, but particularly for those at risk of academic failure. That meant the first charters would most likely be going into neighborhoods where other public schools were perpetually failing and where social and economic needs were greatest. At the same time, however, the law provided charter schools with far less money per student than was allotted to other public schools in the same home district, in large part because the new charter schools would get no sustained state money for school buildings or for rent. How, Fliegel and Newman asked Klinsky, did he think he could make it all work?

Klinsky had already begun studying education reform, and he had started to form some ideas. The charter law required each school to receive 501(c)(3) status from the Internal Revenue Service, designating it a nonprofit corporation, recognized as such for charitable tax deduction purposes. Consistent with the 501(c)(3) rules, each school Klinsky worked with would be run by a school board of community leaders, such as local ministers and teachers, who would serve without pay and who would have ultimate control over the school's policies and personnel, subject to the state's chartering authority. Klinsky, in turn, would create a technical support and advisory group that would seek out the very best of these community leaders, give them the start-up funds and technical advice they needed, and help them start and manage their own schools. The advisory group would work for the schools in the same way a law firm, architectural firm, or consulting firm advised clients in other areas.

When Klinsky sought a name for the new advisory group, the word *victory* came optimistically into his head. *Victory for children! Victory for education reform!* The advisory group would not be a 501(c)(3), any more than a law firm is. It was permitted by law to earn a profit. But in fact Victory would be chiefly mission-driven like a law firm that focused chiefly on pro bono cases. Julie Mikuta's 1997 memo to President Clinton's staff had asked if there was any way to get persons with business acumen and managerial competence to help charter schools. Victory—as an ally, advisor, and resource for the best not-for-profit community leaders—would create one practical way.

Along with start-up funds, Victory would provide charter schools with most of the services that a traditional public school normally received from its local board of education, superintendents, and central administrators. Further, Klinsky hoped Victory could be efficient enough to allow charter schools to pay much less for such services than he thought traditional school districts did (about 20 percent of revenues rather than the estimated 40 percent he thought they paid traditionally). This would enable charter school budgets to balance even though the charter school would receive less public funding per child.

Klinsky was expecting to lose about $1 million for every school that Victory initially supported, and he would fund those losses himself. However, he hoped that if Victory could work for enough schools, it might be able to spread its costs and gain economies of scale. Then, in a best-case scenario, it might be able to build a large in-house staff of the best experts and become both a socially beneficial and financially strong enterprise, like a respected and financially sound newspaper in the golden days of journalism.

Fliegel and Newman listened. They agreed to help him, but they were skeptical about two points. First, they warned him that the entrenched political opposition would be a lot worse than Klinsky could ever expect. Second, the financial losses would be much greater. "You're one of the good guys, and you are going to help a lot of kids," Fliegel said, smiling wisely. "But this is going to be your biggest philanthropy!" Klinsky was undeterred. Even if Victory lost more than he expected, he thought, it could turn out to be the best "charity" he supported. Later, as Klinsky studied the charter application, he realized, in a glass-half-full kind of way, that the application's length and specificity were a blessing in disguise. The long list of questions provided a detailed checklist of all the work that needed to be done. If he answered those questions, he would have his road map.

Working alone at first, Klinsky began to systematically tackle each academic, political, and financial challenge inherent in building a school from scratch. His goal was to create a self-sufficient, replicable, and practical school model that would work consistently, even in America's most impoverished and educationally underserved neighborhoods. The Victory advisory group would help the best local community leaders "create great schools for America's children," on the premise that all children can succeed if they're given a high-quality learning environment.

But how should he answer the school design questions? And which leaders and communities should he support? The first topic he addressed was the curriculum.

Drawing from his six years of success at the after-school centers, Klinsky knew that he wanted to incorporate the GKCCs' interdisciplinary, thematic after-school curriculum approach into an extended day for every student. This would increase learning time and opportunities for higher-level thinking. It would also be a way to add art, music, physical activity, and creativity into the charter school program.

Next, Klinsky began an intensive study to seek out the most research-proven and successful methods for the earlier, more formal part of the traditional school day. Soon he discovered the federal government had itself endorsed a limited number of programs based on proven evidence of success and that a study commissioned by the National Association of Elementary School Principals, the National Association of Secondary School Principals, and the research arms of national teachers' organizations had endorsed programs as well. In particular, the American Federation of Teachers (AFT) had recently issued an extensive report, praising six curriculum approaches that their research had shown to be highly effective. Two of these AFT-endorsed approaches particularly caught Klinsky's attention.

The first was Core Knowledge, a challenging educational approach that had been developed by University of Virginia professor E. D. Hirsch Jr. Core Knowledge was most commonly known in the bookstores as the *What Your First Grader Needs to Know* or the *What Your Second Grader Needs to Know* series. Hirsch's idea was to make sure that, before graduation, students were exposed year by year—systematically and in an organized way—to the hard facts and knowledge that a highly educated young person should know. Students would learn, for instance, the reasons behind the American Revolution in first grade, and they'd learn about King Ashoka and the birth of Buddhism in second grade. One pundit described Core Knowledge as "a gifted curriculum for all kids." It had the kind of high academic expectations Klinsky believed would help at-risk children overcome the stereotypes against them. The curriculum was also exactly the sort of coursework he would have wanted for himself growing up, or for his own children now.

A second approach recommended by the AFT website was Direct Instruction (DI) for math, reading, and English language. The DI program began in the 1960s and had been extensively tested since then, offering years of hard evidence to support its effectiveness. Online testimonials from schools attested to the major leaps they had seen in student scores when DI was properly implemented.

Direct Instruction consisted of a ladder of carefully scripted lessons that would be taught through small group instruction, within which each student proceeded at his or her own speed. Every class in a DI school, for example, would teach reading at the same time of day so that a high-achieving first grader could read with a small group of third graders for that period and then return to her own age group for the rest of the day. Also, DI allowed teachers to track exactly where each child stood on the organized ladder of lessons, so that the school could closely monitor each individual student's progress and make sure that no child ever fell through the cracks or was forgotten.

The major criticism of DI was that it was *too* scripted and thus limited teacher and student creativity. The standard criticism of Core Knowledge was that it taught knowledge and facts but didn't sufficiently emphasize basic skills training. For these reasons, it seemed logical to Klinsky to combine the two (along with the thematic approach of an extended day). In this way, Direct Instruction could be used for teaching basic fundamentals in the morning; the unscripted, high-achieving, conceptual Core Knowledge approach could be used for teaching history, science, and social studies in the afternoon; and a GKCC-style extended-day program would add in art, music, a thematic curriculum, conceptual thinking, and fun at day's end.

Finally, Klinsky thought, it could all be tied together in an inclusionary class management setting, where students wore uniforms, teachers gave each child personal attention, and everyone valued education and had high academic expectations. As part of the equation, too, parents would be treated as clients and offered a level of respect that at the time was unusual in the traditionally failing inner-city system.

As far as he knew, Klinsky was the first to combine the DI and Core Knowledge programs in this way. He would later discover that blending could draw opposition from people who held fierce loyalties to just one of the individual curricula and so viewed alternative approaches as anathema. But at the time Klinsky (who had combined economics with philosophy and law with business in his own education) felt he would've enjoyed learning in this way. The highly experienced educational experts at CEI agreed with his blend of curriculum choices, so he plunged ahead.

As Klinsky got deeper into the charter school project, the work demands on him grew and grew. By March 1999, he had voluntarily moved out of his luxurious office near the center of Forstmann Little's headquarters and into a smaller, more bare-bones side office where he could work long hours, alone and undisturbed.

He was still wrapping up his work with Forstmann Little, including arranging the sale of its last shares in General Instrument, and preparing for his own future private equity fund. He was also now dedicating more than a normal full-time workday to researching schools, writing the charter applications, driving out to inner-city neighborhoods and communities, and establishing alliances with experts and educators.

His became a harried existence of eighty- to one-hundred-hour work-weeks. He gave up going to the boxing gym so he could arrive at the office earlier and earlier. Except for spending time with his family, he cut out almost everything else.

The importance of the project grew in his mind as the days went on and as he witnessed the social ills that a failing education system can help create.

One morning, at about the same time that the *New York Times* and the *Wall Street Journal* were reporting on Forstmann Little's success at General Instrument, Klinsky found himself in a setting that was entirely different from his typical private equity work experience. He sat in a second-floor courtroom in Mt. Vernon, New York, just outside of New York City, waiting for a meeting with local community leaders. As he sat in the back left bench of the court, Klinsky watched a wave of humanity parade by—one police officer wearing an earring, another sporting a walrus mustache—and he watched the young defendants, who looked mostly to be in their twenties. Many of them appeared to be drug users. All seemed to know the courtroom process and each other far too well. "I know Mr. Smith. I'm setting a two-thousand-dollar bail for Mr. Smith," the presiding judge said before Mr. Smith's two-minute arraignment was up. Next in line was a young mother, who also looked to be about twenty. "I know Miss Jones," the judge went on. "She uses drugs. You have to go to window sixteen for a referral. Where is your child, Miss Jones?" As the demoralizing courtroom scene unfolded, Klinsky couldn't help but view it as a tragic, real-life lesson about what happens when social structures break down. For the hundredth time, he told himself that if he ever actually got his charter school up and running, he could never let it fail.

Ultimately, though, Klinsky understood he could only be one small part of a larger group-based success. By then, he had begun assembling a team to join him in trying to launch a charter school and build Victory over time.

Klinsky's starting belief was that Victory should combine the best of the public and private sectors, with a staff that included both traditional educators and socially motivated MBA types. For the MBAs, he called Steve Nelson, the executive director of Harvard Business School's Social Enterprise Initiative, for which Klinsky served on the advisory board. The business school had recently established on-campus organizations for business students interested in socially motivated careers, and Klinsky asked Nelson for help in finding the top MBAs, with a passion for education, who might be interested in joining him after they graduated that summer. Nelson sent along a resume book for the business school's newly established Education Club, and before long Klinsky searched out and called two soon-to-be MBA graduates who looked especially promising. They took their own leaps of faith and agreed to come to New York to meet him.

The first was Erik Heyer, the son of a Syracuse, New York, elementary school teacher. Heyer had earned his bachelor of science degree in systems engineering from the University of Virginia and had worked briefly at Goldman Sachs before moving on to Harvard Business School, where he became president of the Education Club. By coincidence, Heyer came to New York to meet with Klinsky on the same day that Steve was scheduled to have lunch with Jay Cross, the president of business operations for the Miami Heat basketball team. Cross and the Miami Heat wanted to talk to Klinsky about how to replicate the Gary Klinsky Children's Centers in Miami as the Heat's team charity, and Klinsky brought Heyer along for the discussion. As things turned out, the Miami Heat did adopt the GKCC model and went on to help hundreds of kids in the team's own version of the children's centers. And as Klinsky also hoped, Heyer agreed to join him.

At about the same time, another soon-to-be minted Harvard MBA, Emily Lawson, agreed to meet him. Lawson also brought an impressive resume. She had been a prestigious Morehead scholar at the University of North Carolina in Chapel Hill, where she earned undergraduate degrees in economics and history. She had then earned a master's degree in public administration from Harvard's John F. Kennedy School of Government and helped start a charter school in Boston before becoming a Harvard MBA.

Lawson was polite but deeply skeptical in the interview: "Let me get this straight," she said. "You want me to give up all my career options to join with you on your charter school effort, but you haven't won any charters. And you want me to help with your private equity effort, but you haven't raised any private equity. What happens if you don't win any charters, or if you don't raise any funds? What happens if you get neither?" she asked. "Well, then," Klinsky answered, thinking fast, "in that case, you can work for the Gary Klinsky Children's Centers!"

In another leap of faith, Lawson signed on to Klinsky's team as well, but neither she nor Heyer could start work for several months. First they had to finish school and move to New York. In the meantime, by May, Klinsky's education-related responsibilities were too much for Forstmann Little's own traditional administrative staff to handle, so he called a temporary employment agency for emergency secretarial help. The agency's owner knew of a feisty Englishwoman named Cheryl Bell whom she thought might be able to help him. "I know this isn't your thing," she told Bell, "but there's this really interesting man who needs an assistant and is a bit desperate." Bell, a skilled professional manager with a finance background, who had herself been an executive director of nonprofit organizations, was far overqualified to be anyone's secretary. Still, after some hesitation, she finally agreed to talk to Klinsky.

Bell was unimpressed with Klinsky's first job offer. "No, no, I don't want to do administrative stuff," she told him. Still, she was impressed with Klinsky. "He told me about his vision for the schools, and I thought, Here's this private equity guy abandoning everything and going completely out on a limb to do something with great societal benefits. I was blown away that this man was giving up the multizillion dollar thing to undertake opening up a charter school," she explains. "I finally gave in and said I would help out, but only temporarily."

As it turned out, Bell was wrong about the temp part. Two weeks later, after informing Klinsky that she was going on another job interview,

Klinsky offered her a permanent job to work as his chief administrative officer while simultaneously setting up Victory Schools. Bell hired on and wound up staying with Klinsky for four years. Another of her earlier observations, though, was right on target: "You are one really, really brave man," she had cautioned, foreseeing the difficulties ahead.

Simultaneously, Klinsky was building his education team. Because he wasn't a professional educator himself, Klinsky wanted someone with broad senior-level experience who knew the ins and outs of the New York City schools. Soon he hired John Elwell, another school leader from Sy Fliegel's earlier alternative school movement in East Harlem. Klinsky and Elwell knew each other from CEI, and the timing was perfect. Elwell had also recently retired from the New York City school system and was planning to set up his own organization, which would create new, high-quality public schools by replicating what worked in other successful schools. As it turned out, Elwell had a window of time open before his own effort launched, and he signed on to temporarily head up Victory's education team, while cautioning Klinsky to move slowly: "Schools need at least a year to get ready," Elwell advised. "If the state wants you to open this September, don't do it."

Elwell would be Victory's first official chief education officer, but Klinsky also wanted to hire top experts to train teachers in each part of the curriculum. Searching websites, he discovered that one of the nation's most respected Direct Instruction consultants, Jane Feinberg, had been successfully implementing DI in other schools for more than a decade and lived in New York state. So, out of the blue, he called her, telling her he intended to use her beloved DI for (he hoped) New York's first charter school. Soon he was driving out to the Long Island town of Valley Stream to retain her and her daughter Kendra Feinberg as his first DI experts.

By then, Klinsky was networking with everyone he could think of. He began with a nearly blank sheet of paper that listed the names and phone numbers of Sy Fliegel and Harvey Newman and then kept adding more people's names as he met them. Eventually, his spreadsheet grew to be many pages long. He followed up on every lead. Without the strength of the Forstmann Little brand behind him, he was now usually totally unknown to everyone he met, and he had to rely entirely on his own resourcefulness. Often, his introductions sounded more like something you'd expect from a door-to-door salesman than from one of the nation's top corporate acquirers. "Hi, I know you don't know me," he'd usually begin, "but I'm Steve Klinsky, and I'm opening a charter school . . ."

One evening, in what would turn out to be a serendipitous turn of events, he attended a seminar for prospective charter school founders at Columbia University's Teachers College. During a break in the program, he overheard a woman sitting in front of him mention some enticingly familiar words: "Core Knowledge." Klinsky already knew he wanted to use the content-rich program, so he tapped the woman on the shoulder and asked, "Did you say you like Core Knowledge?"

"Yes," she answered, turning away to continue her conversation with the man seated beside her.

When she finished, Klinsky tapped her on the shoulder again, this time opening up the conversation with the well-rehearsed lines ("I know you don't know me . . .") he had used so many times before. The woman, in turn, introduced herself. She was a longtime New York City educator named Laurie Brown, who coincidentally had also been a professional staff developer for Modern Red Schoolhouse, an educational organization that emphasizes rigorous academic standards for all students and a core curriculum, and she was a leader in the city's Core Knowledge movement. After a brief conversation, they agreed to talk again. Within days, they met in the lobby of the World Financial Center near Brown's Battery Park home. "He could have been making it all up," Brown would later recall. "But the minute I saw him face-to-face I knew without a shadow of a doubt that he wanted something better for the kids. I believe all children can reach high standards, regardless of their zip codes. He felt that way, too, and it was almost as if I was looking into a mirror as we were talking about our commitment to the children."

Brown had every intention of opening a charter school herself, but her instincts told her to follow Steve's lead. "It was like all of the pieces were falling into place," she recalled. "Steve was like the Pied Piper, and he said that night he wanted me to come work with him." She did, and Victory had itself a Core Knowledge expert, making Laurie Brown perhaps the first traditional educator to dedicate her career full-time to the New York charter school movement.

Then came the hard part.

If there was one piece of the charter school puzzle that could stop a faint-hearted education reformer in his tracks, it was the real estate maze. Klinsky's initial reaction was that he should look for a community outside of New York City because school-ready real estate in the city was expensive and difficult to find, and school funding per child was *lower* in the city than in some of the surrounding areas, where real estate costs were less pricey. Also, in high-profile New York City, political opposition and media scrutiny would most likely be intense. So as he looked for alternatives, Klinsky studied test scores in the surrounding counties, trying to find a town where a charter school could benefit students and still meet its budget.

For the first few months, Klinsky scoured the neighborhoods alone, looking for a school site in a community with strong local support and leaders to partner with. As his network of relationships grew, one person led to another until finally he was introduced to Marshall Mitchell, a young political strategist and preacher who, as one of the leaders of Parents for School Choice, had mobilized inner-city parents in their push to get the charter law passed. Klinsky and Mitchell met for breakfast one morning at the Marriott Hotel in Brooklyn. Right away, they hit it off.

The two men's interests meshed perfectly. Now that the state had a charter law, Mitchell's next mission was to help get a pioneering school off the ground. Soon he and Klinsky were traveling together in Klinsky's SUV, Klinsky at the wheel with two-year-old Cavan's car seat in the back. Their journey through the inner cities of New York State took them to bodegas, social work offices, and ministries. To a casual observer, the forty-three-year-old, business-suited Klinsky and the twenty-nine-year-old black theologian might have appeared to be a mismatched pair. But over time and over many a conversation about philosophy and theology, they realized that they had more in common than just a mission. They also shared many of the same values, and a genuine friendship between them blossomed. Walking on some difficult streets, Klinsky learned that, as a boy, Mitchell had been trained by his mother to never run when a policeman was nearby; she feared he might be mistaken for a criminal and shot. Mitchell taught Klinsky the substance of some of the most inspirational Christian sermons and homilies he knew. Klinsky also learned that one of Mitchell's great-grandfathers was Jewish and that Mitchell's father was an African American Baptist minister who read and spoke Hebrew and had helped build a kibbutz in Israel. Before long, Klinsky realized that Mitchell was almost as closely connected to the Jewish tradition as he was! And for Steve, the diverse, sincere people and the religious and humanist lessons he was experiencing in his travels on behalf of the education reform movement kept coming together as one unified whole.

The more days they spent traveling together, the more Klinsky and Mitchell grew to respect each other. When New York City parents held a street rally for charter schools, Mitchell and other supporters gathered to paint their pro-charter school signs in Steve and Maureen Klinsky's apartment living room. And on days of good luck and success, Mitchell brought over a six-pack of his newest discovery from Philadelphia—Victory-brand beer—to toast the occasion.

As they crisscrossed one blighted area after another, Mitchell and Klinsky looked at underutilized college campuses, abandoned parochial school buildings, closed-down discotheques, and any other real estate that could possibly be transformed into a schoolhouse on short notice. They enlisted support from just about anybody willing to listen. Most community leaders they met with were welcoming. They sincerely wanted good schools for their children. Others, though, were not so noble. Sitting in one neighborhood kingpin's office, Klinsky explained that he wanted to help open a high-quality school in the community. He talked about how great it would be for the neighborhood and the children. That's not, though, what the high-profile community "leader" had in mind. "But when do I get *my* money?" he demanded in a gruff voice without flinching. "Never," Klinsky said. "You get a great school for the kids. You get jobs for the local people. But you will *never* get any money."

Along with Mitchell, Klinsky also began spending time in the black churches that often served as the most positive force in many minority neighborhoods. These included the Greater Allen African Methodist

Episcopal Cathedral in Queens, led by Rev. Floyd Flake, who—as a for-mer US congressman—was one of the most important African American leaders and Democrats in the city and one of the most consistent voices for grassroots community economic growth and interracial peace. Local Queens community leaders, including Flake and other top-ranking local African American Democrats, would help start Queens' first charter school—the Merrick Children's Academy—with Victory's technical sup-port and start-up funds a year later.

Later, on a more somber day, Klinsky's respect for Mitchell would also lead him to another church, the one in Philadelphia where Mitchell's father, Rev. Frank Mitchell, had served as senior pastor for many years. Funeral eulogies were underway on that day in February 2000 for the senior Mitchell, who had been known as a "minister's minister" and as a teacher and mentor to many of the most influential black pastors of his day. Ten or so of some of the most highly regarded ministers in the nation had come back to Philadelphia from throughout the country to attend Rev. Mitchell's memorial. In one exceptionally eloquent, moving speech after another, they each took to the stage to remember and praise their teacher. Finally, Marshall Mitchell himself was called to the altar. As he addressed the packed church, he delivered a heartfelt speech that soared above all of the others. Klinsky listened to all the orations from the church balcony, where he sat among the mournful parishioners and congregants. But as his eyes wandered around the sanctuary, he spotted Hebrew letters and six-pointed stars in the stained glass windows and ceiling decor. He realized that Rev. Mitchell's church had once been a syn-agogue. Once again, Klinsky's experience was reinforcing his idea that the links between and among supposedly disparate people are strong and can be found everywhere, even in the search for a schoolhouse.

Earlier, in the spring of 1999, the application deadline had loomed closer. As Maureen's due date for their second child also grew closer, and as Klinsky and Marshall Mitchell scoured far-flung neighborhoods out-side of New York City, Klinsky kept his cell phone on and fretted that he'd be too far away to get back for the impending birth.

Klinsky's charter school model and application were shaping up, but he still hadn't found a school site, a community to support it, or a lead applicant. Marshall Mitchell had an idea—but it flew in the face of Klinsky's initial plans to steer clear of New York City. Mitchell mentioned a prominent Baptist preacher, whom he knew from years back, who was a charter school supporter. Maybe, just maybe, Mitchell suggested, this minister might be of some help. A half century earlier, Mitchell's father had preached one of his favorite sermons to a group of college students in Virginia. It was based on the New Testament scripture in which Jesus taught his disciples that the greatest and most important person is the one who does the most service for others. This was the same lesson Marshall Mitchell himself had taught to Klinsky on one of their many days together, and the message had moved Klinsky. More important, the elder Mitchell's words had been a clarion call to the ministry for one young student who, all those years later, was an influential, highly regarded pastor in Harlem and a mentor to Marshall Mitchell.

This minister's church had just finished building a sparkling, new multistory building in Harlem. Why not open the school, Mitchell asked, in the symbolic heart of black America—Harlem? Why not try to team up with the powerful preacher, a leading voice for charter school reform, an icon of the civil rights movement who had once worked alongside Dr. Martin Luther King? Why not go see Rev. Dr. Wyatt Tee Walker?

Ten days later, Klinsky and Mitchell would pay Walker a call.

5

Building a Community

Harlem was still wounded in early 1999. Rudolph Giuliani was mayor. Racial tensions were running high. On February 4 of that year—just weeks before Klinsky arrived to meet Dr. Wyatt Tee Walker—four plain-clothes New York City policemen had mistakenly killed an unarmed African immigrant, Amadou Diallo, in a hail of forty-one gunshots as he stood in the entrance of his apartment building in the Bronx. The controversial shooting was viewed by many as a tragic symbol of a much deeper racial injustice. Hundreds of civic leaders, including Walker and Marshall Mitchell, marched to police headquarters and had themselves arrested and jailed in sympathetic acts of civil disobedience.

The block on which Mitchell, Klinsky, and Walker met that day, 116th Street between Lenox and St. Nicholas Avenue, also had its own notorious history. During the 1960s and 1970s, the neighborhood had been the home base of drug kingpin Frank Lucas, who was later portrayed by actor Denzel Washington in the movie *American Gangster*. "A hundred sixteenth between Seventh and Eighth Avenue was mine," Lucas told writer Mark Jacobson twenty-five years later, according to Jacobson's book *American Gangster: And Other Tales of New York*. "It belonged to me. . . . I bought it. I ran it. I owned it." According to testimony quoted by Jacobson, when a group of US congressmen and local politicians toured the scene, drug dealers told them, "If you're not buying, get out of here."

By 1999, the neighborhood had improved substantially, thanks in large part to Rev. Walker's efforts. The drug trade was no longer visible, but the vicinity was still mainly a collection of old commercial buildings turned to churches or mosques, small bodegas, empty storefronts, and shops. There were almost no white faces anywhere.

Walker's name was quite familiar to Klinsky. Klinsky had studied the "Letter from Birmingham Jail" as a student of political philosophy at the University of Michigan, and he had read the Supreme Court case, *Walker v. City of Birmingham*, at Harvard Law. Klinsky knew of Walker's heroic struggles for civil rights, and that Walker was Chairman of Rev. Al Sharpton's National Action Network, so he recognized that Walker was near the epicenter of just about everything that was happening in Harlem. By this time, Klinsky had also spent substantial time visiting black churches, and he knew Walker's reputation among his fellow ministers: a brilliant man who was adept at sizing people up and who pulled no punches. Walker would know a pretender if he met one and would not be afraid to tell him so.

The Diallo shooting and the accompanying protests had raised the city's racial temperature. So while Klinsky approached the meeting that day with great respect for Walker's intelligence and abilities, he wondered how he—an outsider to Harlem in such a tense time—would be received. He wondered, too, how Walker would perceive him and what kind of person Walker himself would turn out to be. Meanwhile, Walker, for his part, had heard favorable reports about Klinsky from Mitchell. But he still wasn't sure he'd be able to work things out with this "Wall Street guy" just yet.

All in all, though, the lunch went well. The conversation was cordial, and afterward the three retreated to Walker's nearby office at Canaan Baptist Church of Christ. Right away, Klinsky had been impressed by Walker's elegance and his Sean Connery-like good looks. He was even more impressed by the lifetime of memories that filled Walker's cluttered office—tributes like a sixties-era national magazine cover that featured a photo of Walker and Dr. Martin Luther King Jr. and a headline that described Walker as King's key confidante. Looking around the office, Klinsky saw other keepsakes from Walker's many travels around the world, the loving references to his wife ("Lady Ann"), and the mementos showing his obvious passion for writing, photography, and music. Klinsky realized that, for all of Walker's struggles and willingness to fight for what he believed in, the minister was a man who embraced life's joys, rather than being consumed by bitterness or hate. That viewpoint meshed with Klinsky's own outlook, and this realization made him feel even more positive about Walker as a prospective partner.

Klinsky's hopes soared, though, when Walker led him and Mitchell out through the back of the church to the Center for Community Enrichment (CCE), a beautiful new building facing 115th Street. In his months-long search for a charter school site, both with Mitchell and alone, Klinsky thought he had just about seen it all. He had looked at shuttered discos long past their prime, boarded-up schools, dilapidated warehouses—anything that could possibly, or not so possibly, be turned into a school. Nothing had come close in quality to what Klinsky saw at Canaan that day. The church had just finished building the new community center, and almost as if it had been handed down from high, it was a gem. The sparkling, three-story Center for Community Enrichment had more than seventeen thousand square feet of usable space. Its clean, sun-streaked classrooms glistened. It had a commercial kitchen, an elevator, and modern fire alarms, and was already accessible for the physically challenged. In a magnificent, spacious assembly room, Embassy Hall, an entire school community could gather together. Whatever logistical concerns there might be about room configurations or about sharing the building with church congregants could wait. That could all be worked out later. "I thought, 'Wow. This place would be fantastic,'" Klinsky recalled. "It was like looking for that first house to buy for months and months. Finally, you see the right one. It has the garden and the fireplace, and you say, 'This is it.'" Needless to say, Klinsky was encouraged. With Mitchell on board and hopefully Walker too, "maybe," he wrote in his journal at the time, "we'll go far."

For his part, though, Rev. Walker needed to know more. The Center for Community Enrichment had been built under his watchful eye, a labor of love for him, his congregants, and his son, Wyatt T. Walker Jr., who had overseen its construction. Years earlier, when most everyone else looked behind Walker's church, all they saw was a forlorn parking lot strewn with abandoned, mostly stolen, cars. But Walker had a much grander vision. "I see a building edifice," he said one Sunday morning while gazing out an open door from his pulpit, "where we can continue our good works for the community." Back then, Walker knew the building would bene-fit the community, but he didn't yet know the exact specifics of how it would be used. His congregants weren't exactly sure either. But after years of watching and tithing from Canaan's committed congregants, Walker and Canaan's church members had accomplished a feat that all of Harlem could be proud of. When construction crews needed to clear the streets to deliver supplies or bring in equipment, even the neighborhood drug deal-ers had willingly shut down business to make room for Canaan's new proj-ect. So now that the building was finally finished, Walker wasn't about to turn it over to someone without checking him out first.

Walker had his own unique system for sizing people up. Everyone started out with one hundred points. Then, if there was a misstep here, an unkind word there, he started subtracting. One surefire way to lose a bunch of points was for a person to act one way in the wealthier circles of Manhattan and another way in a less affluent place like Harlem, to change their manners, as Walker would say, "when you cross 110th Street."

As it turned out, Klinsky had made a strong first impression on Walker that day, and soon the tables would be turned: Walker would pay Klinsky a visit.

One day, as Klinsky was wrapping up his work at Forstmann Little's luxurious headquarters in midtown Manhattan, a puzzled receptionist walked into his office. "There's a Dr. Walker here who wants to see you," she said. "There is?" Klinsky asked. Walker, who had been in midtown Manhattan for other business, had shown up unannounced. He wanted to talk about the school. And, Klinsky suspected, Walker also wanted to verify that Steve was truly what he seemed to be and that, if the reverend trusted in him, Klinsky wouldn't let the community and the school down.

And so it was that an earnest give-and-take began between church-goers who had sacrificed to pay for a community center, their pastor who desperately wanted good public schools, and an unlikely education reformer asking them all to have faith that together they could confound the skeptics and be a part of creating something great, exciting, and new.

As the discussions began in earnest, Walker enlisted Canaan's able business manager, Judith Price, to help oversee the process for the church. JP, as she was known, was highly organized and had both an intelligent managerial mind and a warm heart. She knew every detail of the new community center's operations and requirements, and soon she and Walker gave Klinsky long lists of questions, which he systematically answered in writing and in a series of face-to-face meetings. They wanted to know more about the school's curriculum, including the merits of Direct Instruction and Core Knowledge. Could Victory customize its curriculum to teach additional lessons about Harlem and African American history? (It could.) What role would the school's board of trustees play? What about staff and budget matters? Real estate issues were also in play. Could the school and Victory afford to fully reimburse the church for the use of the community building? And even though Canaan's congregants had sacrificed to build the center, New York's charter school law didn't allow any special consideration for the children or grandchildren of church members to attend the school. If any of the church's children were to attend, they would need to be picked by lottery, just like everyone else. So how on Earth could the congregation share their building with a school and still get to use it themselves?

With a new state charter law and Klinsky to work with, Walker's own longtime dream of founding a school now seemed practical. So the Harlem minister and the former Michigan public school kid teamed up and began to face the crush of a thousand details. Once everyone decided they could work together, the labors intensified. So did the marathon meetings with Walker, Mitchell, Price, and Klinsky huddling in Price's office at the community center, trying to resolve a long list of issues that seemed to grow longer by the day. No longer was Klinsky answering the application's questions in the abstract. Now that his vision had a schoolhouse and community, everyone was up against the real-life minutiae of building a school from scratch—and they had precious little time to do it.

Some issues were large and strategic; others were the endless and specific planning details that most people take for granted—the materials, the equipment, the furniture that all had to be in place on opening day. Someone had to start thinking about ordering pencils, pens, and bulletin boards. How would safety and security be maintained at the front door? Meanwhile, what about that bulky refrigerator that needed to be moved downstairs? On and on, the meetings went; and if everyone got lucky and the school was awarded a charter, there'd be even more work in store.

One of the application's key requirements was to prove that the proposed charter school had the support of the local community. This was not a simple test in 1999, when most New York parents had never seen or heard of a charter school. Mitchell took the lead here. Using the same kind of political fieldwork he had used to help get the charter law passed, he and a team of teenagers hit the city's neighborhood streets to explain the charter concept to Harlem's citizens, and they convinced hundreds of supporters to sign petitions. Meanwhile, Klinsky also continued reaching out to community leaders, asking them to join him on the proposed school's board, along with Price and Mitchell.

Soon the board took shape. The Brooklyn Bureau's staff, whom Klinsky knew through his work with the Gary Klinsky Children's Centers, introduced him to Melba Butler, the executive director of the Harlem Dowling–West Side Center for Children and Family Services, and she agreed to become a trustee. Klinsky also called on Harlem's city councilman Bill Perkins, and he too joined the board. Others signed on as well, including Charlie King, a leading Democrat and a member of the litigation department of a prestigious New York City law firm, where he also directed its pro bono program. So did attorney Peter Sloane, who was board chairman of the Heckscher Foundation for Children and who was interested in seeing the charter school concept in action. Under the school's proposed bylaws, the president of the school's Parent Teacher Association would become a board member as well, whenever that person was eventually chosen.

Along with this group, Walker also nominated Minnie Goka, a highly respected member of the Canaan congregation who had recently retired from her position as an assistant principal in the New York City system and was passionate about education, teachers, and students. Goka wouldn't hesitate to express honest criticism about any adult's performance when she felt criticism was due, but she would become the most loyal friend, supporter, and board leader any school could have. Eventually she would become the school's—and New York State's—longest serving trustee, chairperson of the board's academic committee from the school's inception, and a true pillar of its success.

The school also needed a formal applicant, and Walker and Price suggested Danielle Moss Lee, a highly capable woman who had grown up in Canaan's congregation. Moss Lee, a young wife and mother, held two master's degrees from Columbia University's prestigious Teachers College, and she had been admitted into its doctoral program. As an educational star in her own right, she symbolized the hopes and aspirations of all of the school's founders and what they hoped to accomplish. Soon she came aboard as a founding trustee and as the lead applicant for the charter application.

Walker also led the way with another choice: the proposed school's name. Walker had been personally involved in the struggle against apartheid in South Africa, and in 1994 when Nelson Mandela made his first trip to the United States as South Africa's president, his first public appearance took place at Canaan Baptist. Walker suggested that the school be named after Mandela's fellow political prisoner and friend, the former deputy president of the African National Congress, Walter Sisulu, and his wife. This marked an auspicious beginning, Klinsky thought; Martin Luther King's former chief of staff was proposing that the school be named after Mandela's close colleague. Everyone agreed with Walker's suggestion, and soon the Sisulu School was born.

Meanwhile, Klinsky and Mitchell were still scouting out other communities for a second, parallel school as a second "proof of concept" site for the charter school movement. They hoped that Victory could spread its operating costs to two sites and thus reduce its losses. Klinsky pored over state test scores and other performance data, trying to determine where schools most needed improving. When it came to academic need, the hamlet of Roosevelt on Long Island fairly jumped off the page.

The beleaguered Roosevelt school district was, to put it bluntly, an educational fiasco. A largely African American and low-income suburban district surrounded by more affluent suburbs, the Roosevelt school system had been failing for years. In 1995, less than 1 percent of Roosevelt's high school graduates earned a Regents diploma—which was more academically rigorous than the other option, the Local diploma—compared to 72 percent in the Jericho school district just a few miles away, and 76 percent in Garden City. Exasperated state education officials ousted Roosevelt's school board in 1996, making Roosevelt the first district in New York's history ever to be taken over by the state. Even so, in 1999, when Klinsky began studying test scores three years after the takeover, local academic achievement was still dismal.

Klinsky contacted Bruce Blakeman, who was then the presiding officer of the Nassau County Legislature, and Blakeman invited Klinsky out to his office to explain the charter school concept to a roomful of local community and political leaders. One of them, Robert Francis, had lived in Roosevelt for thirty years and was the commissioner of planning and economic development for the adjoining town of Hempstead as well as an advisor to the state panel appointed to oversee the Roosevelt school district. Soon Klinsky was meeting with him and other Roosevelt community leaders, hoping they would support a charter school and maybe even agree to serve on its board.

In the meantime, Klinsky and Mitchell were scouring the community block by block, building by building. Finally, they came upon a site in Roosevelt that seemed perfect: a building that had housed a thriving parochial school years before. The empty classrooms had the look of a once-bustling schoolhouse that had died before its time, and the local parish officials initially seemed eager to rent the space to the charter school. The rent would help the parish, Klinsky thought, and with a few repairs here and a little sprucing up there, the school, it seemed, could once again come alive with children.

As local support for the school came together, the board did too. Community leaders, including Francis, who was named the school's lead applicant for its charter application, joined the board. "The Roosevelt schools were not competitive with the surrounding schools," Francis explained. "So when we saw an opportunity that could provide a good education for the children, we jumped on it."

With a second Victory school underway, Klinsky was now working in Harlem, working in Roosevelt, and perfecting applications and school designs for both schools, all while still trying to balance the enormous undertaking with the business and family sides of his life. Most important, on April 22, 1999, the same day as Steve and Maureen's fourth wedding anniversary, he was at Maureen's side for the healthy birth of Kiera, the couple's second child and the first girl born into the Klinsky family in one hundred years. She would be joined by another boy, Owen, and another girl, Ella, in the years that followed.

Days later, Klinsky was back in Harlem, and the details of Sisulu's organizational structure were hammered out over the next few weeks. The school would be located in the Center for Community Enrichment building and would pay $16,000 in rent each month and $4,000 a month for utilities during its first year to allow the church to break even on its building costs. Klinsky, through Victory, would give Sisulu several hundred thousand dollars in advance so that the school could start buying textbooks, furniture, and supplies and could begin to hire and train its staff and teachers before the school doors opened.

The Sisulu School was a not-for-profit organization controlled by its local trustees, who would ultimately select the school director and teachers, and set policy according to the school design approved by the state in the charter school's application. The school could get the services it needed outside of the traditional school day (such as curriculum development, finance and accounting, payroll work, insurance, technology expertise, etc.) from a staff that Victory would hire for this purpose. Sisulu would pay a percentage of its revenue to Victory, which was much less than Victory's cost of providing the services. However, if Victory could share the costs of the staff with other charter schools besides Sisulu, its finances could improve.

As these issues were resolved, another threat raised its head: the risk that the Sisulu application would be rejected for violation of the constitutionally mandated separation of church and state. Charter schools are tax-funded public schools, not parochial or private schools. As public schools, they can rent space from a church, but they cannot be operated by a church or be under its control. Would opponents now argue that, because it was being housed in Canaan's community center and supported by Walker, the Sisulu School violated the US Constitution?

The SUNY trustees would soon be awarding the first charters. They did not want the movement stopped by constitutional law challenges, and, Klinsky learned, they were concerned about Sisulu's potential church-state issues. So, drawing on his own background in constitutional law, he contacted one of the nation's foremost pro bono lawyers on religious freedom and church-state issues, Seamus Hasson of the Becket Fund for Religious Liberty in Washington, DC. Seamus knew Klinsky from Klinsky's past support for religious freedom, and he came to New York to see him. Together, Klinsky and Hasson parsed through earlier court rulings to come up with ways to use the community center as a school while not violating church-state issues. According to the procedures they developed, foot traffic between the church and the school during the day would be prohibited, except in case of fire or safety emergency. In addition, Canaan congregants who used the building for meetings on some nights or on weekends would need to put away all of their materials by the beginning of the next school day. Likewise, Sisulu educators who shared some of the space would have to pack up and store their own materials each afternoon. There could be no crucifixes or religious symbolism on the walls, and the curriculum would be entirely secular. Even so, some political insiders warned Klinsky not to team up with a high-profile religious and community leader like Walker in media-obsessed Manhattan. That would be like waving a red flag in front of opposition groups, they warned. And, they further cautioned, if you try to open the state's first charter school, brace yourself for lawsuits.

Klinsky was unfazed. He had fought plenty of other battles in his life, and he never minded fighting them if he thought his position was the right one. "Wrong to tie up with a church group?" he later mused in a journal. "I'm leaning toward fighting alongside Martin Luther King's chief of staff, the strategist behind Birmingham." Besides, the former constitutional law student joked to himself, "My life's goal about being involved in a Supreme Court case may come true. I just thought I would be the lawyer, not the client."

Klinsky and Hasson knew that some of the most difficult issues would arise if Walker served on the school's board of trustees while also the senior pastor of Canaan. In the beginning, Klinsky had wanted Walker to serve on the board and Walker had wanted to, as well. Walker felt strongly that his role would not violate church-state issues. But if there was one lesson that Walker had learned from his years on the front lines, it was that sometimes in the interest of getting things done, you have to stay focused on the big picture. After so many years of schools failing his community's children, he had no interest in being the cause of a prolonged church-state clash that might derail the school and the entire New York movement. For the sake of the children, he let someone else fill his seat.

But Walker did bestow his blessing on the school in a way that only he could do. By then, he had heard back from his longtime friends, Walter Sisulu and his wife, Albertina. They had agreed that the charter school could be named in their honor, allowing it to serve as an educational symbol of the spirit and values that had driven the lives of Walter Sisulu, Nelson Mandela, Martin Luther King, Wyatt Tee Walker, and so many others.

So Klinsky pressed on. His team of Harvard MBAs hadn't graduated or arrived yet, so, in the spring of 1999, he continued to write and organize Victory's application almost entirely alone, just as he had since January of that year. Knowing how strict the reviewers would be, he drafted the application, redrafted it, and then rewrote it again. He labored away in the Forstmann Little side office while his former partners became more and more excited by the billion-dollar Internet and telecom opportunities they were beginning to pursue without him. At times, it felt to Klinsky like his colleagues were on the *Queen Mary* ocean liner steaming away to glory, while he had chosen to float foolishly alone in a little wooden boat, falling farther and farther behind.

Finally, on May 13, 1999, the day before applications were due, Klinsky placed his months of labor into two Federal Express envelopes: one for an elementary school in Harlem, the other for an elementary school in Roosevelt. Each application was almost one hundred pages, typed and bound, plus more than one hundred pages of additional exhibits and appendices, lists of board members, architectural drawings of the proposed schools, petitions from local parents, and other materials.

Meanwhile, the people charged with deciding who would open New York's first charter schools were moving ahead too.

Initially, many people expected that no charter schools would be authorized until September 2000, after more than a year of preparation. But others believed the delay would also give the law's opponents a year to challenge the charter movement before it began. So, early in 1999, SUNY's charter school committee had made a bold decision: if there were qualified applicants who were ready to launch charter schools and were willing to go through an expedited process, the SUNY trustees would approve their first schools to open just months later, in September 1999. "Every day that a student spends in an underperforming school is a school day that is lost," explained one of the cochairmen at the time, former New York secretary of state Randy Daniels. "I wanted to get them out of those schools as fast as possible." His former cochair, Edward F. Cox, then a senior partner at the law firm of Patterson Belknap Webb & Tyler, added: "The legislative background of the law was a difficult one. We knew we had to administer the law in a completely apolitical manner, according to the letter of the law, and we were helped by the fact that it was generally a well-designed law."

To evaluate the applicants, at the suggestion of SUNY vice chancellor Scott Steffey who headed the university's Charter Schools Institute, the committee brought in experts from around the country who were themselves highly experienced in charter school education, curriculum design, finances, and administration. Sixty applications were submitted to them, including the two that Klinsky had written. Working on weekends, the panels reviewed and ranked these proposals, eventually whittling the list down to fewer than twenty potentially viable options.

The SUNY trustees also decided early on to size up the faces behind the paperwork before giving anyone a charter. Cox and Daniels conducted site visits with the founders of the top applicants at their proposed schools. After interviewing Klinsky and his fellow board leaders, the two liked what they saw. "Klinsky understood organizations," Cox says. "He had the resources and the drive to make it work. . . . He had a business-person's sense to know when mistakes are made to change directions and to do what needs to be done." There were other qualities that Steffey also liked, and given the controversy surrounding the law, they took on added importance. "I was determined that we would fight the battles that needed to be fought. And I felt that if we had to go through trench war-fare, Steve wouldn't back down." Later, when Steffey presented Governor Pataki with a list of a half dozen schools, the governor asked which appli-cations Steffey would pick if, hypothetically, he could only pick two. "The two Klinskys," Steffey answered. "Why is that?" Pataki asked. "Because," Steffey replied, "he'll run through a brick wall to get them opened."

Later, when Steffey saw Governor Pataki at a black-tie event, the gov-ernor brought up charter schools again. "He put his hands on my shoul-ders and pulled me aside," Steffey says. "He said, 'You are the only person who can tell me, not any of the self-interested parties, which schools are most likely to succeed.' And I said, 'The Klinsky schools.'"

But there were other, less cordial moments too. Early on, Steffey recalls, opponents of the charter law, who were trying to thwart the state's charter movement, invited Steffey to be the main speaker at their annual conference. Steffey, who was involved in contract dispute negotiations with them and had confronted them on two major issues, was hesitant to attend. "I was a bit of a lightning rod figure," he says. Eventually, though, he agreed to speak. When he arrived, the room was packed with television and radio cameras, strategically placed to record the event. Steffey was given a flattering introduction, but, he recalls, the meeting came to a less welcoming conclusion when he was served with legal papers to place an injunction on authorizing the first schools—all while the cameras rolled. "Luckily, I had the presence of mind to rip the document in half, know-ing full well that the actual filing had to go to my legal group," he says. "I then dropped it on the floor and said, 'Thank you for the nice introduc-tion, but pieces of paper will not stop me from putting in place reform efforts to change New York's failing schools.'"

By then, the behind-the-scenes feedback on the Sisulu and Roosevelt applications was positive, and the schools appeared to have navigated adeptly through a host of obstacles and challenges. But just when it looked like Klinsky's charter efforts had made a breakthrough and were likely to be successful, he was hit by a new and potentially devastating threat. Indeed, it was the one type of threat that he most secretly feared. Doctors wanted Klinsky's son, barely two years old and inexplicably under the weather, to be tested for cystic fibrosis. It was just a test, doctors said, but Klinsky's concerns rose.

So, at almost the exact moment that the SUNY trustees were making their final decisions, Klinsky was at a cystic fibrosis clinic in Greenwich Village. On a warm spring day, his young son was bundled in heavy sweaters as Klinsky walked and ran the toddler around the block until the boy worked up enough perspiration for the cystic fibrosis sweat test. Klinsky, who tried to make it a policy to never pray for favors, was praying now.

When the results came back, the Klinskys learned their child was fine. And as it turned out, Sisulu and Roosevelt would be too.

On June 15, 1999, as a swarm of media gathered in midtown Manhattan, the SUNY trustees announced their selections. They had approved eight schools to be the state's first charter schools, and Klinsky was the only person to be involved with two of them. The Sisulu Children's Academy would be one of three schools approved to open that year, in the fall of 1999. The Roosevelt Children's Academy was one of five approved to open the second year, in September 2000.

The launch of the charter movement that day was front-page news in the *New York Times*, where Governor Pataki proclaimed it to be "the single greatest improvement in education in state history." Meanwhile, an article in *Newsday* called the arrival of the charter schools "A New Course" and a "historic" breakthrough. "A charter school in Roosevelt won't serve every child," one of *Newsday*'s editorials concluded. "But if it can succeed where public schools have failed, so be it."

As the SUNY press conference wound down and congratulations flowed, Harvey Newman turned to Ed Cox and offered what he thought might be some helpful advice. As it turned out, Cox had been saying the same thing, and he gathered up his fellow trustees so they could hear the message again—this time from the respected, longtime educator.

Approving a charter school is the easy part, Newman warned: "Running the schools will be infinitely more difficult, so now comes the hard part."

So it was back to the charter school crunch full force as Klinsky, still waiting for his skeleton staff to arrive, started down what would be perhaps the most difficult phase. It hadn't been feasible for Sisulu's founders to advertise for a principal or teachers, or to recruit students, before the school officially had a charter. So it was already mid-June 1999, and in just twelve short weeks Klinsky, Walker, Mitchell, Price, and Sisulu's board would need to find a principal, hire teachers, conduct professional development, recruit parents and students, install classrooms, buy supplies and furniture, arrange bus transportation, health facilities, safety systems, computers, food services, and much, much more.

The Sisulu community would have to come together quickly to perform miracles, all under the harsh glare of the charter movement's opponents and the skeptical New York City media.

If New York's first charter school stumbled, everyone would be there to watch it fall.

6

Building a School

July of 1999 was brutal. New York City wilted in the grips of a punishing heat wave. Crippling blackouts left tens of thousands of people without power, and electrical brownouts irritated millions more. As the lights flickered on and off across the city one night that summer, Steve Klinsky and Marshall Mitchell were feeling the heat, and not just from the evening temperature.

Over the summer, the two had set up a series of open houses in Sisulu's lower-level meeting room, known as Embassy Hall. They were attempting to convince hundreds of parents to entrust their children to a new kind of school that most had never heard of. By then, the Center for Community Enrichment glistened like a new home, waiting for children to arrive. It wasn't perfect, though. The schoolhouse-to-be didn't have a separate gymnasium or stand-alone library. It didn't have a staff of teachers yet either. Nor did it have a track record. But on those scorching summer evenings, parents ventured in and out, all with the same burning question in mind: Should we buy into a reform movement that offers hope—but no proven track record in New York?

Folding metal chairs were set up in rows across the bare room, and Judith Price and Rebecca King of Canaan Baptist made sure a refreshment table was well stocked along the side wall. Often, Mrs. King's own grandson, seven-year-old Mzuri King, would come with his grandmother, also helping to set up refreshments, patiently hearing the presentation again and again, and once even figuring out how to get the video system to operate. As the parents listened, Klinsky and Mitchell stood in front of the room and took turns speaking about their vision of what great schools are and why they believed this school had a chance to become one of them. They explained that Sisulu's students would wear uniforms and benefit from a longer school day. They also described the school's three-pronged curriculum of Direct Instruction, Core Knowledge, and Thematic Learning, explaining the logic for each and discussing their unique approach to blending the three instructional programs. Klinsky and Mitchell were enthusiastic. But as they spoke, the two made something else clear. They couldn't—and wouldn't—promise too much.

There wasn't enough money or physical space, at least in the beginning, to provide state-of-the-art technology, or arts or sports programs. As a new venture, they warned, the school would have many bumps and difficult challenges along the way. What Klinsky and Mitchell did promise, though, struck a chord with many parents: Sisulu would focus on academics, and whenever problems arose, everyone would work together to make sure that the children succeeded. Students would be taught to read at high levels. They would be taught to excel at math and develop high-level, critical thinking skills. Perhaps most important, they would experience something that was in short supply in many nearby public schools in those days: whatever problems the children had, wherever their talents took them, educators working to build brighter futures for them would respect and value them all.

Like their children, the parents had traveled different pathways to arrive at that moment. Some were college educated and highly successful. Others had never finished high school. Their concerns ran the gamut too. Some wanted to know about class sizes, technology instruction, and programs for academically advanced children. Others asked about the free lunch program, after-school care, and special education for those who struggled. One parent, whose son attended a nearby public school, made a request that was both humble and startling for what it revealed. She desperately wanted a school with enough textbooks, she told a reporter for the *New York Post*, so that her son's assignments wouldn't have to be photocopied. That way, he could have homework even when the copy machine broke down.

Everyone had their own reasons for being there that night, but they all had one thing in common: an unflinching desire to give their children the best education available—even if they hadn't had it for themselves.

As the open houses concluded and everyone stepped back out into the unbearably hot nights, no one knew for sure which of these parents or children they'd ever see again. Some parents left empty-handed, still not convinced that what they heard that night was any different than what they'd heard so many times before—grandiose ideas today, broken promises tomorrow. Others, though, picked up applications. "I'm just looking for something more challenging," one parent explained in a July 9, 1999, article in the *New York Post*. "It's a new school—a fresh start," said another. Some, already sold on charter schools, were hoping against hope that their children would win the entrance lottery and get into the school. Even though no one wanted to say it, no one knew for sure that there would be enough takers to need a student lottery. And if there was a lottery, who'd end up getting picked to go to Sisulu?

It had taken a full-throttle effort to reach this point. In recent weeks, community leaders and volunteers had been talking up the new school on the block; and true to form, Mitchell was back at work, recruiting a schoolhouse full of students on short notice. Throughout the summer, Mitchell sent teams of young people out into the community, where they stood on street corners, handing out thousands of handbills announcing Sisulu's arrival. Mitchell took to the streets himself. He hopped on subways, knocked on apartment doors, and visited nearby housing projects to spread the word. He set up milk crates and played dominoes on the street corners, skillfully redirecting the conversation to charter schools whenever he could. On some days, he even resorted to playing poker on the streets of Harlem, betting that he could convince his newfound card-playing pals to send their children, grandchildren, nieces, and nephews to a brand new kind of school.

By then Klinsky had taken on another unfamiliar role. A low-key and private person by nature, he decided to be a public face for charter schools, at least temporarily. Klinsky didn't want the reform effort to be discredited by false stereotypes before it had a full chance to begin. So he temporarily took on an uncharacteristically high-profile role to challenge the misconceptions about charter schools and to explain the reform effort statewide. He gave interviews to wide-ranging national newspapers and other publications, including the *New York Times*, the *New York Post*, the *New York Daily News*, and *Newsday*. He made the case for the new type of public schools on national television and radio broadcasts, including Fox News, WNBC, public radio, and C-SPAN. Even more audaciously, he pledged that the nascent Harlem charter school would beat local test scores, ushering in the kind of achievement some communities hadn't seen for decades.

As Sisulu's fortunes rose, however, Klinsky's own position in the world seemed to be heading down fast—perhaps permanently. On July 1, he left Forstmann Little forever. Filling a cardboard box with family photographs and a few personal papers, he and Cheryl Bell (formerly his temp secretary and now his new chief administrative officer) set off to walk to Victory's founding headquarters, two drab rooms on a floor of rent-an-office-by-the-month spaces in a nearby building. Another education reform–minded Harvard MBA, Josh Solomon, who also sought to help the charter experiment, joined them and helped carry the box down Fifth Avenue. Their journey was only from Fifty-Ninth Street to Fifty-Second, but the threesome might as well have been heading off to another planet. Klinsky was walking away from his status as a senior-level partner at one of the most successful financial firms in the world, leaving behind Gulfstream jets, Sikorsky helicopters, private chefs, drivers, and celebrity Aspen weekends, all for hard work in Harlem and Roosevelt, zero pay, and the need to start again. "Here was Steve walking away from his big-time investment job to this miserable temporary rented office," Bell recalls. "It was a cathartic event," she says, "very symbolic."

There were no friendly faces to welcome Klinsky and Bell at Fifty-Second Street, just a small room with a bare metal desk, a swivel chair, and a file cabinet for Klinsky, and another just like it down the hallway for Bell. Klinsky unpacked his family photographs, proudly propped them up where they would always be in his view, and got back to his list of tasks.

Klinsky and Bell's new abode was itself a symbol of American capitalism in that go-go Internet year. Bare individual rooms filled the entire floor of a large Midtown office building, lining a long hallway that wrapped around the central elevator bank. It seemed that each office contained a small-time entrepreneur dreaming of his future rise, suffering from a recent fall, or remaining stuck in a perpetual rut. The floor had one conference room, and tenants could rent it by the hour for a hefty fee in order to appear presentable when potential clients visited. Fax and phone services were available through the landlord, also at a high price. To Klinsky, it seemed that just when a tenant had settled in long enough to print up business cards and make it difficult to move again, the already-high monthly rent would be raised. As time went on, Klinsky came to think of the entire setup as the equivalent of the Appalachian company store brought into the Internet age.

Years later, Klinsky was asked by at least one skeptical person why he didn't seek a more luxurious traditional office space. He did in fact move his team into regular offices within a year; but at that moment in time, in the early summer of 1999, his focus was elsewhere. He was consumed with setting up the schools and establishing the next phase of his life. His staff and future firm didn't yet exist as much more than a vision. The rent-an-office was simple and available, like a hotel or motel room for a busy man to live and work in until there was time to think about a truly permanent home.

As Klinsky and Bell settled in, they found that their new neighbors were colorful in their own ways. In one room, an irascible older stockbroker worked with a frowzy secretary invariably sitting by his side. The broker kept his office door open and could regularly be heard shouting obscenities at an unknown foe via his telephone. "I'm gonna sue you! I'm gonna sue you!" he would scream before slamming down the receiver, his conversation reverberating down the hallway. A lone pharmaceutical salesman, apparently abandoned by his overseas home office, roamed the hallway late at night with his hands alongside his frantic face, looking like a living, silent version of Edvard Munch's *The Scream*.

Before long, Emily Lawson and Erik Heyer arrived, and Klinsky found another disconnected room on the hall for the two new MBAs to share.

Their office had a window, but that just meant their bleak, closet-sized interior room had an opening that looked into *another* gray space, whose only inhabitant was a pathetic-looking, human-sized artificial potted plant. "We had to carefully maneuver in our seats," Heyer later reminisced with fondness. "Otherwise, we would be running into each other." Eventually, two more administrators—Trish Belfiore and Deborah Cox—arrived and were shoehorned into Victory's three-office headquarters as well. Together, the growing team divvied up Klinsky's ever-growing list of assignments.

A few weeks earlier, on Bell's first day on the job, Klinsky had handed her a list of ninety-seven jobs excerpted from the handwritten to-do lists on one of his ubiquitous yellow legal pads. Bell would need to set up Victory's central office, which, among other things, meant setting up the entire financial structure of both Victory and Sisulu, staffing the office, creating administrative and accounting systems, figuring out the technology infrastructure, and setting up health benefits, insurance, and pension plans. In July, when Lawson arrived, she was given a different, equally long list under the heading, "Open Sisulu School Successfully on September 8." She helped recruit staff and students, lined up vendors for food and other services, and worked on the logistics of furnishing the building and setting up transportation. Then when Heyer reported for work in August, he took on some of the workload and began putting together applications and working on real estate, financial, and budget issues.

As they worked together, Klinsky's admiration continued to grow for the people who had joined him on his quest. Emily, Erik, Cheryl, Deborah, and Trish excelled in their own spheres; and educators and community leaders like Wyatt Tee Walker, Laurie Brown, Marshall Mitchell, Judith Price, Minnie Goka, Sy Fliegel, Harvey Newman, and the Sisulu trustees were among the most exceptional people Klinsky had ever met. The importance and newness of the charter school ideal, he realized, attracted people who were both kind and smart. He was proud to be associated with them, and in general he considered them to be more fundamentally spiritual and noble than he was. In most cases they were dedicating their entire careers to helping others, while he was planning to dedicate just a part of his life to the schools before reviving his traditional career.

Events at the school were moving rapidly, demanding everyone's full attention. Sisulu's board of trustees had organized, and Mitchell was chosen to be its first board chair. Klinsky served as an ex officio founding board member of both the Sisulu and Roosevelt charter schools, while Walker supported the effort from alongside. The Sisulu board, in turn, set up committees for academics, business, and finance, appointing trustees to each committee who were knowledgeable in those areas. Their list of tasks was long, but first things came first: the board's most pressing responsibility was to find Sisulu a principal.

A selection committee was created, whose original members included Mitchell, Goka, Klinsky, and several other board members. Working with Victory and the Center for Educational Innovation, the committee quickly began to identify and interview good candidates. Among them was an idealistic educator named Berthe Faustin. A longtime New York City educator, Faustin was the assistant principal of PS 189, a bilingual school for kindergarten through eighth grade in the Crown Heights section of Brooklyn. Hers was a gem of a school, where many children came in speaking very little English, but left as eighth graders who spoke the language fluently and were accomplished learners. Twelve hundred students were enrolled at PS 189, but somehow the school's staff managed to nurture them. Every year, though, when Faustin sent another class of eighth graders off to high school, she worried about what would happen to them next.

At her interview, Faustin thought about how rewarding it would be to teach at a smaller school like Sisulu, which was set to start with fewer than 250 children. And if the school ever grew to a K–12 model, as some trustees and parents hoped it would, it would be wonderful to teach students for all thirteen years before sending most of them off to college. What appealed to her most, though, was the raw excitement of the educational mission she saw that day. "We all shared the same vision and goals for the school, and the energy was really, really impressive," Faustin said. "I saw the school as a way to do good for the children. I was very excited, and I started to dream about what would happen there." Just as she had hoped, Faustin was hired as Sisulu's first principal.

But there were problems. Applications were only trickling in. By mid-July, fewer than a hundred had been turned in. "It is not the overwhelming demand we had hoped for," Klinsky wrote in his notes at the time.

Then tensions in the public arena flared. One of the most serious challenges had surfaced just days after the SUNY trustees had approved the first charters: a group of legislators and education officials claimed that the SUNY vote violated the state's new charter law.

"CHARTER VOTE IS ASSAILED AS ILLEGAL," a *New York Times* headline blared as a vitriolic back-and-forth took place that threatened to stop the state's first three charter schools, including Sisulu, in their tracks. The group claimed that the SUNY trustees hadn't followed a requirement in the charter law because they hadn't sought input from local school districts and communities before granting the charters. Some of the most outspoken criticism came from state assemblyman Steven Sanders, who chaired the state assembly's Education Committee and had voted in favor of the law.

Claiming, according to the June 20, 1999, article, that the charters' approval had been marked by troubling secrecy, Sanders was also quoted as saying: "No one is suggesting that these schools ought not at some point be allowed to open up. . . . But it is now clearly precipitous for that to happen this fall."

Two weeks later, as the rhetoric intensified, a *New York Post* article carrying the headline "LEGAL THREAT HANGS OVER HARLEM CHARTER SCHOOLS" quoted Sanders as saying that if the law were to be followed "there's no way a charter school can be opened up in September. . . . If they don't do this the right way, they'll never open up."

Klinsky publicly defended the school in that same article. "Our school will absolutely open this September," he said. "No technical challenge now can keep the children and parents of New York City from getting the better educational choices they clearly want."

SUNY officials responded to the approval process challenges by saying it wasn't too late for public comment, according to the *New York Times* article, and that they hadn't violated the law. Describing the fracas as "nothing more than a red herring," Charles Deister, a spokesman for Governor Pataki, told the *New York Times* that summer: "Unfortunately, there are always going to be defenders of the status quo who oppose innovative ideas in education."

Just to be on the safe side, though, the SUNY trustees voted again to approve the same charters, even though they claimed they weren't required to do so. No subsequent legal action followed, and the schools did open that fall.

Years later, Sanders declared in a May 13, 2010, essay published in the *New York Daily News* that the "jury has returned and the verdict is clear: Charter schools, and the energy and innovation that accompanies them, have overwhelmingly been a great success."

In a 2013 interview for this book, Sanders explained that he was never opposed to the concept of charter schools and that, if the schools are properly constructed, school choice is beneficial. But he still maintains that the first charter schools were rushed. "I felt there was not sufficient community input, as the law envisioned," he says. "I'm always very zealous of protecting the legislative process because when a law is passed, there's a process that needs to be adhered to.

"I felt strongly that prematurely opening the first schools was not consistent with the law. If it wasn't technically illegal, it wasn't respectful of the law," he continues. "From my vantage point it always seemed to me that they were pushed too fast. History bore out my concerns that they were all being rushed. Just witness the litany of problems that occurred."

During the summer of 1999, Marshall Mitchell grew concerned about another potential threat as well. With strong constituencies lined up in favor of Sisulu, there was never any doubt in his mind that the school would open. He worried, though, that charter school opponents would try to sabotage the school by interfering with the required inspection and licensing processes, forcing Sisulu to open a few weeks late. So on his own initiative, he reached out to the power brokers and community leaders he knew, invoking Dr. Walker's name. One such conversation, Mitchell recalls, ended like this: "Mitch," the political leader said, leaning back in his chair, "you've got my support. Harlem needs good schools, and this school needs to open."

By August, the city's heat wave was breaking, and over at the Center for Community Enrichment, excitement was building. The school community and Canaan had worked feverishly to get the building ready, and by late summer, things were finally coming together. Boxes were arriving with gleaming art supplies, never-before-used textbooks, and science equipment, all paid for by Klinsky's advance. Meanwhile, Walker arranged for friends to donate furniture from their upstate school, which was closing. At the same time, the team worked to find enough classroom space in their nontraditional school building and to make accommodations so that the building could also be used by the church during nonschool hours.

Sisulu's teaching staff had come together too—sometimes in utterly unexpected ways. Consider, if you will, Michelle Haynes. She was the young Harlem girl who years earlier had been a stellar student until her insatiable interest in learning was nearly snuffed out by years of uninspired traditional public schooling. She was the child whose mother, Madeline Haynes, had enrolled her in a different school every time she found out that another learning community was doing something better. Michelle was now a promising college student, and when her mother read about Sisulu in the newspaper, she suggested that Michelle investigate it. One day that summer, Haynes walked over to the school, and she was intrigued by what she saw. "I liked the idea that a new school was opening, and I could start out fresh right from the very beginning," she explains. "I wasn't sure what a charter school was, but it really appealed to me." Sisulu's staff saw something special in her too. They hired Haynes as one of the school's first teacher's assistants. In time, she would come to represent the very best of Sisulu.

Somehow, in a way no one completely understood, all of these small stories added up to a big one. All of the hard work had paid off; Harlem had bought into the Sisulu promise. By the end of July, after an initially slow start, hundreds of Harlem parents had signed their children up for one of the school's slots. Sisulu was going to have a schoolhouse full of children. And with many more applicants than the school could accommodate, it would need to hold a student lottery. Who would be picked? Who would be sent away? Those answers would come by luck and by chance.

The parents who gathered for the lottery on the evening of August 2, 1999, had about as many reasons for gambling on charter schools as there were children applying. Some had children already on their way to becoming academic superstars, and they needed a school where they could excel. Sisulu's flexible instructional program would suit them well, some of those parents thought, because students could work at their own pace, even if it meant studying with children in older grades for part of the day. Other families had children who needed a gentle push to reach their potential. And parents of children with special needs were told that Sisulu would welcome such students and would seek to mainstream them as much as possible with the general population, rather than warehousing them in special education settings. They saw in Sisulu a school that promised to welcome all children in an equally warm and inclusive way.

But, almost to a person, there was another reason motivating these inner-city parents to rally around charter schools: they had all but given up on traditional public schools. Many had attended neighborhood public schools themselves, or they were the parents of other children who had. The neighborhood buzz, backed by decades of hard data and experience, was that too many nearby traditional public schools weren't working.

Padora Vincent, a Harlem mother and lifelong resident of New York City, was among the parents who knew New York City's schools inside out. As a child, she had attended public schools in the Bronx and felt that students were poorly educated there. "Some teachers tried to teach, and their students learned," she recalled. "But others were just there to get a paycheck." Vincent now worked as a school aide in the city public school system, and she knew that she wanted a disciplined school for her son, Traiquan Payne, who was finishing up preschool. "I didn't want to put him in a regular public school," she said. "I wanted a different environment."

One day, a friend told her that a new school was coming to the neighborhood. "I heard talk about how the charter schools were going to really teach kids how to read and write," she said, "and I wanted him there." At the time, Traiquan was a shy, sensitive boy, but already he was showing signs of unusual artistic promise. Even as a toddler, he was drawing, and his artwork was exceptional for a young child. Clearly, Traiquan had a creative spark. It would be great, his mother thought, if she could find a school that would ignite it.

Gladys Lamb was another hopeful parent, a young Harlem mother who had experienced firsthand both the good and bad sides of Harlem's schools. Twenty years earlier, as an inquisitive, bright kindergartner, she had enrolled in an elementary school a few blocks away. Typical of the financially strapped schools, hers was short on teaching supplies, but it was a disciplined school, and in fifth grade she was placed in a rigorous class for high-achieving students. Her no-nonsense teacher expected his students to excel, and he wasn't afraid to tackle new challenges, like teaching them German. Most important, though, he instilled in his students a love of learning.

In junior high school, Lamb was placed into another top academic class, an oasis of learning in a school where many of the other classes were chaotic. But the following year, Lamb did something that caught almost everyone by surprise: she quit going to school. "I was smart," she explained, "but I forgot about being smart."

Eventually, she returned, but she had lost her spot in the top class and lost access to the disciplined classroom and high expectations that came with it. She fought back, though. She later transferred to another school, and by tenth grade she was enrolled in the city's business enterprise high school for students interested in business careers. One day, she ran into a guidance counselor in the hallway who told her, "I don't think this is a good school for you. You don't take school seriously, and no one else takes you seriously either."

Right then and there, Lamb decided she would prove the guidance counselor wrong. And she did. At her graduation ceremonies in June 1994, she waited while the teachers handed out that year's academic awards to her classmates. "The math teacher started talking about this great student who is so diligent and who works so hard. The teacher was saying she is so focused, and she is this and that. Then he called out the name, 'Gladys Lamb.' I couldn't believe it." The accolade, a math award, was the first of six she won that day.

By the summer of 1999, Lamb had a preschooler named Mylaecha Aska. Mylaecha had blossomed at her private preschool, and Lamb was

Nelson Mandela (left) and Walter Sisulu (right) in Robben Island prison, South Africa. SOURCE/CREDIT: EXPRESS NEWSPAPERS VIA AP IMAGES

Dr. Wyatt Tee Walker (standing center) with Dr. Martin Luther King Jr. in Birmingham, Alabama, 1963. SOURCE/CREDIT: ERNST HAAS / ERNST HAAS COLLECTION / GETTY IMAGES

Dr. Wyatt Tee Walker (left) with Dr. Martin Luther King Jr. at Canaan Church, Harlem, 1968. CREDIT: BETTMAN/CORBIS IMAGES

Walter Sisulu (left) and Dr. Wyatt Tee Walker (right) at ANC headquarters, South Africa. SOURCE/CREDIT: COURTESY OF DR. WYATT TEE WALKER ARCHIVES

Teacher Kathleen Sherry (left) with her daughter Maureen (right).

PHOTOGRAPHER: OWEN KLINSKY

Sy Fliegel (left) and Harvey Newman (right).

PHOTOGRAPHER: CRISTIAN SORIANO

Dr. Wyatt Tee Walker preaching to a stadium of thousands, Japan, 1991.

PHOTOGRAPHER: WYATT TEE WALKER JR. SOURCE/CREDIT: COURTESY OF DR. WYATT TEE WALKER ARCHIVES

Principal and former teacher Michelle Haynes.

Gary Klinsky (left) with Steve Klinsky (center) and their mother, Constance, and brother Richard around the time when Gary was helping to teach Steve to read.

Ed Cox (left) and Scott Steffey (right) with Steve Klinsky (center) at Sisulu-Walker on opening day, September 8, 1999. PHOTOGRAPHER: CHERYL BELL

Sisulu opening day: September 8, 1999. Charlie King (left), Marshall Mitchell (center), and Steve Klinsky (right). PHOTOGRAPHER: CHERYL BELL

Steve Klinsky (left) and Marshall Mitchell (right) welcome the first ever kindergartners to a New York charter school on September 8, 1999. PHOTOGRAPHER: CHERYL BELL

Some of school's early founders and supporters (left to right): Zvia Schoenberg, Peter Sloane, Melba Butler, John Faso, Charlie King, Marshall Mitchell, Steve Klinsky, Rev. Floyd Flake, (unidentified), Ed Cox, Scott Steffey, Bernard West. PHOTOGRAPHER: CHERYL BELL

The Victory team with Dr. Walker circa 2001: (left to right): James Stovall, Cheryl Bell, Erik Heyer, Melissa Jeria-Couvillion, Steve Klinsky, Dr. Wyatt Tee Walker, Dr. Margaret Harrington, Laurie Brown, Trish Belfiore-Molyneux.

PHOTOGRAPHER: CONRAD GLOOS

Dr. Wyatt Tee Walker (left) and Steve Klinsky (right), circa 2001.

PHOTOGRAPHER: CONRAD GLOOS

Tenth anniversary celebration cake for Sisulu-Walker, 2009.

PHOTOGRAPHER: JAMES STOVALL

Sisulu-Walker at the Center for
Community Enrichment building,
125 W. 115th Street, circa 2013.

PHOTOGRAPHER: DAVID STEWART BROWN

Sisulu-Walker student.

PHOTOGRAPHER: DAVID STEWART BROWN

active in its parent-teacher organization. But from what Lamb was hearing from her friends, many of the neighborhood schools weren't much better than they had been when Gladys was a child. In all of those years, Lamb hadn't forgotten the exhilaration that came from being a high-achieving student. Nor had she forgotten the frustrations of being derailed by peer pressure, low-performing schools, and even lower expectations. Those were frustrations she didn't want her daughter to face.

Lamb wasn't sure how she would afford a private school, but she was looking for options that summer, hoping that Mylaecha could get some kind of scholarship. Then tragedy struck. On June 16, 1999, her other daughter, a five-week-old infant named Tamar, died in her sleep of sudden infant death syndrome. Lamb was overwhelmed by grief. Still, she managed to attend one of Sisulu's open houses with Mitchell and Klinsky later that summer, still determined to find the right school for Mylaecha. She didn't know much about charter schools, but she liked what she had heard: Sisulu would focus on academics, and its class sizes would be manageable. Her instincts told her something else just as appealing, something especially important. "I sensed that the teachers would care about their students," Lamb says, "and expect every one of them to do their very best." Sisulu's teachers, she believed, would be more like the inspirational educators she'd had as an eager young student, and less like the guidance counselor in the hallway.

As the date for the lottery approached, board chair Mitchell felt strongly that the history-making lottery should mirror the importance of the moment and that, whatever the outcome, everyone should leave that night feeling the process had been fair. So he and a friend, Bernard West, picked up three gigantic, wire Bingo-style canisters in Brooklyn to use for the drawing, returning over the Williamsburg Bridge in the middle of rush-hour traffic. As some of the parents arrived, the two set up the equipment in plain sight in cavernous Embassy Hall, where that summer's open houses had been held. In time, Embassy Hall would become the physical heart of Sisulu, the gathering spot where assemblies were held, where students would study, sing, dance, and enrich each other's lives, and families would celebrate their children's milestones. Already, it had its own distinctive sense of place. Towering above the room, a ceiling-high ring of brilliantly colored African flags flew. Walker and his wife, Theresa Ann, had spearheaded the project, and at their insistence only those flags representing democratic countries were flown.

As the lottery began, a hush fell over Embassy Hall. Some families let out screams of joy when their children's names were announced. Others quietly embraced, brushing back tears. Still others, like Vincent, leapt into the air as if reaching for the heavens when the spinner spewed out her son's name.

Vincent, after being briefly caught up in the excitement, quickly turned her thoughts to someone else. The friend who had first told her about Sisulu now sat anxiously beside her, with no word yet about whether her own son would be chosen. The minutes seemed like hours until finally her friend's son's name was drawn. "They finally called out his name," Vincent said, "and then we all started jumping up and down together."

But not everyone left happy. At the end of the night, dozens of families whose children had not been chosen quietly filed out, disappointed to know that they probably would never set foot in Sisulu again. Some who had lost out fought back tears. Others unleashed them. It was a sad scene that no one relished, but just as state law required, the lottery had been above reproach. Sisulu's founders had taken great care to ensure that the lottery was fair. One child who wasn't chosen was a young girl everyone had just assumed would be a member of Sisulu's first class. She was the grandchild of someone very influential; but, true to form, her grandfather wasn't about to compromise the fairness of the lottery by pulling strings to get her in. She was the granddaughter of Rev. Dr. Wyatt Tee Walker.

As for Gladys Lamb, she hadn't attended the lottery, but received her own good news when she opened a letter telling her that Mylaecha had won a spot at Sisulu. It was a godsend, a glimmer of hope in an otherwise sorrowful summer. "When I read the letter I was so very, very happy," Lamb recalled. "I really felt that it was going to be good, and all I could think about was that Mylaecha finally had a school."

By late August, Sisulu's roster was set. All in all, 247 children in kindergarten through second grade were coming to Sisulu. A few days before opening day, Sisulu's staff gathered for an inspirational dinner at Sylvia's

Restaurant, the legendary soul food restaurant in the heart of Harlem. The restaurant was the perfect place for launching big dreams. Its owner, the late Sylvia Woods, was a self-made woman who had opened her first small, one-counter luncheonette in 1962 after borrowing money from her mother, who had scraped it together by mortgaging the family farm. By 1999, Sylvia's restaurant occupied almost an entire city block and attracted celebrities, sports stars, and famous diners, like President Bill Clinton and South African president Nelson Mandela.

The night was an emotional one. Meeting in a private room off to the side, Klinsky spoke of everyone's pride in the new staff, the importance of the school to the children and to the charter movement, and the additional meaning that the effort gave all of their lives. Many problems would arise along the way, he predicted, but everyone in the room that evening would work to overcome them. Principal Berthe Faustin spoke too, as did the teachers. Some of them were young. Others had been teaching for years. Some talked about how they already felt at home at Sisulu. Others said they were taking a gamble on charter schools because they sensed something very positive about them that was different from what they had experienced at traditional public schools. One teacher was especially poignant. "I've been praying on this," she said.

School, after all, was opening tomorrow.

7

Year One

As Laurie Brown headed to Sisulu on September 8, 1999, the first day of school, a very small incident told her a very big story.

Brown, Victory's curriculum director, was in a cab stopped at a traffic light in Manhattan rush-hour traffic when something caught her eye. Waiting for the light to change, Brown watched a frantic mother, grasping her young daughter's hand, dart across the crowded intersection just seconds before the light changed. The little girl was impeccably dressed in a blue-and-white school uniform. Her hair was flying. Obviously, the two were in a hurry to get to someplace important.

Within minutes after arriving at Sisulu eighteen blocks away, Brown was stunned to see two familiar faces—the same little girl and her mother. She realized then that they had been rushing to Sisulu. At that moment the human side of what was about to take place really struck home. "When I saw them, I realized that they hadn't been running late. They were just in a hurry to get to Sisulu," Brown recalled. "Then I thought, 'Oh, I feel guilty. If I had only known where they were going, I would have picked them up.' It really hit me then just how exciting it all was."

A crowd of students, families, and well-wishers had begun arriving well before the appointed hour. So did the news media. Steve Klinsky handed a polished brass school bell to the very first student to arrive at Sisulu's doors—a redheaded kindergartner named Carter, who sounded it, ringing in a new era in education reform in New York State. Sisulu had become the first charter school in New York to open its doors.

Even before the school bell sounded, a crowd of dignitaries had gathered. Some, like SUNY trustee Edward Cox and SUNY vice chancellor Scott Steffey, were on hand to see what they had helped create. Politicians of every stripe, including Assemblyman John Faso, a Republican, and Democratic politician and civic leader Charlie King joined them. Dignitaries smiled for photos, holding a prominent banner proclaiming, "Welcome to Sisulu Children's Academy—A Victory School," which Marshall Mitchell had ordered for the occasion.

Everyone was caught up in the moment. For most, like kindergartner Mylaecha Aska, the journey had begun at daybreak. Mylaecha woke up early that morning and, without prodding, slipped into her crisp blue-and-white uniform. Together, she and her mom, Gladys Lamb, walked over to Sisulu, and when they got there Mylaecha reported to the K Red class.

Traiquan Payne settled in quickly too. Unlike some children, who whimpered when their families said good-bye, Traiquan ran right in. Having been in preschool for a few years, Traiquan didn't surprise his mom, Padora Vincent, with his independence. But she, like Laurie Brown, was in for an unexpected encounter of her own. Vincent, who worked as an aide in a New York City Department of Education office, had seen firsthand how education could empower students, even those who had temporarily veered off track. So wherever she was, whether at work, in the grocery store, or anywhere in the community, Vincent never passed up an opportunity to talk up her office's programs. Years earlier she had often run into an unusually bright teenager in her neighborhood, and even years later Vincent had never forgotten her. "She was always very smart," Vincent recalls, "but she was undecided at the time about what she wanted to do."

Whenever Vincent saw the teenager, she would tell her about some of the continuing education courses she should think about taking, classes in nursing, computer technology, keyboarding, or emergency medical technician training. In her heart, Vincent always thought the teenager would find her way to one of the helping professions. She'd probably be a nurse, Vincent thought. But time flew by, and Vincent didn't see the young woman for years—until the day she dropped Traiquan off at Sisulu. "I just looked at her," Vincent later recalls, "and asked, 'What are you doing here?'" The teenager, now a grown woman, was a teacher's assistant and soon to be a college graduate as well: Michelle Haynes. "I was so surprised to see her there," Vincent says, "but I was so very, very happy for her."

As the reunions wound down and the crowds cleared out, the nuts and bolts of educating 247 children began. Putting together a ninety-three-page application for a groundbreaking school on short notice had been difficult. Finding a schoolhouse had been even more trying. But just as longtime educator Harvey Newman had warned on the day Sisulu got its charter, running the school was going to be the hardest part of all. As it turned out, Sisulu's early challenges would prove him right.

Despite the smiles, handshakes, and inspirational speeches, there were startup glitches and obstacles. City buses got lost, stranding some students. Paperwork requirements hit like an avalanche. Sisulu didn't have a traditional playground, a separate lunchroom, or a full-fledged gymnasium, so everyone had to improvise. The kindergarten teachers faced the most daunting challenges of all. Kindergarten classes in Sisulu's first year were being held in Embassy Hall, which was split up into classrooms by rolling partitions. The classrooms had to be disassembled, and teachers had to pack up their instructional materials at the end of every school day for cleanup and in case church members needed to use the space for meetings at night or on weekends. By the time students arrived the next morning, the congregants had to remove their materials, and school officials had to put everything back in place.

Because the school shared the space with the church, even principal Berthe Faustin had limited access to the building. This was something she hadn't dealt with in her previous jobs; then, if she had needed to work nights or weekends, she could come and go as she pleased. "It was a beautiful building," she said, "but we were tenants, rather than owners, of the building, and in the beginning it was very, very rough."

As all of these difficulties hit home within the first few weeks, a handful of teachers threw in the towel. It had been hard enough finding high-quality educators willing to trust their careers to a fledgling, new kind of school on short notice over the summer. Finding well-qualified teachers to fill in gaps *after* the school year had begun proved even more daunting. Sisulu's and Victory's staffs searched everywhere for certified replacements, and then Klinsky learned that he had a teacher with a valid certification close to home. Klinsky's mother-in-law—Kathleen Sherry— was the experienced, warmhearted teacher who had taught for years in traditional Harlem elementary schools before leaving to raise her own children. Now with her four children grown, she agreed to help Sisulu as a temporary teacher, on an emergency basis, expecting to stay for a very short time as an unpaid volunteer. She would quickly prove to be one of Sisulu's strongest teachers, however, and the school staff persuaded her to stay on full-time for the year. Michelle Haynes was assigned to be her teaching assistant, and "Ms. Cherry," as Sherry's students called her, became Haynes's senior teacher and mentor. The two, working together, developed a close friendship as Haynes became a gifted teacher in her own right.

Right from the beginning, clashes erupted over educational philosophies at Sisulu, centering mostly on the Direct Instruction prong of Sisulu's curriculum. Some teachers liked DI's highly structured and scripted program and the results it produced. Others, though, quickly decided it was too old-fashioned, too skills-based, and too rigid. Sisulu's original charter application had stressed balancing Direct Instruction's rigidity with the offsetting strengths of Core Knowledge and a theme-based extended day. However, some teachers complained that DI was being overemphasized. Meanwhile, the outside experts hired to train the school in DI thought the school wasn't implementing DI's philosophy aggressively enough and resigned from the charter school project in its initial months.

As philosophical and operational challenges arose, there was little time to quietly work things out. Sisulu was New York's first charter school, so it remained under intense media and regulatory scrutiny. Just a month after the school opened, members of New York State's Board of Regents came to inspect the school personally, a visit that was akin to the Joint Chiefs of Staff coming to review an army unit four weeks after it was formed. The regents had decided not to approve any charter schools for a 1999 opening, and some charter supporters thought they were more skeptical about the charter movement than their SUNY counterparts. On their tour, the regents expressed concerns about Sisulu's nontraditional building and highlighted the fact that one teacher had, as reported in the *New York Times*, apparently "misspelled the word *strawberry* three times on a chalkboard," thereby raising doubts among some about the school's staff and its academic quality in general.

Meanwhile, Sisulu's students and their families faced their own challenges. The great majority of them, by virtue of their incomes, qualified for the federal free or reduced-price lunch program, and many had to overcome problems like asthma that were endemic to their inner-city neighborhoods.

A few weeks later, Klinsky faced another type of threat. At dusk on a fall evening, Klinsky waited on a dimly lit and mostly empty subway platform at Lenox and 116th Street to head home after another long day at Sisulu. A gaunt, wild-eyed man came unexpectedly out of the shadows and placed the sharp tip of a long knife directly against Klinsky's heart. At first, Klinsky thought he was being robbed. Then, as he looked into the man's eyes, he sensed instead that the stranger was insane, which, Klinsky thought, might make him even more dangerous.

Klinsky had no idea what to do. He just stood stiffly and silently until, thankfully, the man, apparently driven by his own demons, seemed to lose interest and wandered off. A train arrived, and Klinsky and a teenager who was also on the platform safely boarded.

As the train pulled away, Klinsky realized that almost exactly one year earlier, he had been in a Gulfstream jet heading to Forstmann's annual celebrity retreat in Aspen. "I can see my obituary now," he thought to himself as the train rattled home. "Charter school *idiot* dies in New York subway!"

Spiritually, though, he was content with his school reform work. And to avoid alarming his family and school team, he did not tell them about the incident.

But even in Sisulu's challenging early weeks, exceptional examples of success began to emerge. Many students began making measurable progress with Sisulu's three-part curriculum. Older students who came in working below grade level were catching up. Kindergarteners were making rapid reading progress. Others whose unruly behavior had gone unchecked in their previous schools were better behaved. One of them was a young boy who had come to Sisulu after having problems at another school the previous year. The troubled child barely spoke, and on most days, he just shut down. If he interacted with the other children at all, it was usually to bother them. Before long, however, the boy blossomed into a pretty normal schoolkid, interacting with his peers and working on grade level. One day, Klinsky ran into the boy's father. "My son has really turned around this year," the father said. That kind of life-changing progress is never measured on any kind of standardized test, but it reminded Klinsky once again that his decision to attempt the charter schools had been the right one.

By then, Victory's staff was working feverishly to launch the two other charter schools it would help open the following year. Working with the local boards there, they were building and training staff, readying their schoolhouses, and building community support in hopes of filling up those schools, too.

Some of Sisulu's best-run classrooms, like the one run by Kathleen Sherry and Michelle Haynes, were becoming wondrous laboratories of learning. Unlike the high school where Haynes had once languished or some of the other classrooms in Sherry's former inner-city school, theirs was a classroom where textbook lessons came alive. When their first graders studied ancient Egyptian civilization, the children didn't just read about mummies, pyramids, and pharaohs. They made their own Egyptian flags and shiny gold bibs decorated with jewels like the ones the ancient Egyptians wore. They also made their own passports. At first, some of the students thought they were really flying to Egypt, but, of course, the class took an imaginary trip there instead.

The students' knowledge was impressive. The children competed in an Egypt-themed game in the style of *Jeopardy* when their parents came for visiting day, using terms like *canopic jar* and explaining how silt washes down a river by studying the Nile River Valley. A visiting reporter gave the school's leaders the ultimate compliment. "Do you have any more schools like this?" he asked. "I'd love to have one for my own kid." The reporter's surprise was echoed again by employees of the Metropolitan

Museum of Art when the Sisulu first graders took a field trip to the Egyptian wing there, and one of the children asked, "Now, where's the sarcophagus?" On another day, a writer for a national newspaper who was touring the school didn't believe that these first graders could possibly understand their American history lesson about the original thirteen colonies, as taught in the Core Knowledge curriculum. "There's no way a first grader even knows what a colony is," he told Klinsky. "Ask one," said Klinsky. The reporter did, and after a young boy explained in great detail just what a colony was, the writer was taken aback. "Oh, that's pretty good," he said. "He kinda does know what a colony is."

Sisulu had an even more high-profile visitor that fall—future US president and then Texas governor George Bush. Like Clinton before him, and Obama after him, Bush viewed education as one of his signature issues and supported charter schools. On October 5, 1999, as he campaigned in New York, Bush, along with hordes of media, descended on the school. As Bush's limousine arrived for his well-planned visit, a line of dignitaries greeted the future president. "I'm Dr. Wyatt Tee Walker," said the minister, recalling his conversation with Bush. "And I'm George *Walker* Bush," the future president replied. Meanwhile, even well-rehearsed drills sometimes took on a childlike spontaneity of their own. Before Bush's visit, Principal Faustin had emphasized to her students that Bush was a governor and not yet a president. She had worked with them so that when Bush entered Embassy Hall they would chant in unison, "Good morning, *Governor* Bush." Faustin thought she had made her point, but as often happens with children, things didn't quite go as planned. When Bush stepped inside Embassy Hall, Faustin was taken aback by the children's response: "Good morning, *President* Bush," they said in unison. Bush was quick with a comeback, as Faustin recalled it. "Principal Faustin," he joked, "I like what you're teaching these kids!"

Later that day, in a major campaign policy speech on education issues at New York City's Manhattan Institute for Policy Research, Bush praised Sisulu as an important symbol of the charter school approach. He spoke in glowing terms about Sisulu and charter schools. "It is a reform movement that welcomes diversity, but demands excellence," he said. "And this is the essence of real reform." Bush went on to say that charter schools push traditional public schools to do better. "As president," he promised, "I want to fan the spark of charter schools into a flame." Later, President Obama, Bush's successor, would energetically promote charter schools as well.

Sisulu, though, wasn't just about hosting high-profile visitors or teaching facts and figures. Its staff knew all too well that sometimes children arrived at school with other problems that had to be addressed. In its very early days, Sisulu depended on a network of social service and medical clinic allies around the neighborhood to help support its students' needs. So if students had problems and needed to be referred to the appropriate social services agencies, if they had emergencies and their parents couldn't be reached by phone, or if firsthand help was required, Principal Faustin personally visited their homes. "I guess I simply wanted to do right by the kids," she recalled.

Meanwhile, Klinsky continued to build his staff of educators. Victory made a major addition to its team that fall: Dr. Margaret R. "Peg" Harrington, who was just retiring as chief executive of K–12 school programs and support services for the entire New York City public school system. Harrington had started as a classroom teacher and then risen to be a principal and eventually superintendent of high schools in Queens. She was the educator who had created smaller thematic schools inside mammoth high schools in the 1980s and '90s when few educators were doing that. She had been awarded nineteen educator of the year awards or similar honors, and she could add the experience and quality that Victory-supported schools and the charter school movement would need. At first, Harrington agreed to work part-time only, but soon the consultancy would grow to full-time work and more. "She's going from 1.1 million kids to 247," Klinsky often said when introducing her, "and that's about the right ratio of talent to students."

Harrington knew how to raise Victory and Sisulu's professionalism, and right away she turned her attention to regulatory compliance. Neighborhood schools had been slow to give Sisulu the records for their former students, and Sisulu didn't have the kinds of attendance, immunization, and permanent records that a school typically maintains from year to year. Necessary papers weren't getting filed, and state-mandated special education files weren't in place. "The school staff was focused on the kids and the parents and not on the systems," Harrington explained. "I would ask for something, and they would say, 'I did that. Now where is that?'"

Harrington rolled up her sleeves and took a hands-on approach to addressing the problem. Several days a week, she filled her car with milk crates full of manila folders and other supplies and drove from her home on Staten Island to Sisulu. She created files and set up record keeping where none existed. She made her own copies and answered phones. Before long, she had created organization out of chaos. "I'm not a prima donna," she said, "and as a leader I had to show that I was willing to do whatever it took."

Others took up the cause as well. Early on, as school issues and the crush of questions from parents felt like a tidal wave, Klinsky's wife, Maureen, along with his sister-in-law Carron Sherry Hogan and family friend Paula Cleary, volunteered to do whatever it took to get things going. Parents pitched in too, helping out during the school lunch hour, in the office or wherever they were needed. Community leaders encouraged other parents to sign their children up for the next school year. Meanwhile, Sisulu's board of trustees worked to build the school from scratch, defining along the way just what it was that a charter school's board was supposed to do. Board chair Marshall Mitchell visited Sisulu frequently, providing guidance on many matters. Other trustees and parents, including future board chair Melba Butler, academic committee chairperson Minnie Goka, PTA leaders, and trustee and parent Sonja Herbert and her husband, Michael, put in countless hours to make the Sisulu vision a reality, as would future board chair William Allen, when he later joined in 2003.

By early 2000, at the turn of the millennium, the overnight Internet fortunes that had captivated many of Klinsky's business friends were going bust. But the fledging school on West 115th Street was beginning to thrive. Education reform had settled in, and the day-to-day details of running a good school were falling into place. Sisulu's operational systems had been strengthened. Buses were running, and the central office was getting organized. A full staff was in place, and children were engaged in learning. Sisulu was getting stronger by the day. The school's parents were pleased. An overwhelming 98 percent of those who responded to Sisulu's first parent survey were either satisfied or very satisfied with the school. Eighty-nine percent said they would recommend the charter school to a friend; only 4 percent said they wouldn't. Meanwhile, one of the parent demands was for *more* homework.

Through it all, there was high-spirited camaraderie and examples of people going above and beyond the call of duty in the way that often occurs from being at the forefront of something new and important. When Erik Heyer was finishing up applications for several more charter schools that were due the next day, he ran out in the wee hours of the night to make thousands of pages of copies and returned, drenched from an early morning rain, just as everyone else was reporting for work. When Sisulu's extended school day meant less in-school planning time for teachers, they put in extra hours, and when kindergartners in Embassy Hall had to learn in a less-than-perfect space, they found a way to achieve.

Across town at Victory's headquarters, education reform was moving at a fast clip too. The group moved into larger and more permanent offices in early 2000, and Harrington joined Victory full-time as its chief operating officer. In the coming fall, Victory would also be helping two more charter schools to open: the long-awaited Roosevelt Children's Academy in Roosevelt and the Merrick Academy, the elementary school in Queens supported by some of the borough's most prominent African American Democratic Party leaders.

But on the financial side, the picture wasn't as promising. By early 2000, it was clear that Victory was going to lose more money than Klinsky had hoped. After the local Direct Instruction team resigned, Klinsky felt he owed it to the school to find top-quality replacements, which led him to bring in DI experts from out-of-state at a much higher cost. Similarly, when new information showed that Canaan could not break even with the rent that was originally agreed on, Klinsky decided that the school should fairly reimburse the church for its building's costs, even though he knew that, for the school to pay the rent, it couldn't also pay him or Victory. Klinsky quickly accepted that Victory would be, in practice, his largest-ever charitable pursuit. Still, he kept investing more to raise Victory's quality and achieve its social mission. He was soon hiring additional strong internal operations people such as Jacques Couvillion, who had been with the Federal Reserve; professional academic developers like Mary Ranero-Cordero; and, later, financial experts like Paul Augello. He also continued to recruit other top-quality MBAs into the education reform field, including Marc Sternberg, who held a master's degree in education and an MBA from Harvard and who subsequently became deputy chancellor of the New York City public school system and then director of systemic K–12 education reform at the Walton Family Foundation.

And so it was that Sisulu's first year ended on a high note. As the kindergartners finished the year, some were performing at a second- or third-grade level. Results from Sisulu's first standardized test, the Iowa Test of Basic Skills—a widely administered standardized test that measures students' reading, language, and math skills—showed that students had gained ground. There were behind-the-scenes personal triumphs too. Working with Sherry, Michelle Haynes was becoming the natural-born teacher everyone knew she'd be. Students like Traiquan Payne and Mylaecha Aska blossomed. And just so everyone would keep reading over the summer, Klinsky and Victory gave every student their own copy of educator E. D. Hirsch's grade-by-grade series, *What Every Child Needs to Know*, to take home.

Klinsky learned a lot that first year. More than ever, he came to believe that teacher quality and staff development would be the key to any school's success, as the tale of Sisulu's two second-grade classrooms showed. Earlier in the year, one of Sisulu's classrooms was filled with the so-called bad, hard-to-control kids whose academic work was weak. Next door were the so-called good kids, achieving at high levels. After a while, school leaders swapped the two teachers, and soon the classroom with the "bad" kids had become the well-behaved, high-performing class. Discipline and test scores in the formerly high-achieving classroom declined. "If you want to predict results, don't tell me the names of the kids," Klinsky concluded. "Tell me the name of the teacher."

Secondly, he came to believe that his own role, or the role of any single individual at the school, would always be limited when it came to achieving ultimate success or failure for the school. He and Victory could support a board of community leaders with resources and technical systems, but at the end of the day the board would ultimately decide who would be the principal. The principal would be the key to attracting, training, and retaining teachers; and those teachers would ultimately make the difference. To Klinsky, schools were not like the General Instrument Corporation, which could invent a new digital compression cable television box and then mass-produce millions of units of the same design. Rather, Klinsky now realized, education would always come down to the granular level of teacher and student, classroom by classroom. Success would be a group effort, not an individual effort made by him or anyone else.

As the school year ended, Sisulu held a stepping-up ceremony for its kindergartners who were moving on to first grade. Media outlets, including the city's twenty-four-hour news channel, sang Sisulu's praises. Its first year had been, parents told the *New York Post*, "a rousing success." The most important stamp of approval, though, came from the community. Sisulu was opening up ninety new spaces the following year, and four hundred students had applied for those spots. Future New York charters could now open after Sisulu with positive community support, thanks in part to Sisulu's successful start.

Finally, that summer, a savvy mom, Gail Whiteman, got some good news. Her daughter Tori Saldivia was already a promising student, and from what Whiteman was hearing, she didn't want to trust Tori's education to traditional public schools. So when it came time for kindergarten, Whiteman initially enrolled Tori in a Catholic school near her work in Queens. "I thought it was worth it, even though paying the tuition was going to be a hardship," Whiteman said. Whiteman also signed Tori up for the Sisulu lottery for its second year beginning in September 2000, and when she learned that Tori had been selected, she enrolled her there. Sisulu was much closer to her home, and the more Whiteman learned about Sisulu, the more she liked it. She couldn't have known it then, but one day Tori would be a star there.

Despite many obstacles, the fledgling Sisulu School had made it through its first year in good form. The state's other inaugural charter schools were struggling, however, and the toughest battles were still to come.

8

Battles

By the fall of 2000, the euphoria that had greeted the arrival of the state's inaugural charter schools had waned, colliding with the on-the-ground realities of education reform. Two other charter schools—the John A. Reisenbach Charter School in Harlem and the New Covenant Charter School in Albany—had opened up in 1999, just days after Sisulu. Now, barely a year later, both were fighting for survival.

Like Sisulu, the Reisenbach School had been launched in Harlem with the best of intentions. Named after a young advertising executive who had been fatally shot in a random mugging on a New York City street, the school had been created by a philanthropic foundation set up to memorialize him. Like Sisulu, the Reisenbach School was to be a beacon of hope across Harlem's otherwise bleak educational landscape.

Reisenbach opened in September 1999 with 121 students in two grades—kindergarten and fifth grades—and it intended to add two additional classrooms each year until it eventually served 600 students each year in grades K through 9. Right from the start, however, the Reisenbach School ran into problems. Not surprisingly, New York City real estate was among them.

In its second year, Reisenbach rented and renovated space in a seven-story building on West 117th Street, a few blocks from Sisulu. Like other charter schools trying to solve the vexing real estate piece of the charter school puzzle, the project soon went over budget, according to reports by

SUNY's Charter School Institute (CSI), and school leaders had to come up with additional funding. Up against financial shortfalls, Reisenbach cut back on enrollment and scaled back its popular extended-day hours.

From then on, Reisenbach never seemed to get completely back on track. According to the Charter Schools Institute report, the school was plagued by chronic staff turnover, ongoing discipline problems, some chaotic classrooms, and a curriculum that was never fully developed.

In time, Reisenbach's students made academic gains in some grades, but its standardized test scores were mostly disappointing, especially those of its eighth graders, who took the state's tests for the first time in 2003. Only 13 percent of those eighth graders were proficient in English language arts, and their math scores were even worse, with just 7 percent meeting state standards. Even more troubling, the CSI report stated, the eighth graders' scores were lower than those for the surrounding traditional public schools in its school district, one of the lowest-performing districts in the city. In math, the 2003 eighth-grade scores came close to hitting the benchmark for the state's lowest-achieving group, schools under registration review (SURR), which charter schools were supposed to easily outperform.

Reisenbach's scores rose the following year. But by then it had descended into troubled waters, and eventually the school was shut down.

The third of the three pioneering charter schools to open in 1999—the New Covenant Charter School in Albany—hit problems immediately as well. New Covenant was founded in 1999 by a group of Albany community leaders, including the then president of the local Urban League chapter. The school was established in a disadvantaged Albany neighborhood near the New York State capitol, where, not quite a year earlier, the state's charter law had passed in the wee hours of the morning. Like Reisenbach, New Covenant was intended to be a promising model for improving urban education. Those hopes, though, soon dimmed.

Construction woes and heavy rains delayed the school's opening by several days, and when the school doors did open, its elementary-grade students were housed in temporary modular facilities that were overcrowded and in disrepair. An August 18, 2000, report in the *New York Times* quoted an Education Department report saying that some classes spilled out into hallways.

By the end of its first year, accusations of financial mismanagement had surfaced. According to the *New York Times* report, a quarter of its students and two principals had left. So had its management company and its founder. Not surprisingly, New Covenant's fourth-grade standardized exam scores for English language arts were among New York's lowest.

New Covenant was placed on probation after just one year, leading some to believe that, rather than being a model for transforming public education, it was instead a real-life example of how treacherous the uncharted waters of education reform would be for the state's first charter schools.

In the fall of 2000, a new and highly visible education company, Edison Schools, was hired to manage New Covenant. But even though New Covenant would make some progress and later get off probation, the roller-coaster atmosphere that had come to define the school continued. Eventually, at the five-year renewal stage, its elementary school's charter was renewed, but its middle school was closed. According to a 2006 report by SUNY's Charter Schools Institute, many of the school's problems had persisted year after year: low academic performance, inadequate financial oversight, and unacceptably high turnover among students, teachers, and administrators, including ten principals in the first seven years.

Eventually, a strong drumbeat began to build—even among some traditionally charter-friendly supporters and in some local newspapers—that New Covenant had outlived its time and should be closed.

As New Covenant and Reisenbach struggled, many wondered what had gone wrong. Meager or nonexistent public funding for buildings was the primary culprit, many charter proponents believed, while critics blamed the inaugural schools' problems on the push to open the first charter schools just three months after they were awarded their charters. But to the movement's most die-hard critics, the schools' struggles meant that the charter movement was inherently flawed and doomed to fail.

So, even early on, it looked like it was up to the Sisulu School to prove that the charter movement could succeed as its proponents had predicted. Meanwhile, other education reformers were stepping forward as well. By September 2000, not quite two years after the state's charter law passed, twenty-three charter schools were up and running, including the fruit of Klinsky's other successful school application from 1999, the Roosevelt Children's Academy, or RCA.

RCA was the state's first public charter school on Long Island and New York's first charter school in a small suburban district rather than in a large city. While this made RCA an important education pioneer in its own way, the situation also created its own set of political obstacles and challenges.

For many in the Roosevelt community, the charter school was a godsend, the perfect antidote to the community's chronically ailing schools. "CAN'T WAIT TO GET GOING," Long Island's newspaper, *Newsday,* proclaimed in front-page headlines, reflecting the excitement many felt as opening day approached.

Officials within Roosevelt's traditional school district didn't share this enthusiasm, however. Although the Roosevelt public school system was legendary for its failure—it was the first school district to be taken over by New York State—local school officials wanted to maintain their monopoly on the district's schools and the funding that came with them. Some of the tax dollars that would otherwise have been spent on students by the Roosevelt district would follow students to the Roosevelt charter school if they chose to go there. While a big-city district might be more likely to overlook this sharing of funds, opposition would likely be more intense in smaller towns. So, despite the dismal legacy of their own schools' performance, many traditional educators in Roosevelt viewed the charter school as their adversary and decided to fight it.

Not fully realizing how hard opponents would push back, Victory and the RCA charter community focused at first on recruiting teachers and students, and parents signed on by the hundreds. One of them, Reginald Brinson, had worked for fourteen years as an electrician for the New York City Transit Authority when he got wind that a new school might be opening up nearby. The older of his two children, Regine, was about to start kindergarten that year. He didn't know much about charter schools, but from what he'd heard about Roosevelt's traditional public schools, he knew he wanted something different for elementary school for his daughter. Not only did Brinson sign Regine up for the Children's Academy, he also took a job as the school's first building supervisor, where he could help build a different kind of school for his kids and for others.

Students shared his enthusiasm. Kathleen Sherry, who had left Sisulu after one year to work as part of Victory Schools' central staff, was giving a reading test to one of the new school's prospective students one day. As she worked with the young boy, he leaned over in his chair, obviously distracted by something else. She was puzzled until he explained that he wasn't daydreaming—he was praying: "I have to pray that we'll get the school," he told her.

Educators, including principal Dr. Terry Tchaconas, who agreed to become RCA's first principal, took their own leaps of faith. Tchaconas had begun his teaching career thirty years earlier at a traditional public elementary school in Harlem. Five years later, he moved to a K–8 school in Astoria, Queens, where he started the school's first Greek bilingual program, taught for eleven years, and served as assistant principal for a decade. From there, Tchaconas became principal of two elementary schools on Long Island. He was poised to retire in 2000 when a new opportunity piqued his interest—the new charter school in Roosevelt.

Tchaconas was intrigued by the idea of charter schools. After spending three decades as an educator in less innovative traditional public schools, he liked the idea that a charter school would offer him more leeway to mold the school into what he thought a good school should be and more freedom to hire teachers who shared his vision. It was also the perfect bookend to his public school career, which had begun in Harlem. "I had started out working with minorities, a lot of whom were at-risk students," he recalled, "so it seemed like a great opportunity to add an exclamation point to my career and to work with them again."

Meanwhile, educators like Catherine Jackvony signed on too. Jackvony was working at a nearby elementary/preschool when she first heard that the charter school might open. Jackvony liked the idea of being on the cutting edge of something new that might make a difference in the community. Even though the new charter school couldn't afford a gymnasium or art and music rooms right away, she knew from her years in parochial schools that fancy facilities don't necessarily make great schools. Educators do. So she hired on, but not before being warned by educators and administrators at traditional school districts on Long Island, "It's going to be a lot harder to ever get a teaching job in a traditional public school if you do this."

Right away, local school officials launched a courtroom attack against the charter school and asked for an injunction to block the school's opening. A state supreme court judge turned them down, but they appealed. The Roosevelt district also filed a lawsuit attacking the state's charter school law itself, claiming it was unconstitutional. If that lawsuit prevailed, the entire statewide charter movement could be legally invalidated. The Roosevelt Charter Academy had become a symbol and test case for the charter school movement even before it opened, and Klinsky decided that he and Victory couldn't let the school die, especially since Reisenbach and New Covenant were facing the possibility of closing for other reasons. Pro-charter groups across the state banded together to fight the lawsuit, and Victory paid for the school to hire its own lawyers. In the end, the education reformers succeeded in defeating the lawsuit, and the state's charter law was upheld. However, the financial cost of legal victory was high.

Simultaneously, thorny real estate issues surfaced, just as they had at some of the state's other early charter schools. Initially, the school planned to rent an unused parochial school building from the local diocese. But just as Victory staffers thought the lease was about to be finalized, diocese officials informed Victory that another bidder had appeared at the last minute and had offered to buy the building for what seemed to Victory like an incredibly high price. Victory suspected the mysterious bidder was the Roosevelt school district itself, seeking to sabotage the charter school, and the bid never came to pass. Still, the rental agreement was off, and Victory and the RCA were left with few practical alternatives and little time to open. To keep the school alive, Victory advanced RCA money to buy land on a lovely tree-lined residential street and build an eight-room schoolhouse that the school would own itself.

The building funds were used to purchase pre-constructed classrooms that could be moved to the site, one room at a time, and assembled into a single, traditional-looking flat-roofed building. The school leaders chose this modular method because such classrooms were made by a very well-known manufacturer and were widely used in school districts all over the country. Therefore, among other positive features, they already came equipped with built-in electrical wiring and fire prevention systems that had been proven to meet fire and safety building codes for schools nationwide.

Even so, once the construction was done and the school sought a certificate of occupancy to open its doors, local Roosevelt officials ordered the school to put in what seemed to Victory officials to be an entirely redundant second fire system. The school did this. Then the officials ordered the school to install a *third* system. The school put this in too. Meanwhile, costs kept rising, and the deadline to get the building open for the children loomed closer and closer.

In the summer of 2000, just weeks before the school's scheduled opening, Steve, Maureen, and their children were in Quantico, Virginia, to watch Maureen's younger brother, Brian, graduate from the Marine Corps Officer Candidates School (OCS). Brian Sherry had left a high-paying post on Wall Street to volunteer for the Marines about one year prior to the 9/11 attacks. He would later fight in Iraq and then return to join the FBI. Brian's family was there to honor him and his fellow OCS graduates that day.

As Steve sat in the stands, watching the Marines march, he received an emergency call on his cell phone. He went off and stood beneath the eaves of a nearby barracks to answer it.

The caller was one of the top staffers in the state's political hierarchy, and he had an unexpected request.

"We want you to pull the Roosevelt application and not open," the caller said. "This building problem is too hot politically. We don't want the controversy."

"You can't do that," Klinsky said. "The kids are already enrolled. The teachers are already hired. They have nowhere to go. You can't switch now."

The debate continued, but Klinsky would not back down. Later that day, the new Marine officers and their families retired to the mess hall. Painted on the mess hall wall, in giant letters, was a classic Marine battlefield saying: "Retreat, Hell! We Just Got Here."

Klinsky, admiring this fighting spirit, snapped a photo of the motto. When he got back to New York, he gave a copy to each Victory member fighting for the school's opening. The Marines' motto became their unofficial motto as well.

In September 2000, the Roosevelt Children's Academy opened its doors to 147 students. To adjust to the building code delays, the school was initially housed in two fallback locations—a Police Athletic League gymnasium and the basement of a local church. Even with those adjustments, though, the opening went down to the wire. Students and teachers were greeted on opening day by a small group of protestors. Then, as they stood outside, teachers learned that local officials had not yet approved the certificate of occupancy for the church. So, ever open to improvisation and mindful that the school's curriculum included a unit called "Know Your Community," some of the Roosevelt teachers led their pioneering young students on a field trip, a walking tour of the community, until the school got a certificate of occupancy an hour or so later.

The strained relationship between RCA and the school district continued even after the school opened. When Catherine Jackvony went to introduce herself to the school district special education staff, she was greeted warmly—until it became clear where she was working. "Now where did you say you're from?" came the question. When Jackvony answered that she was from the charter school, a pall fell over the room. She got to talk to staff members there, but what was intended as a friendly get-acquainted session was, in her words, "chillingly cordial."

And then, in a last-ditch maneuver that could've ultimately killed the charter school, district officials unleashed the most potentially damaging weapon in their arsenal: they didn't pay up.

In New York, tax dollars for charter schools went first to the local school districts; the local districts were then legally required to pass them on to the charter schools. But there were no penalties or fines in the law to punish a district that *refused* to pay. Within months, the Roosevelt district owed the charter school more than $600,000; eventually, that figure rose to close to $2 million. Tax dollars weren't coming in to RCA to pay for its ongoing expenses, such as teacher salaries, books, food service, and facility costs. Local officials claimed that the charter school would drain money from their schools and they needed to confirm RCA's enrollment figures. This was a blatant violation of the law, some charter proponents thought. To them, it seemed that the Roosevelt district had found a foolproof way to destroy any charter school, and perhaps the charter movement, once and for all.

Fortunately for the Children's Academy, Klinsky and Victory had the financial strength to fight back. Klinsky was determined not to break his promise to the families, kids, and school community or to the state's nascent charter school movement, even if the cost was high. "This wasn't a business issue," Klinsky recalled. "If we had shut Roosevelt down, that would have shown that anybody can kill a charter school just by holding up the check. We decided we weren't going to let the ship go down if there was any way to save it." So Victory Schools began to pump millions of dollars into yet another school, advancing money, interest free, to pay every bill, teacher's salary, and benefit on time and to keep the school open. Finally, by mid-November, the brand-new schoolhouse was open and ready. Klinsky, through Victory, personally kept the Roosevelt school solvent for most of the next two years.

While these financial and legal battles continued outside the schoolhouse in the early days, principal Terry Tchaconas traveled back and forth between buildings, working to implement the school's curriculum, the same combination of Core Knowledge, Direct Instruction, and thematic learning that Sisulu used. He expected every child to achieve at his or her own highest levels, and most did. In his trademark soft-spoken way, Tchaconas created an environment where teachers were eager to do whatever he asked of them. Sometimes, that was a lot. Before the building was ready, when the temporary classrooms had to be cleared out each day so the space could be used by others at the church and the PAL building, teachers packed up their materials in video cassette containers and mail crates and stored them until the next morning. Inconveniences like that could have demoralized a less committed staff. Instead, the Roosevelt staff pulled together and grew closer.

After teachers in the temporary classrooms packed up each day, Reginald Brinson, the RCA building supervisor, and a coworker disassembled everything else in the classrooms. Then they showed up early the next morning and put everything back before the children arrived. Once the new schoolhouse opened, Brinson took care of the building and the people within it as only someone who cared deeply about a school would do.

When teachers organized baby showers for each other, he helped set up. He helped scout out other real estate properties where the school might be able to grow. It made for some sixteen-hour workdays, but he felt it was worth it. The educational gift he gave the children, Brinson thought, would be a lasting one.

Finally, in the battle over funding, the New York State Education Department began to gear up to force the Roosevelt district to follow the charter law and pay up. Tax dollars began to trickle in. But even then, more than eighteen months passed before the Children's Academy received all of the money it was legally owed.

The biggest payoff for struggling through all of these obstacles with such determination went, of course, to the parents and children of RCA. In a survey of parents during RCA's first year, every one of them said they were either satisfied or very satisfied with the school, and 99 percent of the students would be returning the next year. Meanwhile, 142 students had applied for 48 openings the next year.

As RCA's first year wound down, the school had some normal growing pains to address: academic expectations among teachers were uneven, according to its initial SUNY inspection, and space, especially for offices (including Tchaconas's closet-sized office where two people could barely fit), was cramped. But academics had flourished. When students arrived at Roosevelt in the fall of 2000, only 13 percent of them scored at or above the fiftieth percentile on the Iowa Test of Basic Skills. By the end of the school year, 55 percent did so.

Soon enough, this strength began to show up on the state exams. By 2003, the two schools Victory had helped found in 2000—the Merrick Academy, which was sponsored by African American Democratic political leaders in Queens, and Roosevelt—ranked second and third, respectively, among all new New York charter schools on the state fourth-grade English language arts (ELA) exam.

A year later, by June 2004, with academic training and support from Victory, Roosevelt ranked first among the state's charter schools, with 87 percent proficiency on the English language arts test, while Merrick ranked sixth among the state's charter schools on the same test. That trend continued into 2005, when 87 percent of students at Roosevelt and

70 percent at Merrick were proficient in English language arts. During the same year, 92 percent of Roosevelt's students and 72 percent of Merrick's students exceeded state standards in math.

Based on the 2003–04 and 2004–05 scores, Roosevelt and Merrick were recognized by the Board of Regents and the New York State Education Department as "high performing/gap closing" schools, an honor bestowed on only two other charter schools in the state in 2005. And by then both schools were financially and academically strong enough to proceed without Victory's financial help. The Roosevelt school began to manage itself without Victory's advice beginning in 2007, and continued to grow and succeed for some years following.

As for Brinson's daughter, Regine, her spirits were never dampened by building woes, payment snafus, or protests. She fell in love with the Roosevelt Children's Academy as soon as she showed up for kindergarten. Regine enjoyed learning. As a kindergartner, she read Dr. Seuss and Berenstain Bears books, and by the end of the year she was reading at a second-grade level. That summer, she and her teacher became pen pals, exchanging letters as they would for many years to come. "Our teachers did everything to help us learn," she said, "so we could start out right."

"She enjoyed school so much she never wanted to go home," Brinson said. So on most afternoons, Regine stayed after school, tackling her homework, helping out whenever she could, and, best of all, enjoying something new. "I loved the school," she said, "and I loved being with my dad."

For them and others, the battle for Roosevelt had been won.

9

In the Valley

Back in 2001 much of the news about New York's charter schools, including Sisulu, Roosevelt, and Merrick, felt like a fairy tale where everyone would live happily ever after. The Sisulu School had ended its first year on a high note, and by the fall of 2001 Merrick Academy and the Roosevelt Children's Academy were thriving. Empowered by these and other early successes, a new wave of eager charter operators was following right behind. Mayor-elect Michael Bloomberg, a pro-charter mayor, was about to take office in New York City. The future looked bright.

In the real world of education reform, though, the battles are never fully over. Sisulu was about to experience its own worst difficulties, and for a time it was far from certain whether even this, the most successful of the three inaugural 1999 schools, would survive.

By 2001, Klinsky—who, beginning in 1999, had been one of the hardest-working and most unlikely hands-on inner-city school reformers anywhere—had shifted his attentions back to rebuilding his traditional business career. He still felt deeply committed to the importance of educational opportunity, and he tracked the charter movement closely. But just as he had always intended, a team of trained educators and professionals was now in place at the schools and at Victory, and he had turned over the day-to-day operations to them.

Dr. Peg Harrington continued as Victory's chief operating officer and ran school operations and academics. Erik Heyer, the teacher's son and the former student leader of Harvard Business School's social enterprise effort in education, focused on running business operations and helping community groups start new schools. And James Stovall, an idealistic, young Howard-educated lawyer who had been introduced to Klinsky by Marshall Mitchell, handled Victory's legal and regulatory work, on his way to eventually becoming Victory's CEO. Together, they were supported by a team of staff members that at its peak numbered around thirty professionals (many with PhDs or master's degrees), plus outside consultants and experts as well.

Victory's goal was to blend the best skills from the private and the public sectors to further all aspects of education reform. From day one, Klinsky had made it clear that Victory's mission was to be *for* children and not against anyone. And Victory's team sought to work for any education constituency that sincerely wanted better public schools, whether in the traditional system or in charter schools, and whether the schools were unionized or nonunion.

In 2001, for example, Victory was retained by the City of Baltimore's public school system, with the support of the Baltimore Teachers Union, and worked in close partnership with the city and the union to save Baltimore's unionized (and then failing) Westport Academy from a state takeover. Victory's work helped to dramatically improve Westport's academic scores and save more than forty union jobs (while helping the teachers get an 11 percent pay raise because of their improved academic performance). Later, the head of the Baltimore Teachers Union praised Victory's work while giving a keynote address in New York City. Similarly, beginning in 2002, Victory worked for the Philadelphia school district, alongside its traditional unions, to turn around six traditional, unionized public schools. This work was favorably featured in *Time* magazine, and researchers from the Harvard Kennedy School deemed the entire project, of which Victory's work was one part, to be highly successful. Meanwhile, Victory continued to support a wide range of smaller, grassroots citizen efforts to help communities realize their own local charter school goals.

On many a morning, Harrington, Stovall, and Heyer piled into Harrington's 1999 Mercury Sable—nicknamed the Victory Taxi—and set off for work. Or they boarded a train for Baltimore or Philadelphia. Often they crisscrossed the city's neighborhoods, fine-tuning new schools that Victory was helping to open. But even with these emerging successes, their attention was drawn back again and again to a new set of seemingly intractable problems in the place where it had all begun—the Sisulu Children's Academy in Harlem.

By its third year, beginning in September 2001, Sisulu was facing a difficult set of challenges, caused mainly by the real estate issues confronting almost all New York City charter schools.

When the school's first year ended in June 2000, Sisulu's students were thriving academically, and parent satisfaction was high. But the Center for Community Enrichment building on 115th Street was filled to capacity, especially in Embassy Hall where the three kindergarten classes shared space and were separated only by temporary (and imperfectly soundproofed) room dividers on wheels. Unless the school found more space, there would be no room to add new grades or accommodate the hundreds of children on the waiting list whose parents were clamoring to get them in. At the same time, the New York charter school law provided no sustained state money for charter school real estate development, and Manhattan (including Harlem) was one of the most expensive and space-constrained real estate markets in the nation.

Sisulu's board members, with Victory's assistance, had begun a search for additional space even during Sisulu's first year, but had run into one dead end after another. One affordable and seemingly workable building met the city's general fire codes but not the specific fire codes for schools. A former laundry building looked like it might work but was eventually ruled out because potentially hazardous chemicals had been used there.

Finally, after a months-long search, the school's leaders had begun talks with the Police Athletic League, a nonprofit recreational, educational, and support program for New York City's youth. PAL, as it was often called, had just constructed a modern new building on Manhattan Avenue at West 118th Street, about a fifteen-minute walk northwest of Sisulu. The PAL building had classrooms and a full gymnasium, and it met the necessary regulatory and fire codes. Best of all, it was mainly used by PAL's students *after* school, so it was available earlier in the day, during regular school hours.

Finally it seemed Sisulu had found a place where it could grow and build on its success. With the PAL space added, the plan was for the kindergarten, first-grade, and second-grade classes to stay in the original Canaan community center building on 115th Street. Embassy Hall would no longer be needed for classroom space and could be used for physical education activities, lunch, and school-wide assemblies. Meanwhile, Sisulu's third graders would be taught at PAL, and new students would be recruited so that Sisulu could afford the extra PAL rent. Sisulu would grow with the older grades at the PAL building where they would have use of the full PAL gymnasium and ample meeting space.

The increase in the school's rental costs from the new space exceeded the rise in revenues from the new students, however, so the school's budget worsened. This meant that Victory (which had already advanced substantial startup funds and which still had not been paid anything for the work it had done over the years) was even further away from being compensated for the services it had provided. Still, Klinsky was supportive of the move if it would help the school, and Sisulu's board approved the plan.

But all of these good intentions backfired terribly. It soon became painfully clear that the addition of the new PAL site was a disaster. The expense of the extra space had been expected. The greater harm, though, was that the healthy and close-knit school culture of Sisulu's first year was unraveling, and its academic progress appeared to be coming undone.

The new students recruited for the additional space at PAL came straight from the neighborhood's failing traditional public schools. Sisulu scrupulously followed the charter law and admitted all children equally, even if they were emotionally troubled or academically weak and even if they had been encouraged by educators at their traditional schools to enroll in a charter school for those reasons.

Meanwhile, the fifteen-minute walk between the two sites meant that Sisulu no longer felt like one unified school. When problems broke out at one location, it inevitably felt like the principal was at the other. With the addition of the new, older students, discipline problems arose at the PAL building. Some previously successful students and families at Sisulu began to withdraw from the school for this reason and were replaced by new students from outside Sisulu. Many were less academically prepared, and some brought behavioral problems as well.

More and more, it seemed that Sisulu had become divided into two separate worlds: the still well-run, happy, and academically strong K–2 school at the original location on West 115th Street and a much weaker school in the PAL building that was spiraling downward.

The contrasts between the troubled PAL classrooms and Victory's other schools couldn't have been starker. Klinsky was impressed during his occasional visits to Merrick Academy and the Roosevelt Children's Academy, which both ranked among the state's top three new charter schools on the 2003 fourth-grade English language arts exam. He was encouraged when he visited Baltimore and when he walked through Sisulu's original building on West 115th Street and watched the students work or saw the quality of their essays on the walls. But Klinsky's spirits sank whenever he visited the PAL building, only to find an undisciplined fourth-grade class nearing a tipping point, a newly hired teacher not yet fully trained for the task, and the principal often forced to be blocks away, addressing other matters.

Even so, there were always some bright moments at Sisulu.

On one of those days early on, Edward Cox, the cochairman of the SUNY charter schools committee that had awarded Sisulu its original charter, and his wife, Tricia Nixon Cox, came to read to the children. As they sat on a rug in a first-grade classroom, Tricia, the daughter of President Richard Nixon, asked, "Who here would like to be president someday?" All of the students raised their hands. She then talked about her own childhood in the White House. Sisulu's students were enthralled. They asked insightful questions. The first graders were even more impressive when they passed around and read fluently from the advanced-level book the Coxes had brought to read to them. After listening to them read, Ed Cox paid the students a well-deserved compliment: "I thought I was supposed to be reading this book to you," he said, "but *you're* the ones reading to *me*."

The professional development of Sisulu's teachers also highlighted the school's progress. Michelle Haynes, the lifelong Harlem resident who had started out as one of Sisulu's first teaching assistants in Kathleen Sherry's room, had gone on to earn her teaching credentials. There was no way she was going to let her own students fall through the cracks. So Haynes ran her classroom using a highly individualized approach to learning, likening herself to, of all things, a chef. "That's the analogy I use," Haynes says. "When you cook food or make a dish, you don't just use one ingredient. You use lots of ingredients. In teaching, I use whatever teaching strategies will create success." Through hands-on science projects, lively history lessons, and her own passion for literature, Haynes brought her lessons to life.

As Michelle was growing up, her mom, Madeline Haynes, had filled their Harlem apartment with pictures, her beloved books, and piles of newspaper clippings she thought worth saving. Now Michelle was passing down her own love of learning to another generation. Hers was a classroom crammed full of reading materials, projects, and artwork, and when space ran out inside her room, she hung more of her students' schoolwork outside in the hallways. But everything wasn't all fun and games. A tall, imposing woman, Haynes ran an orderly, disciplined classroom that was a wondrous mix of serious study, delightful teaching, practical life lessons, and old-fashioned nurturing. She expected her students to respect her and to respect each other. Most important, she expected her students to respect themselves, and—as the embodiment of Victory and Sisulu's educational philosophy—she never gave up until each child was performing at his or her own highest levels, whatever they might be.

There were bright spots among the children as well. There was, for example, the young boy whose mother was seriously ill and awaiting major surgery. He had come in as a second grader, lagging behind academically and acting out, both at school and at home, but soon he had made a dramatic turnaround.

There were the siblings who left their home in the city at 5:45 AM each day and traveled with their mom for nearly two hours by subway and bus to get to Sisulu. Then, at the end of the day, they made the trip again. Somehow, despite the exhausting commute, they managed to succeed.

There was Traiquan Payne, whose mom had encouraged Michelle Haynes to continue her education back when Michelle was a teenager. Now, Traiquan was one of Haynes's students, and in an odd twist of fate, Haynes was encouraging *him* to pursue his own lofty dreams. Traiquan was a natural-born writer and artist, and Haynes nurtured his gifts, encouraging him to do extra artwork, giving him the job of designing covers for booklets, and then hanging up his artwork for all to see. "She kept telling me how talented I am," Traiquan recalls. "Finally, it sunk in." One day, those talents would take Traiquan to exciting places beyond Sisulu.

And perhaps most encouraging, every year promising new students like Tori Saldivia arrived at Sisulu. When Tori enrolled in the fall of 2000, it soon became apparent that she had been well prepared academically. As things turned out, Sisulu's academic program suited her well. Using the Direct Instruction curriculum, all the school's classrooms taught reading simultaneously, allowing an advanced kindergartner like Tori to be placed with a first-grade class for the ninety-minute morning reading session. Before long, Tori moved up a grade, not just for reading, but for all of her academics.

At first, some on Sisulu's staff worried about the social implications of Tori skipping a grade, but her mom, Gail Whiteman, decided the move would be best. "I knew that I had to do what I had to do for my child and that she should try it," she said. So Tori advanced to first grade, and it worked. Again, she excelled, making excellent grades and acing standardized tests along the way. But her successes weren't measured only in test scores and grades. Her teachers made it work in other ways as well. They made sure she was included when her former kindergarten class held its stepping-up ceremony at the end of the year. They even picked her as student of the year.

In another school, with less nurturing and more rigid teachers, Tori might have grown bored. She might have floundered. Instead, at Sisulu she rose quickly to accomplish her full potential.

But, for all the positive signs at Sisulu, the structural flaws inherent in operating in two different buildings and the problems they created in the upper grades at the PAL site soon became obvious. Meanwhile, by Sisulu's third year, Principal Faustin had returned to the traditional public school system and a new principal from a charter school in Cambridge, Massachusetts, had been hired.

The make-or-break tests that were crucial in evaluating schools that year were the state's standardized fourth-grade tests: the dreaded English language arts (ELA) and math exams. To everyone's disappointment, when Sisulu's fourth graders at the PAL building took the tests for the first time in 2002, they scored about as poorly as students in the nearby traditional public schools from which many had recently come. In one sense, it wasn't surprising that only 24 percent of them were reading at or above grade level; most of them had received some, if not most, of their K–3 education at low-performing public schools. Still, it was a deep blow to the school's self-confidence to have any poor test scores at all.

By the following year, the fourth graders' scores had improved but were still far below the school's own lofty expectations. After hearing about the weak scores, Klinsky felt heartsick, and he authorized Victory to increase its financial losses even more and pour additional educational resources into the school. Victory paid to bring in more and more staff trainers and specialists.

Despite all of these efforts, however, problems at the PAL building seemed just as unsolvable as ever. Some members of the school community began to blame the teachers at PAL, while some of the teachers there, as well as others in the school community, began blaming the school's curriculum instead.

Educators are often passionate about curriculum choices, frequently favoring whatever methods they learned at their original teachers' college or from their first mentors. A change of curriculum at any charter school can be complicated because the school's authorizers have specifically approved the curriculum described in the school's application, and because the school's parents, in essence, voted for that curriculum when they selected the charter school for their children. Some parents might object if the school changed its curriculum after their children were enrolled there. Even so, teachers, principals, and board trustees who disagree with a school's original curriculum choice don't want to feel forever straitjacketed by a charter school proposal that they didn't write and that they now believe may not be working.

The Core Knowledge and Direct Instruction programs at Sisulu were two of the most researched and highly recommended curricula in the country, supported by national studies and by the AFT and others. Still, it seemed to some that the curriculum was not succeeding, and

Sisulu's leaders were concerned that when the school's charter came up for renewal in a year or so, Sisulu could be shut down by the state.

The Direct Instruction piece of the curriculum came in for the harshest attack. Klinsky's original application had coupled the structured, scripted DI program with the content-rich Core Knowledge program, and a thematic, creative extended day. But even though DI's supporters say that studies show it also teaches higher-order thinking skills, some DI critics thought its scripted nature was demeaning to the teachers and students. "Why is Sisulu using DI if the elite private schools don't?" some of them asked. "Is it out of disrespect for our teachers or our children? Is it racism?"

Parental satisfaction on surveys at Sisulu continued to run high. Even in the school's troubled third year, 96 percent of its parents said they were either satisfied or very satisfied with the school. Some trustees had harbored doubts about the original curriculum since the beginning, however; and as time went on and new board members joined, dissatisfaction with the curriculum became stronger. No particular hostility was directed at Klinsky personally, who was generally seen to be well intentioned, but there was a clear intellectual split of opinion. The school was not just dividing into two separate physical buildings; it also threatened to devolve into two separate philosophical camps.

Victory staff developers and regional directors continued to work at the school, but they often reported back in frustration, "They're just not listening to us. . . . They're not implementing the program." The same combination of DI, Core Knowledge, and thematic learning was producing outstanding results at Victory's Merrick and Roosevelt charter schools, which had similar student populations and ranked at that time as the state's second- and third-highest-performing charter schools. Victory's staff cited those statistics as proof that DI was not to blame for Sisulu's troubles, but critics of the curriculum couldn't be persuaded.

Klinsky felt deeply and personally responsible to the families that he had helped attract to the school in 1999. As the problems grew, he found himself coming back to the school more and more frequently. He received reports from the field and complaints from some of Sisulu's trustees and others, and he found himself lying awake at night, wondering what to do. In the meantime, he learned that several of the first families he had helped to recruit in the summer of 1999 were now planning to leave. He arranged to see them at the school, and he told them about all of the extra staff and resources that Victory was pouring into the school. He asked them to hold on. They all knew, however, that each year of education is incredibly important in a child's life. The parents couldn't be persuaded to stay.

The authorizers' decision to either renew Sisulu's charter or close the school down was looming. Klinsky felt he could see the school's underlying progress, and he never lost faith in the kids, the families, or the school. However, he knew that some at the school had certainly lost faith in Victory and in him.

It was also clear to him that his own role at Sisulu had changed and diminished with time. Despite all his efforts as a founder, application writer, and initial funder of the school, the New York charter law made clear that Sisulu was controlled by its board of community leaders, not him. Victory was ultimately just an advisory firm, like a law firm, architect, or consultant; ultimately, key decisions lay in the board's hands. From the board's point of view, Victory was essentially just an employee (even if it had, in fact, never been paid)—and so, therefore, was Klinsky.

In the early days, Marshall Mitchell had chaired the school's board, and Dr. Wyatt Tee Walker had been a strong physical presence as Klinsky's cofounder and spiritual ally. But Marshall Mitchell had stepped down from the board after Sisulu's first year to pursue a career opportunity. Judith Price, Melba Butler, Peter Sloane, and Charlie King—some of whom had put in hundreds of hours of high-quality volunteer service—had also departed or would soon leave the board. The founding board members had, in essence, endorsed the charter application when submitting it; but the new board members who replaced them, while they were equally outstanding as leaders, had not endorsed the original application and didn't really know Klinsky. And some of the original trustees who remained on the board had harbored issues about the curriculum from day one. Klinsky felt more and more isolated and unwelcome as the board evolved.

Then came the saddest development of all.

One day, as Klinsky was returning from a business trip, his staff passed on some terrible news: Rev. Walker had been felled by a series of strokes and was in critical condition. It wasn't clear when, or even if, he would ever regain his powers of speech or movement. To Klinsky, Walker's very vibrancy and passion for life made his strokes an even greater shock and blow.

By this time, the unlikely alliance and friendship between Walker and Klinsky had grown into something that transcended Sisulu. During their years-long partnership, Klinsky had seen Walker's keen intelligence and exceptional capabilities firsthand. He had come to greatly admire Walker for those abilities, for his fundamentally joyous heart, and for the key role he had played in many of the most crucial moments of the civil rights era and the succeeding decades.

For his part, Walker had seen with his own eyes how the young students in the Center for Community Enrichment building were thriving. He had come to respect Klinsky's sincerity and integrity, and he had become enthusiastic about helping Victory open more top-quality charter schools to help other communities.

As the years had gone on, Walker (who had a passion for music, among his other interests) had begun to invite Klinsky to some of the concerts he organized, which frequently featured the Three Sopranos, a trio of singers with angelic voices, who were Canaan's own version of opera's Three Tenors. When Klinsky was honored at the Center for Educational Innovation's annual formal dinner, Walker agreed to introduce him. And when Walker asked Klinsky to serve on the board of a local Harlem hospital that Walker was trying to save, Klinsky said yes.

Eventually, Walker had agreed to become national chairman of Victory to help promote better public schools nationwide. He was in his seventies by then, but remained energetic and strong. He had come to Klinsky's office to discuss their next steps, and as Victory's staff snapped group photos of him with the entire team, Walker had described for Klinsky the active weight lifting and exercise regimen that kept him fit. Now, though, Dr. Walker was laid low and would need to begin his own hard fight to recovery.

As Sisulu neared the end of its third academic year, bad luck seemed to be descending everywhere. Walker had been struck down. Marshall Mitchell had left the board. Test scores—at least those that were available for the state exams—appeared to be poor. Morale was low.

It was the worst of all worlds, Klinsky thought. So much effort, so much expense, and so many good intentions—all seemed to be for naught. The school could fail. The families who trusted him could be hurt. Klinsky could now see that he might go down in local history as just another con man who had come up to Harlem and lied.

Late one evening, Klinsky found himself called to the school for a special board meeting. The board members asked him to defend Victory and the school's performance. As calmly and as clearly as he could, Klinsky explained the facts as he knew them; he described the emerging success of many of the children who had started their own educations at Sisulu and the positive results that Victory's curriculum had produced at other charter schools. The board members seemed unconvinced.

Finally, Klinsky was excused from the meeting and told to wait outside while the board considered Victory's future in executive session. Having nowhere else to go, he wandered toward the back of the school and through the fire escape exit that led to Canaan. As he entered the sanctuary, he saw that the cavernous church was empty, except for its choir, which was practicing late into the night. Feeling about as low as he'd ever felt, Klinsky took a seat, unobserved and alone in the back row of the darkened room, lost in his own thoughts.

Canaan's storied choir, one of the most beautiful and honored church choirs in America, began to sing, practicing the songs that had lifted listeners' spirits for generations. Eventually, Klinsky couldn't help but turn his attention to the music, and soon he felt his own spirits rising too. For the first time, he understood in his bones just how much comfort this church must have brought to so many people over the years.

The choir sang out its words of hope, that out of darkness and despair comes a new and better day. "That's right," Klinsky thought, "that's right." Sisulu would persevere. Walker's hope would persevere. All of their hopes would persevere.

Better days were coming.

10

A Light Shines

It was 2003, during the New York charter movement's fourth academic year, when Victory's senior management team—James Stovall, Margaret Harrington, and Erik Heyer—gathered in Klinsky's office to suggest the unthinkable: maybe, they said, it was time to walk away from Sisulu.

By any rational analysis, the logical decision would be to quit. Sisulu's problems were mounting, and no matter how hard Victory's professionals tried, they seemed to be caught up in a no-win situation. Victory was pouring more and more time, people, and money into the project, and increasingly, they felt their advice was being ignored or disregarded. Still, if Sisulu fell, Victory would take the blame. "What do you think we should do?" they asked Klinsky,

As the three spoke, Klinsky rocked back in his chair. He didn't say much. He just listened, knowing that Victory's on-the-ground leaders were simply trying to be realistic. Still, it was clear that his mind was already made up.

"What our reputation is really built on," Klinsky explained, "is being committed partners and standing up for what we believe in. I'll do my part. I'll work for free. I'll do whatever it takes to make things work, but we will never let Sisulu fail if there is any way we can save it." Besides, he explained, it wasn't just Victory's reputation that was at stake. It was more fundamental than that. It was a moment for all of them to define their inner values and what—in hindsight—their lives would prove to have been about.

"This," he said, "is tombstone stuff."

For Stovall, it was a defining moment. Back when he was interviewing for jobs, Stovall had decided to join Victory not only as a way to practice law but also as a way to positively impact young lives. Again, he realized his decision had been the right one. "After that day, there was no doubt in my mind that we were going to make it work. It was my cue that Steve was willing to put his reputation on the line and do everything within his power to save Sisulu. It was like a pregame speech for me," Stovall says, "and I left there fired up."

Still, Klinsky was experienced enough to know that noble sentiments weren't enough to fix Sisulu's ills. He believed that wonderful things were happening for the students who had begun their academic careers at Sisulu, but those students were still too young to take the make-or-break fourth-grade state exams. Before those children were tested, the SUNY trustees would have to decide whether or not to renew Sisulu's charter. Sisulu's state scores to date were weak, and SUNY's Charter Schools Institute staff was determined to show that they were serious about closing weak charter schools. So the clock was ticking, and the school could soon be lost.

When Klinsky had returned to the board meeting after listening to Canaan's choir practice, he had faced a roomful of concerns and uncertainties from some of Sisulu's board members. Victory continued to work for Sisulu, but the board's issues and concerns remained.

Klinsky believed that unity was key to Sisulu's survival, so he and Victory would now move to pull all the parts of the school community back together and move forward as one unified whole. The clearest way forward was for him and Victory to make some major changes in order to achieve this unity, even though Klinsky felt the changes were not what he would've chosen in an ideal world, and even though those changes might be painful to Victory and to himself.

On the financial side, Klinsky instructed his staff to reach out to Sisulu's board and formally waive all of the unpaid fees still technically owed to Victory for its work, going back to day one. Since Sisulu's beginning, Victory had never taken *any* cash payments from the school. Instead, it had poured money into Sisulu for its startup and emergency needs. However, the unpaid and uncollected fees had built up on Sisulu's financial statements, making the school's balance sheet look weak. Formally wiping the slate clean, with no chance for future payment of those past bills, left the school highly solvent. Once Victory forgave those debts formally and forever, it gave Sisulu a strong financial position, helping its chances for the renewal of its charter. This gift, in addition to the funds Klinsky had spent on behalf of Victory's other early charter schools, meant that he had given approximately $3 million of his own money to help launch the reform movement and create better schools. But working for free would make clear to any skeptics, once and for all, that Victory put the kids ahead of its own finances and had no intentions of walking away from Sisulu or its founding families.

Additionally, Klinsky instructed Victory to support the removal of Direct Instruction from Sisulu's main curriculum. Klinsky never blamed DI for Sisulu's troubles. The same curriculum was performing beautifully at the Roosevelt charter school, at Merrick, and at many, many other schools across the country at that time. And Klinsky worried whether it was right to change a curriculum that Sisulu's parents had, in effect, chosen when they had selected Sisulu, and which was in the charter application that SUNY had specifically approved. But DI had become an insolubly divisive issue and the need for unity outweighed these doubts.

Over the years, Klinsky had concluded that many curricula could succeed, not just one. He had long since given up on the idea that he or anyone else could hit upon the one and only school design that was the right one. Successful schools, he had come to realize, were the ultimate group experience and the consummate example of what can be achieved when a community works together. The most important need was to get everyone back together on the same emotional page and move the entire school forward together.

With these financial and curriculum changes made, Sisulu's leaders could focus on a third key change—winding down operations at the PAL building and returning Sisulu to its roots: a small and cohesive school community, all in one place at the original Center for Community

Enrichment building on West 115th Street. Classes would continue at the PAL site until Sisulu's fifth graders finished there and could move smoothly into middle schools. But no new students would be enrolled at the PAL building, and the number of students at the CCE building would be kept at the existing levels so that Embassy Hall wouldn't be needed for classroom space.

Now that Victory had explicitly donated all of the fees owed to it, Sisulu could better afford to make those potentially budget-straining changes. But at least for the time being, Sisulu's leaders would have to give up on one of their longtime dreams—adding a grade to Sisulu every year and expanding Sisulu from a K–5 school to a K–12 school someday.

With these strategic changes in place, it would once again be possible for a highly qualified principal to succeed, and Sisulu recruited Norma Figueroa-Hurwitz. Selection of the principal is usually the single most important factor for school success, since a good principal attracts, trains, and retains good teachers. Figueroa-Hurwitz came to Sisulu with an enviable track record. For years, she had been principal of an East Harlem school that was one of the city's top-performing public elementary schools. She knew how to run a good school. She'd do it at Sisulu.

Beyond the classroom, other behind-the-scenes changes were put in place by the spring of 2004. Sisulu's board had elected William Allen as its new chairperson. Allen had earned a bachelor's degree from City College of New York, where he was president of the graduating class. He earned a master's degree in urban affairs from Hunter College, where he was president of the graduate students' association, and then earned a master's degree in public administration from John Jay College, where he became an adjunct professor and member of the faculty senate. In later years, Allen headed up Communities in Schools of New Jersey, a network of after-school programs. He was also a parent at the school, a Harlem resident, and a Harlem community leader who had made history when he became the youngest person in the state ever appointed to be a trustee of a community school district. Now he would be making his mark on education reform at Sisulu, in the neighborhood where he himself had grown up.

With all of this done, Sisulu began its fifth year of operation, 2003–04, with renewed optimism and confidence that its growing pains were a thing of the past. The school had a strong board and a dynamic principal in place. Its finances were in order, and real estate issues weren't as pressing. That meant that everyone—from Principal Figueroa-Hurwitz and her educators, to Sisulu's trustees, and Victory and its staff—could focus on academics and on winning Sisulu's charter renewal.

Parents at the school pitched in to win a renewal for the school that many of them had helped create five years before. They appeared at board meetings. They talked about how desperate they were for good schools and how, after all of the decades of broken education promises, they had found real promise at Sisulu. They wrote heartfelt letters to the Charter Schools Institute at SUNY, hoping to touch a nerve. For the mother of one fourth grader, Sisulu had been a nostalgic journey: "The first seven years of a child's life are important," she wrote. "That is when a child's personality is molded. Sisulu has played a big role in those years for my son." For another mother, Sisulu had been a joyful adventure: "I beam with delight as my seven-year-old (who performs above his grade level in many areas) tells me about the Great Wall of China, asks me did I ever hear of the Trojan War and then commences to tell me about it."

For one grandmother, the journey marked the end of a decades-long search for good schools. Like many Sisulu parents, she had attended city schools. Her child did too. "I have witnessed the failure of the public school system to educate the children of this community adequately," the grandmother wrote, knowing all too well what she was saying. The grandmother had been longing for good schools for three generations—first for herself, then for her child, and finally for her grandchild. At long last, her family had found one. "My granddaughter has developed a love of learning," she wrote, "that I hope will continue to grow at the school she loves."

In January of 2004, the SUNY charter school trustees, still led by Ed Cox and Randy Daniels, faced a decision. The initial Sisulu kindergartners were now fourth graders, but their fourth-grade state exam performance was still unknown because the school year was only half over, and the test scores were not yet in. If SUNY gave Sisulu a full five-year renewal, it would be ignoring the weakness at PAL. But if SUNY gave no renewal, a full shutdown would ignore the progress of the younger Sisulu grades and ignore the fact that Sisulu had outperformed the local schools over-all the prior year, with a reunified school culture and leadership. In a Solomonic decision, SUNY granted a two-year probationary extension to allow the school to continue its progress. Sisulu was the only one of the state's three charter schools up for renewal that year to have all of its grades renewed. New Covenant Charter School in Albany had its elementary grades renewed, but its middle school was closed. The hard-fighting John A. Reisenbach Charter School in Harlem was shut down altogether. From the beginning, SUNY was making it clear that New York's charter schools would be held accountable for delivering the results they promised—and would be closed down if they did not.

In the case of Sisulu, it quickly turned out that SUNY's faith was well placed. A few months later, when the ELA test scores for that year's fourth graders arrived, they were strong. Sisulu ranked as the highest-performing charter school in all of Manhattan and ranked fifth among the state's charter schools overall (while Roosevelt ranked first among the state's charter schools and Merrick ranked sixth, making Merrick the highest-scoring new charter school in Queens). Sisulu's 55 percent ELA passing rate exceeded the 50 percent rate for New York City's public schools as a whole, and was about 1.8 times higher than the 31 percent passing rate for New York City's School District Five from which Sisulu drew most of its students. Saying he was "extremely pleased" with the results and the success of Sisulu's students and teachers, William Allen, chairman of Sisulu's board of trustees, added: "This year's fourth-grade is the first class of students to begin at Sisulu as kindergarteners and are therefore the best test of Sisulu's educational quality. Sisulu's faculty, board and administrative team have continuously worked to supplement and strengthen the school's instructional program. The result has been a consistent improvement as students, staff and parents build experience with the instructional model."

"When Sisulu began in 1999, the school's founders pledged to deliver a high-quality public education alternative with superior academic results," Latasha Fields, the president of Sisulu's parent-teacher organization, said at the time. "These promises have now been met. The hard work and dedication of everyone involved has paid off."

Sisulu's students had also learned much more than just how to pass standardized tests. They had studied biology, the Great Wall of China, geometry, the Greek gods, and the US Constitution. They had picked pumpkins, ice skated, and experienced the thrills of Rye Playland, one of the country's oldest amusement parks. They had watched caterpillars grow into beautiful butterflies, and then they had trekked over to Central Park and released the brilliantly colored painted ladies into the sky.

Many of these students had their own inspirational stories to tell. The boy who had come to Sisulu barely speaking had continued to progress. Another boy had arrived as a second grader with physical and developmental disabilities that might have doomed him at another school. He couldn't read, but his teachers worked with him. His classmates did too. He now read as well as some of his peers did, and by the time he left Sisulu he was reading at grade level.

And there was Traiquan Payne. For years, Traiquan's classmates had been captivated by his mature, expressive artwork, which Michelle Haynes had displayed all over their classroom. It was his passionate writing, though, that one day brought them to tears.

Reading had been a staple of everyday life in Haynes's class, one of the most revered activities of the day. Sometimes, students read different books, each at his or her own pace. Sometimes, they studied the same one. One of the books they had all read ended way too tragically and abruptly when a young boy's beloved dog died. The book had left a lot of questions unanswered, so for their next writing assignment, Haynes asked her students to write their own endings. All of their writing was admirable. But when Traiquan began reading his final chapter aloud, a somber hush fell over the classroom. In elegant, beautifully written prose, he described how the heartbroken boy picked up his dog's lifeless body, and even more movingly, Traiquan detailed the boy's last emotional moments with his loyal pet before he was buried. Traiquan hadn't planned to evoke such strong emotions from his classmates. He had just written from his heart. But his writing was so moving that it had touched them and made some of them cry. His words brought tears to Michelle Haynes's eyes, too.

As results came in from more schools, Victory began to receive some positive recognition. In April 2004, the US Department of Education cited Victory's success and dedicated a full feature article to its work in the department's national publication, the *Education Innovator*.

"Every time a child learns, it is a victory—a victory over ignorance, a victory over poverty, and a victory for opening a world of knowledge. This is the goal of Victory Schools," the article said.

It cited Victory's work with charter schools in New York, including the successes of Sisulu, Roosevelt, and Merrick. It mentioned that on the 2003 fourth-grade ELA exams Merrick Academy and Roosevelt Children's Academy ranked first and second in comparison to New York's new charter schools that were educating high-need children. The article reported on Victory's partnership with the Baltimore school system and the Baltimore Teachers Union to turn around Baltimore's Westport Academy. It discussed the success in Philadelphia, where *Time* magazine ranked Victory as the best school management services provider in the Philadelphia experiment. The Department of Education's *The Education Innovator* quoted a local community leader as saying, "We have found [Victory Schools] to epitomize what we would like the public schools in our community to be."

In May 2004, Pearson Scott Foresman, a well-known elementary publisher in all subject areas, selected Victory to pilot a national demonstration model for literacy education. And that same month, the Maryland State Education Department honored Victory's Westport Academy for the second time in two years based on its academic gains on the Maryland School Performance Assessment Program (MSPAP). With the combined effort of the Baltimore school system, the Baltimore Teachers Union, and Victory, the number of Westport eighth graders accepted into competitive application high schools in Baltimore had risen from 43 percent in 2001–02 to 55 percent in 2002–03 and then 66 percent in 2003–04.

So, academically, the school year ending in June 2004 had been a good one for Victory and Sisulu-Walker, but, along with that good news, Klinsky and Sisulu's leaders wanted to make sure one key contributor to the school would not be forgotten: Rev. Dr. Wyatt Tee Walker.

Walker was now recovering from his strokes, and he had retired from Canaan and Harlem to Chester, Virginia. He would be returning to Harlem in the fall of the 2004–05 school year, however, for an appreciation dinner being put on by the community in his honor. Klinsky was invited to be one of the speakers at the dinner, which would be held at the Alhambra Ballroom on Adam Clayton Powell Jr. Boulevard. On that night, Walker's civil rights, human rights, artistic, and ministerial accomplishments were described by a host of speakers. Then, when Klinsky spoke, he told the audience how the Sisulu School, and perhaps the entire New York charter school law, would never have happened if it hadn't been for Walker. "When you applaud Dr. Walker's role in civil rights and housing and theology, remember his triumphs in education as well," Klinsky said. And then he added a surprise.

"Now bringing fresh honors to Dr. Walker is a little like bringing water to the ocean. It is no easy task." Five years earlier, Klinsky told the audience, Walker had himself contacted the Sisulu family in South Africa for permission to name the school after Nelson Mandela's close friend, Walter Sisulu, and his wife. "But," Klinsky continued, "now that the school has gotten older and is doing so well, that Sisulu name seems a little lonely all by itself. . . . It seems to us that the name of Martin Luther King's great friend and advisor should be included as well. And so, Dr. Walker and Mrs. Walker, if you consent, your friends are proposing that New York State's first public charter school should be renamed the Sisulu-Walker Charter School of Harlem."

Across the room, Walker, still impaired from his strokes, silently nodded his approval. At a board meeting a few months later, Walker's longtime close friend and colleague, school trustee Minnie Goka, put forth a motion to officially rename the school. The Sisulu board unanimously approved the motion, and the school now had a proud new name.

That school year, ending on June 22, 2005, would prove to be even better.

Now, Sisulu's original kindergarteners, who had enrolled at Sisulu in September 1999, were graduating as fifth graders from the Sisulu-Walker School. They had made progress, and as fifth graders their scores jumped again. A full 90 percent of them tested at or above grade level on the city's fifth-grade ELA exams, while 77 percent scored at or above grade level in math. These 2005 reading scores were almost two times higher than those at the nearby traditional public schools, and Sisulu-Walker's math scores were more than double those of the nearby neighborhood public schools. They exceeded the scores of the more prosperous New York City public school system as a whole. And Sisulu-Walker—the Harlem school that some had thought would never survive—posted the highest scores of any charter school in New York City!

As graduation day approached in the spring of 2005, the fifth-grade students had the bittersweet realization that they would soon be leaving for middle school and exiting Sisulu-Walker for good. Six years earlier, on their first day as kindergartners, they had been greeted with raucous fanfare and media attention as New York ushered in a new era of education reform. Now, seventy-two Sisulu-Walker fifth-grade students had made it to Sisulu's graduation day.

By then, Sisulu-Walker had become like family, a close-knit, intergenerational community of people whose lives had intersected at a crucial time in the children's lives. Some of the parents had known each other since childhood. Some of the grandparents had too. Many of them thought of Sisulu-Walker's children almost as their own. Many of the teachers did too. When students excelled, their teachers bragged about them. When they didn't, educators worked that much harder to make sure those students did better.

Michelle Haynes had looped up with her students to the end of the line—advancing a grade-level with the same students each year, teaching them until the fifth grade. She'd had years to put her imprint on her students. They had had six years to teach her some things too. Day in and day out, week after week, year after year, Haynes had taught her students to value education. She had encouraged them to take academic risks, and had assured them that, if they did, their efforts could take them to places they never dreamed they'd go. Every year, they'd grown as students. Every year, she'd grown as a teacher.

One of her students, Tori Saldivia, had excelled, just as everyone knew she would almost from the moment she had shown up for school. Another of her students, Traiquan Payne, the once quiet, shy kindergartner, was now a confident, accomplished young artist and writer. No one doubted his talents would take him places. He knew that now too.

Haynes was proud of what Traiquan and all of his fellow fifth graders had accomplished. Sisulu-Walker's soon-to-be graduates had never given up, even when it would have been easier to spend their early school years in the anonymity of one of the neighborhood's traditional public schools. Even as the crowds swelled and the cameras rolled on their first day of school, they had trudged on inside, set up shop in their makeshift classrooms, and gotten down to business. Even when there were whispers that their school's fate might be up in the air, some wrote their first (though, hopefully not their last) letters to key decision makers, hoping they might make a difference. Then, even when their school's initial test scores weren't as high as everyone would've liked, they just kept on working. Soon they would learn it had all paid off in a big way.

Most everyone, it seemed, had found themselves another good home. Many of Sisulu-Walker's graduates were now going on to some of the city's best schools: some were headed to parochial and private schools; many had been chosen to go to the city's most selective public schools; others were bound for other charter schools.

As for Tori Saldivia, she had been chosen to attend one of the city's selective public schools. Everyone knew she would benefit from her new school's rigorous academic program. She'd also get to pursue dancing, acting, and singing there. Traiquan Payne had also landed on his feet. He was going to another selective public school, one that also offered a wonderful performing arts program. Everyone figured he'd also find a way to be a star there.

Just as everyone had expected, Mylaecha Aska had rebounded academically that year, after spending third and fourth grades at another school. Her fifth-grade scores were stellar, and she would be going to another charter school, where she would continue to build on her successes from Sisulu-Walker. It was proof once again that her mom had done right by Mylaecha six summers earlier when she had taken a gamble on charter schools. Gladys Lamb hadn't known exactly what a charter school was back then, but she was sold on them now. Mylaecha and her classmates were too. One day, as Lamb entered a classroom, she saw Mylaecha sitting with Tori Saldivia, diligently collaborating on something. At first, Lamb wasn't sure what they were working on, but as she looked more closely, she saw they were composing a simple song, one that said so much about their time at Sisulu:

The Sisulu-Walker Charter School of Harlem
It is the best and the first of them all.
Since 1999, the school continues to strive,
For achievement, honor and service are our motto.

Mylaecha and Tori worked hard on their song. They kept working on it until they got it just right, and then they sang it for Lamb. After they finished, Lamb was moved. "I was so unbelievably proud," she recalled. No one had insisted that Mylaecha and Tori write a song about Sisulu-Walker. No one had made them say good things about their school. Their song had been their own work. But it seemed they shouldn't sing it just to themselves and a few others, because there were so many others who shared their pride. As it turned out, they would get to sing it to them too.

As the school year wound down, everyone was sentimental. "It was going to be a big transition, and I felt sad about it all," Lamb recalls. "They started out here together, so I was emotional about them leaving, not just about Mylaecha, but for all of them." Mostly, though, she and others were just thankful that they'd had Sisulu-Walker for as long as they did. "My decision to put Tori in this school was one of the best choices I have made in all of my life," says her mom, Gail Whiteman. "The school prepared her well, and it helped shape her into the young person she is today." And in their own ways the parents and children of Sisulu-Walker had all left an indelible imprint on education reform in New York.

As could be expected, when the fifth graders' graduation ceremony and final day at Sisulu-Walker finally arrived on June 22, 2005, emotions ran high. People began arriving early, long before the appointed hour, and Canaan's sanctuary—the former grand movie theater where Dr. Wyatt Tee Walker, Dr. Martin Luther King Jr., and Nelson Mandela had spoken so many powerful words—was packed. There were heartfelt remarks from those who had been with the school from the very beginning. There was praise from William Allen, who was now leading Sisulu-Walker as its board chairman.

True to Harlem's history, the music was lively, inspirational enough to move some of the audience to tears. But when a small group of singers stepped up to the front to perform a piece of music no one had ever heard of, the room fell quiet. It was a special moment. It wasn't just that the voices were lovely or that the lyrics struck a nerve. It was that the song had been written by two young girls one afternoon after school. It was "The Sisulu-Walker Song," and those two girls, Tori and Mylaecha, along with several of their classmates, were singing it for hundreds of people.

Soon it was time to hear another speech, this one from Sisulu-Walker's top graduate—its valedictorian. She was articulate. She was poised beyond her years. She was, to no one's great surprise, Tori Saldivia.

Sisulu's two fifth-grade teachers—Michelle Haynes and Leslie Fuller-Hope—were introduced, and they were cheered like rock stars. Then, one by one, the children approached the podium to get their diplomas, an age-old symbol of completing one step and starting another. There were many smiles that day. There were many tears. And finally as Steve Klinsky approached the podium for his own good-bye, he felt honored to be standing at the same altar where so many great people had stood and to be part of this school community. He couldn't help but feel awed by the beautiful young people and the families and teachers in front of him and how much they had accomplished.

"Thank you so much for allowing me to address you this morning in this beautiful church on this great and happy day," he began. "There is no place I would rather be and no group I am prouder to be with than the students, parents, teachers, and friends of the Sisulu-Walker Charter School."

He reminded them of their accomplishments that could be measured. He reminded them, too, of those that could not be. "And far beyond test scores, you have proven that there is a divine and joyful spark in you, and you have let it shine," he said.

Klinsky spoke of the great things that the Sisulu School hoped would be in their future, the ones who would become doctors and ministers, judges, firemen, policemen, scientists—maybe even great teachers like Michelle Haynes and the others they had learned from at Sisulu-Walker.

And then he ended with a small request, offered as part of the hopes and dreams shared by all of the hundreds of people who had joined together to create this Harlem school. "Thirty-eight years from now, you will be forty-nine like I am now, and I will be eighty-seven," he told them. "Write me a letter and say, 'Dear Old Man Klinsky, I am a graduate of the Sisulu-Walker Charter School of Harlem, class of 2005. I am one of the first students in the first charter school in the history of New York. My parents helped me grow, and my teachers taught me well. I've faced many challenges and passed many tests. I never gave up, and here is how I've helped my world.'

"Tell me what you've done," he asked them. "Tell me that your light still shines."

11

Evolution: Coming of Age

It was September 30, 2009. As occasional wafts of cool air signified the end of summer and the beginning of another school year, hundreds of parents, children, teachers, education reformers, and government leaders assembled to commemorate the end of the first decade of New York's charter schools, and the beginning of the second. Quite fittingly, the celebration was held in the place where it had all begun—the Sisulu-Walker Charter School of Harlem.

As the program unfolded, Mayor Michael Bloomberg rose to speak. Although he hadn't been elected when Sisulu was founded in 1999, since taking office he had become one of the nation's most ardent champions of public charter schools and of improving the traditional public school system. Standing at Canaan's pulpit, he marked the occasion by giving a key educational policy address.

"When I was first elected, many people thought our public school system was hopeless," Bloomberg said. "They [the city's Board of Education] talked about doing a lot of things, but nothing ever changed. Test scores remained abysmal. Graduation rates remained flat. Dropout rates kept going up. School violence remained out of control, and the bureaucracy kept getting bigger and bigger.

"Well, I'm glad to say those days are over."

When Bloomberg took office in 2002, New York City boasted seventeen nascent charter schools, including Sisulu. Eight years later, as Sisulu-Walker celebrated its first decade, the city had ninety-nine. Those schools were educating about thirty thousand students, and about forty thousand more children were stranded on wait lists, hoping to get into one. Against that backdrop, Bloomberg said he planned to create one hundred more charter schools in New York City in the next four years, doubling their numbers, and he called for the state to raise its cap on the number of charter schools that were allowed to operate.

Pointing to rising test scores in English and math as proof that the city's educational winds were moving in the right direction, he said the city was closing the "unacceptable achievement gap" that had been allowed to exist for far too long between students of different ethnicities.

"I strongly support charter schools for a very simple reason," he said. "They work."

■ ■ ■ ■ ■

By 2013, the state had raised its charter school cap to 460 schools; and 183 charter schools, educating seventy thousand students, were up and operating in New York City. During that time, their popularity had only increased. There were about four times as many applicants as openings in New York City that year; more than fifty thousand students (not including returning students) were placed on waiting lists. Currently those charter schools are mostly outperforming the traditional public schools in their neighborhoods, and the best of them are doing so by substantial margins. An analysis of the charter schools' performance (both for New York and elsewhere) and the issues facing them will be presented in the next chapter, along with areas of ongoing skepticism and debate. This chapter will seek to give some sense of their wide diversity.

■ ■ ■ ■ ■

Across New York City, charter schools fulfill many specific niches. The New York French American Charter School, for example, is the nation's first free bilingual French/English charter school; its educational program draws from the best American and French approaches, and both its board chair and parent coordinator are fluent in six languages. The New York Center for Autism Charter School, the state's first charter school to exclusively teach students with autism, focuses on defining how to best educate public school students with autism and other pervasive developmental disorders. Meanwhile, the Equity Project Charter School is attempting to prove, as extensive research suggests, that teacher quality is the single most important factor in whether or not a school's students, especially those from low-income families, succeed academically. The school pays its master teachers substantially higher salaries than traditional public schools, with the potential to earn bonuses, and it does so, the school maintains, because the productivity and quality of its teachers allow it to save costs elsewhere.

Still other charter schools, such as Success Academy, started out with a single school and a vision, but have since rapidly expanded. Several blocks from Sisulu-Walker, a former New York City councilwoman and teacher, who was also a public school parent, opened Success Academy's first charter school in Harlem in 2006, creating a culture where students (called scholars) are expected to graduate from highly selective colleges. Success Academy's curriculum is rigorous. Students arrive between 7:15 and 7:45 AM and depart at 4:30 PM, and on a typical day they are immersed in reading, math, and writing studies, hands-on science, project-based learning, and an array of specialized subjects, including the arts, physical exercise, and chess. While its practice of sharing space within existing traditional public school buildings is controversial, its program works. Success Academy consistently outperforms its neighborhood's traditional public schools, and in 2013 the school scored in the highest 1 percent of all New York schools in math, and in the top 7 percent in English language arts. In its eight years, Success Academy has grown not only in terms of numbers but in scope as well. A summer program started in 2011 trains new teachers, and in 2012, Success Academy launched a program to train leaders in fields other than education to be future leaders of schools. With twenty-two schools educating nearly sixty-seven hundred scholars, it's now New York City's largest charter school network.

Perhaps New York City's best-known operator of charter schools is the Harlem Children's Zone (HCZ). In the early 1990s, the HCZ operated a pilot program in a one-block area of Harlem that aimed to break the cycle of poverty by providing an all-encompassing range of services. Today, it blankets about a hundred blocks of Harlem, and its "cradle to college to community" programs include workshops for expectant parents and parents of young children (from newborns to three-year-olds), pre-school and after-school programs, and health and obesity programs. Several years after Sisulu began, HCZ also established its own Promise Academy charter schools, which now educate more than a thousand students in kindergarten through high school.

Like many of the city's charter schools, Promise Academy schools have an extended day and school year. But what sets HCZ's educational effort apart is that it also supports kids who attend traditional public schools in the zone, or who live in the zone and go to school elsewhere, by providing in-class assistants (called peacemakers) and after-school programs. Its work has been featured on the *Oprah Winfrey Show* and other national media outlets, including *60 Minutes*, National Public Radio, *Nightline*, and the widely acclaimed movie *Waiting for Superman*. Communities across the country have been awarded millions of dollars in federal funds to create Promise Neighborhoods of their own, and in early 2014 President Obama named five Promise Zones where the federal government will assist local communities and businesses in creating jobs and improving education, housing, and public safety. While academic achievement of some of its charter students has been mixed at times, its far-reaching programs and high-profile founder Geoffrey Canada are being closely watched to see how much of a long-term impact HCZ's "whatever it takes" attitude will have on low-income children.

Other charter networks are also taking what works in one place and replicating it in others. The Knowledge Is Power Program, for instance, started out in 1994 when two former Teach for America teachers launched their first program for forty-seven inner-city Houston fifth graders. KIPP, as it's more commonly known, has grown to educate more than fifty thousand students in a network of 141 charter schools that stretches across twenty states and Washington, DC.

Still other networks, like Los Angeles–based Green Dot Public Schools, are not only running their own charter schools, they're also taking over failed public schools and turning them around. After Green Dot took over one of the worst public high schools in California, students there became substantially more likely to graduate than students at neighborhood schools, and they were almost four times more likely to be prepared to attend college. Green Dot has since succeeded in turning around other schools.

School staff employees at the network's California schools, except for principals and assistant principals, are unionized, and Green Dot has expressed support for teachers' unions, again showing that there is no inherent conflict between unions and the charter school ideal.

Perhaps one of the most heartening developments today is that charter schools have matured to the point where they're now learning from each other. Throughout the country, charter operators are modeling their schools after other successful charter schools, borrowing this idea and sharing that one. Some are even sharing what they've learned with traditional public schools.

Achievement First is one such charter network. Achievement First was established in 2003 by the founders of a highly successful charter school in New Haven, Connecticut, that had opened four years earlier to address the persistent achievement gap between low-income, inner-city students and more affluent ones. After achieving dramatic academic gains there, the school's leaders decided that to have the kind of impact that the inequities cried out for, they would take what had been learned at the charter school in New Haven and apply it elsewhere. They opened more charter schools and have since partnered with other reform-minded organizations, including traditional public school districts. Achievement First has since worked with the New Haven Public Schools to launch the Residency Program for School Leadership, modeled after the medical school rotation system. The program, which expanded to two additional city school districts in Connecticut, is designed to recruit and train leaders for high-need schools, using the best practices of both charter schools and traditional public schools.

As the years went on and the number and types of charter schools proliferated, the Sisulu-Walker School persevered.

Its test scores had high years and low years, but Sisulu-Walker consistently outperformed the local traditional comparison schools in central

Harlem's District Five, which has a similar student profile and where many of Sisulu's students live. (Sisulu is technically on the northern, or Harlem, border of District Three, which chiefly includes the affluent Upper West Side of Manhattan and only a small sliver of central Harlem. Therefore, Sisulu—which primarily seeks to serve less affluent students from central Harlem—has always been compared to the neighborhood schools in Harlem District Five.)

Sisulu-Walker's high point came when the original kindergartners graduated as fifth graders in 2005. In that year, the Sisulu school ranked highest among all of the charter school fifth grades in New York City, with a 90 percent proficiency rate in English language arts (ELA) and 77 percent in math—roughly two times the scores of the local traditional schools. The school stayed strong for a number of years, but then declined as the school's leadership changed and teacher turnover increased. Happily, Michelle Haynes—the teacher who had helped lead the school to its stellar scores in 2005—was recruited back to Sisulu to be its principal after spending the previous four years working as a senior-level education person at Victory and as acting principal at the now high-scoring Academy charter school in Hempstead, Long Island, that Victory also served. Her first full year was the year that ended June 2013. In that year, all New York State scores took a drastic decline as Common Core standards were introduced statewide and as the grading and nature of the exam were changed to raise the passing score. In 2013 in the three grades in which Sisulu-Walker's students were tested, it outscored its local traditional schools by a factor of about 1.5 in ELA and more than doubled the local schools' math scores; however, in those same grades, the traditional schools had proficiency rates of only 12 percent and 14 percent. Sisulu's graduating fifth graders scored 24 percent in ELA, compared to about 11 percent in District Five; they scored 20 percent in math, compared to about 9 percent in District Five. The average proficiency rate among all the city's charter schools was 35 percent in math and 25 percent on the ELA, compared to Sisulu-Walker's 27 percent in math and 18 percent in ELA for its three test-taking grades. However, according to the New York City Charter School Center, New York City charter schools as a whole outperformed their district and charter peer schools 79 percent of the time in math and 54 percent of the time in ELA in 2012–13, while Sisulu-Walker did outperform its comparison district in that same year, and generally outperformed in prior years. As this book went to press, Principal Haynes was in her second full year as school head, and there were many positive signs of forward progress. Time will tell whether Sisulu rises back to the top of the charter school rankings again or remains merely a higher-achieving alternative to its own local neighborhood schools.

Whatever its test scores are in any given year, though, the Sisulu-Walker Charter School has made important contributions to other charter schools in a number of ways. First, of course, it was the first charter school to open in the state and is the only survivor of the pioneering class of 1999. Its initial success opened the path for the schools that followed, and even now there are those who believe that if Sisulu-Walker hadn't survived, the state's charter movement would've been significantly slowed down or stopped in its tracks. But perhaps just as important, Sisulu-Walker is the forerunner of a group of charter schools that are led and controlled by local community leaders themselves, that reflect the wide diversity and dreams of those local leaders, and that have not received special funding or facility support to achieve their results.

Many of the best-known charter school groups today supplement their public funding with large institutional-style fundraising and philanthropic campaigns. Millions of dollars are raised each year from wealthy board members or grant-making organizations who come from outside the community and who may control or significantly influence the organizations' policies, as well as from parallel institutionalized organizations such as the Robin Hood Foundation in New York City. Sisulu-Walker, in contrast, receives relatively little of such funds and controls its destiny at the local board level.

The Harlem Children's Zone, for example, recently received a rather staggering amount of gifts and grants to build a $100 million school building and community center in Harlem, near Sisulu, which opened in 2013. These funds included a $20 million gift from Goldman Sachs Gives, a $6 million gift from Google, and $60 million from the New York City Department of Education's charter school facilities matching-grant program. Similarly, Success Academy raised $7 million in one evening's gala. In comparison, Sisulu has received less than $21,000 in gifts and donations over the last two years.

Some charter schools also receive rent-free space in traditional public school buildings. This has been an important part of the Success Academy's financial model, for example, along with its private fundraising. Such free space for charter schools has led to complaints of political favoritism and has at times been contentious with the traditional school communities.

No rent-free space was ever available for Sisulu-Walker, and Sisulu now pays almost $500,000 a year in rent. Klinsky's $3 million gift in 2003 averages out to just $210,000 per year over the schools' fourteen-year history. While generous by any individual's standards, that's just a fraction of one year's rent, and it's considerably less financial assistance over many years than the value of rent-free space that many other New York City charter schools receive each year. Some of them, too, raise millions of dollars in private funds year after year. Klinsky's initial donation is also significantly less than what the charter schools would have received if they had been given state facilities funding comparable to what traditional public schools are given. At its heart, the Sisulu School remains a small, community-led organization competing against much larger, much better funded, and more politically connected groups and institutions. The community-led and financially self-sufficient model that Sisulu represents has been successfully replicated by other New York charter schools. Some of these were also started with Victory's help, and today some rank among the highest-performing charter schools in the state.

Several miles north and east of Harlem, in Yonkers, is the Charter School for Educational Excellence (CSEE). Its leading founder was Eduardo LaGuerre, a Hispanic and Democratic community and political leader in the South Bronx with long personal roots in the Yonkers community. The school has never required any substantial outside gifts or grants, relying only on the public charter funding and occasional loans or mortgages that it has repaid as they come due. It is governed entirely by local community leaders and Yonkers citizens, independent of any controlling overseer or outside institutional board. Its principal,

Dr. Catalina Castillo, provides its day-to-day leadership, and Victory provides technical services as needed.

CSEE now occupies two school buildings that it built or renovated, and serves about 650 children each day in grades K through 8. It is the first school ever to be chartered in Westchester County, and its student population is about 95 percent black or Hispanic, chiefly from Yonkers with some from the South Bronx. Over 80 percent of the students qualify for free or reduced-cost lunch based on income.

In 2013, CSEE's students more than doubled the ELA proficiency scores for the traditional Yonkers public school district in the same test-taking grades, and they tripled those proficiency rates in math.

The scores for CSEE's low-income minority population were far higher than the state's scores overall and higher than New York City's overall. For fourth-grade ELA, CSEE scored approximately 49 percent proficient; the corresponding figures for New York State and New York City were about 30 percent and 27 percent, respectively. According to statistics from the New York City Charter School Center, CSEE would have ranked as the eleventh highest out of the seventy-three New York City charter schools tested in fourth-grade ELA and seventeenth highest in math.

At eighth grade, CSEE continued to significantly outscore the traditional Yonkers schools, even though the traditional Yonkers public schools had more funding per child, more facility resources, and a higher-income student population than did CSEE.

About thirty miles east of Sisulu is the Academy Charter School in Hempstead, Long Island. This school was also founded and led by highly capable local community leaders; in this case, the lead founder was a longtime Hempstead minister, Barrington Goldson, who was elevated to bishop in his church soon after the school began.

The school has relied on no significant gifts or philanthropy, and—with Victory's technical advice and local Hempstead leadership—has proved both academically successful and financially sound. Students gather in a gleaming, highly attractive building that the school itself renovated from a former automobile showroom. In 2013 the school's scores were almost four times higher than those of its local district, with about a 33 percent proficiency rate in ELA; more highly funded and resource-rich

ELA Scores for CSEE

CSEE

Grade	Tested	CSEE Level 3+4 #	%	YONKERS Level 3+4 #	%	NYS Level 3+4 #	%
3	74	36	48.7%	321	16.9%		31.1%
4	69	34	49.3%	308	16.8%		30.3%
5	76	35	46.1%	285	15.8%		30.2%
6	62	34	54.8%	293	15.7%		29.6%
7	54	19	35.2%	328	18.2%		31.4%
8	54	12	22.3%	259	14.8%		33.7%
Total	389	170	43.7%	1,793	16.4%		

Math Scores for CSEE

CSEE

Grade	Tested	CSEE Level 3+4 #	%	YONKERS Level 3+4 #	%	NYS Level 3+4 #	%
3	73	27	37.0%	321	16.8%		34.2%
4	69	38	55.1%	392	21.1%		36.3%
5	77	29	37.7%	266	14.6%		29.9%
6	62	41	66.1%	319	17.0%		30.6%
7	54	11	20.4%	167	9.2%		27.7%
8	54	23	42.4%	143	8.1%		27.5%
Total	389	169	43.4%	1,608	14.6%		

traditional Hempstead schools demonstrated only about 9 percent proficiency. The Academy scored about 41 percent in math, compared to about 10 percent for Hempstead overall.

One mile due north of Sisulu, in the South Bronx, sits the Bronx Global Learning Institute for Girls (BGLIG or "Big League"). This highly innovative school was chiefly the vision of local Bronx leader Shirley Remeneski and other mostly Hispanic and women leaders in the Bronx. The school is now led day to day by BGLIG's principal Celia Domenech, who left the very wealthy traditional Southampton school district for this assignment and who is supported with technical services from Victory.

BGLIG is an all-girls charter school (now grades K–6), offering local South Bronx girls the type of education generally only available in the most expensive private schools. The school is dual language, with lessons taught one day all in English and then all in Spanish on the following day. Each girl is trained in ballet and taught a stringed instrument so that visitors to the school are serenaded with classical music from a school-wide orchestra composed of violins, violas, basses, and cellos. BGLIG does receive free use of space in a traditional public school building but has received almost no private gifts or grants. Even with less funding than nearby traditional schools, the charter school has outscored the traditional schools by more than 2.5 times, with an ELA score of about 24 percent in 2013 versus about 10 percent for the same three grades in Bronx District Seven, and a math score of about 33 percent, compared to approximately 11 percent for District Seven.

In a 2010 article, "Forget Superman, Charter Schools Are Waiting for Oprah," *Fortune* magazine's Scott Olster wrote about some of the major private gifts in the K–12 education space, such as a $100 million donation that Facebook's Mark Zuckerberg made to all types of Newark, New Jersey, public schools; Oprah Winfrey's $6 million gift to six charter organizations; and the Charter School Growth Fund's commitments of $80 million that includes gifts from the Walton Family Foundation. He also cited the chief development officer of a Houston charter network who was seeking private funding of about $12 million for the organization's $42 million annual budget.

According to Olster, "achieving sustainability, a point at which charters will be able to operate schools without seeking private investment, is considered by many as the holy grail for the charter movement, the major proof point that charters are realistic, affordable alternatives to traditional public education." He added, though, that it was not yet certain if sustainability was "any more than a pipe dream" for the majority of charter schools.

The Sisulu-Walker/Victory–style schools may be achieving this holy grail more consistently and in more schools (and may have been doing so for more years) than any other group. And they have empowered the local community members themselves.

As of 2013, Victory supported fifteen public charter schools in Philadelphia, Newark, Chicago, and New York State, including eight in New York City. It provided academic and instructional support to six of these New York charter schools.

On the 2012–13 New York State math exams, 100 percent of these six New York charter schools (including Sisulu-Walker) outperformed their home comparison districts even though none of the six received any significant private funding or philanthropy. A total of 83 percent of these schools (five of six) outperformed on the ELA.

More comprehensively, if you think of every grade level in every charter school as another test case, then over the last five years (ending in 2013), charter schools that Victory helped establish have outperformed their local comparison districts 89 percent of the time in ELA (seventy-eight out of eighty-eight times) and 97 percent of the time in math (eighty-five out of eighty-eight times).

This performance record appears to compare well even to some of the best national charter networks, such as the highly regarded KIPP network. According to KIPP's "2012 Report Card," the following statistics show the percentages of students in a particular city who outperformed their peers in the same grade.

Reading	
3rd grade	78%
4th grade	80%
5th grade	43%
6th grade	78%
7th grade	91%
8th grade	96%
Math	
3rd grade	67%
4th grade	80%
5th grade	62%
6th grade	88%
7th grade	96%
8th grade	92%

These thriving, economically sustainable, community charter schools are the direct outgrowth of the Sisulu/Victory model that Klinsky and Walker established years ago. They are the wildflowers of charter school reform, growing up from the communities themselves in a cost efficient and replicable way. At Sisulu's ten-year anniversary celebration in 2009, the school's current board chair Martez Moore said in his own moving speech, "So that has been the mission of Sisulu from day one, to be a place where dreams come true."

The dream of a replicable model for self-sufficient, community-led schools that outperform wealthier traditional and charter schools may one day come true as well.

12

What Have We Learned?

What are the nation's leading educational reform thinkers saying about charter schools today? What is academic research telling us? What are some of the broader lessons that have been learned from the early round of charter schools, and what else can they teach us? As the nation's charter movement enters its third decade, some findings and observations are emerging.

High-quality education is a fundamental right that isn't being met for many children.

It's easy to forget these days that Harlem, like many of the nation's most economically disadvantaged communities, had languished near educational despair when it gave birth to Sisulu-Walker and the New York charter school movement. Racial tensions had reached a near tipping point in the community when police in the Bronx shot and killed an unarmed African immigrant, Amadou Diallo; and the map was filled with so-called educational dead zones, where academic failure seemed perpetual and unending. Still, underneath it all stood a basic ethical imperative to give the children in these districts a better education and a fairer chance at life. Dr. Wyatt Tee Walker made this point powerfully, tying the educational reform and charter school movement back to Dr. Martin Luther King, and Steve Klinsky and others echoed this call as well. "To me, the charter school movement is not *against* anyone or anything. It is *for* giving all kids a quality education and a fair chance at life," Klinsky has said, reflecting the spirit of Walker. "The issue is a human rights issue, and it is an absolutely fundamental one."

Charter schools can work, and some have proven they can very substantially raise academic performance, even in America's most economically disadvantaged neighborhoods.

The success of the original Sisulu-Walker kindergartners is one anecdotal indicator of this, as is the record of the Succcess Academy network and other schools. However, important academic research shows the potential of charter schools more broadly and systematically.

The gold standard of charter school research is sometimes said to be the work of Stanford professor Caroline M. Hoxby, who, along with her colleagues, studied standardized test scores for New York City's charter students over an eight-year period, ending in 2008. The study was extensive, covering 93 percent of all New York City charter school students in test-taking grades three through twelve from the 2000–01 school year through 2007–08.

Most important, Professor Hoxby's study was built on an apples-to-apples analysis, where the scores of charter students were compared over time to those of other students who had applied to enter charter schools at the same time, but had lost out in the admissions lottery and attended traditional Board of Ed public schools instead. It could be argued that the children and families of these lotteried-out students were just as motivated as those whose children won seats at charter schools. Any difference in results would be attributable to the schools and not the type of parents or children.

Hoxby found that the differences over time for charter school lottery winners and lottery losers were substantial. The students studied were more likely to be black and poor than New York's City's traditional public school students overall, but Hoxby found that, on average, a student who attended a charter school from kindergarten through eighth grade "would close about 86 percent of the 'Scarsdale-Harlem achievement gap' in math, and about 66 percent of the achievement gap in English." Test scores for those who attended a charter school for a shorter period of time improved by a "commensurately smaller amount." Meanwhile, the lotteried-out students who attended traditional public schools from kindergarten through eighth grades, on average, didn't close the Scarsdale-Harlem gap by much, although they stayed on grade level.

That upward pathway of the charter students continued through high school. Compared to lotteried-out students, charter students scored about three points higher on the New York Regents subject exams for every year that they attended a charter high school prior to taking the test. Those same charter high school students were more likely to earn a New York Regents diploma by the time they turned twenty.

Hoxby's study centered on New York City, but the New Orleans school system has become another one of the most dramatic charter school laboratories in the United States. The public school system there had been dysfunctional for as long as most people could remember; but after Hurricane Katrina destroyed huge swaths of the embattled city, New Orleans had a unique opportunity to rebuild its entire public school system virtually from the ground up. Charter schools made up the backbone of that effort.

By 2013, 79 percent of New Orleans's students were attending charter schools, the largest percentage of any city in the nation, according to the National Alliance for Public Charter Schools, and recent studies show that the schools have been generally effective. In a six-year study by Stanford University's Center for Research on Education Outcomes that measured achievement from the 2005–06 school year through 2010–11, New Orleans's charter students' scores improved, on average, by "four months per year of additional learning in reading and five months for math" compared to students at traditional public schools. "As their peers' growth has declined, so have the charter students' scores improved," the study noted.

Charter schools might also improve the traditional public schools around them.

Some research shows that charter schools help not only the test scores of children who attend them, but also those of children who remain in traditional schools, perhaps by instilling the benefits of competition or by attracting lower-performing children away from the traditional schools to the charter schools.

Marcus A. Winters, senior fellow of the Manhattan Institute for Policy Research, has examined this question for New York City. In a 2009 report titled "Everyone Wins: How Charter Schools Benefit All New York City Public School Students," he argued that an "analysis of student-level data provided by the New York City Department of Education, which runs the nation's largest public school system, reveals that students benefit academically when their public school is exposed to competition from a charter. Specifically, for every 1 percent of public school students who leave for a charter, reading proficiency among those who remain increases by about 0.02 standard deviations. Math performance is unaffected. However, the lowest-performing students in a school benefit from charter-school competition in both math and reading."

Parents in disadvantaged neighborhoods clearly want charter schools for their children.

In New York City, and elsewhere, thousands of students remain on waiting lists, wanting to enroll in charter schools. Total charter enrollment in New York City has grown from a few hundred in 1999 when Sisulu-Walker began to seventy thousand in 2014 and is projected by the New York City Charter School Center to exceed one hundred thousand over time. There were almost eight thousand applicants for 2,709 seats in Harlem, more than thirteen thousand applicants for 2,627 seats in the South Bronx, and more than eighteen thousand applicants for 6,495 seats in Central Brooklyn, according to the charter school center. Families are often the best judge of how their neighborhood schools are performing, and their support for charter schools in traditionally underserved communities is strong.

Total Enrollment in NYC Charter Schools (Historic and Projected)

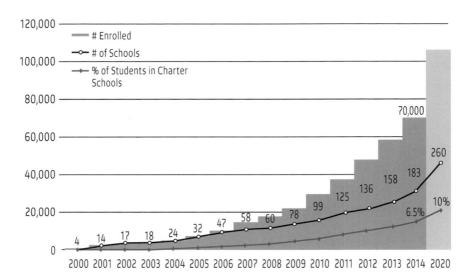

Source: New York City Charter School Center

NYC Charter School Applicants and Seats, by Neighborhood
(estimated, 2013–14)

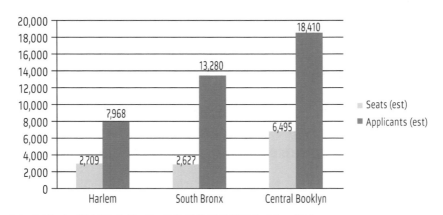

Harlem is defined as CSD 4, 5; Central Brooklyn 13, 14, 16, 17, 18, 19, 23, 32; South Bronx 7, 8, 9.
Source: New York City Charter School Center

But while charter schools can work, they can also fail.

While the charter school movement in New York City is considered among the strongest educational reform movements in the nation, if not *the* strongest, some individual charter schools still struggle or fail in New York; and throughout the country some charter schools have shown weak or mixed results. Reformers argue that the weaker charters will be shut down by strict authorizers and replaced with better models. To them, the ability for charter schools to be closed or to rapidly evolve and improve, may be one of the charter concept's key strengths.

The opposition to charter schools remains.

Although charter schools have been around for more than two decades now, many of the same arguments and skepticism that marked their arrival are still present. Critics allege that they take money away from traditional schools, harm traditional public schools, and skim off the best students, rather than encouraging special education and English language learners to apply. An entrenched me-versus-them competitive lens continues to be applied; one traditional school official recently equated the attitude to the "Coke versus Pepsi" debate. Through the years many of the arguments against charters have become more muted, but the charter movement still has its share of vocal critics.

As the charter school movement grows, supporters say, it can open up avenues for teachers with nontraditional backgrounds and raise the pay of teachers and principals.

Charter schools offer nontraditional paths to teaching, and many of their teachers come to them through Teach for America and other such programs. Because they're flexible, many charter schools can set their own pay scales or even team up with top universities to offer new paths to teaching degrees and master's degrees in education. Some charter schools seek to pay more than traditional public schools.

Charter schools didn't end up being dominated by supporters on just one side of the economic or political spectrum.

Politically, charter schools have widespread support among Democrats, Republicans, and Independents. President Barack Obama and his education secretary, Arne Duncan, have made charter schools a centerpiece of their Race to the Top competition, in which millions of dollars have been awarded to the states with the most innovative ideas for improving public schools.

Nor is the movement inherently antiunion. In New York City and other places, teachers' unions have opened charter schools of their own. Teachers at some of New York City's charter schools have formed their own unions, and Victory has worked with teachers' unions in Baltimore and Philadelphia to turn around failing schools there.

Funding and real estate access for charter schools should be fair. They should receive the same public school funds per student and equal funding for buildings as traditional public schools, and all types of charter schools should be treated equally.

More than a decade after New York's charter law passed, the state's charter schools still receive no sustained state money for buildings, and whenever the nation's charter advocates are asked what change is most needed, equality of funding and facilities almost always tops the list.

In recent years, the New York City school district has given free space in traditional public schools to some charter schools, but not all. When favorable co-location space has been given to charter schools, such as for the Success Academy Charter Schools, it has raised tensions with traditional schools that have lost the space. At the same time, the process for giving free space has appeared arbitrary to some school operators, who believe that the charter schools without free space often appear to be the single-school, independently run, and community-led charter schools that most lack political connections and clout.

The economic differences between charter schools with free space and without it can be stark. Sisulu-Walker, for example, pays about $500,000 in rent for its private space each year and has been unable to obtain free space from the city despite past attempts. If Sisulu-Walker had received years of free space like some other charter schools, it would have had millions more in funding to enhance its services and quality and to raise teachers' salaries.

By early 2014, when Bloomberg's successor, Bill de Blasio, took office, the tensions between the traditional schools and the rent-free charters erupted into a full-scale battle. Just weeks after taking office, Mayor de Blasio reversed an earlier decision by Bloomberg that would have given free public school space to three Success Academy schools, two of them new schools and the other an existing high-achieving school. De Blasio, who had already expressed anti-charter sentiments and had been at odds with Success Academy founder Eva Moskowitz, said, as reported by the *New York Times*, that the co-locations were ill advised because they would've put younger students with high school students or would have taken space needed for special education programs.

Success Academy, bolstered by its enviable academic track record, refused to back down. Thousands of supporters gathered at a rally at the state capitol in Albany, where New York governor Andrew Cuomo vowed to help "save" charter schools. The *New York Post* weighed in, too, proclaiming in its headline: CHARTER SCHOOLS NEED AFFORDABLE HOUSING, TOO.

Then in the final days of state budget negotiations, Governor Cuomo pushed through an agreement requiring the city to reinstate free public school space for Success Academy's three uprooted schools. The city would also be required to provide free school space to new and expanding charter schools and for other charters that already have it. If space isn't available, the city is to pay much of the schools' costs to rent private facilities.

The budget agreement was a victory for those charter schools, but it gave no building funds to the rent-paying schools, like Sisulu-Walker, which will continue paying the same rent for its private space as before.

(New York City's charter schools without free space paid average rental costs of about $2,350 per student in 2011–12 according to a New York City Charter School Center report.) The new budget "is a victory largely for the large charter management companies that already mostly have space in traditional public schools," the CEI-PEA's Harvey Newman explains. "But it's a major defeat for the already existing independent charter schools that often do not have free space. It causes greater stress for them, and it has exacerbated the divide between the two groups."

"Is it fair?" he asks. "If you're the recipient of a nice gift, it's very fair. If you're not, it's a piece of the pie you're not getting, and if you're doing commensurate jobs, it seems inherently unfair." In the end, "It was the governor versus the mayor and the rich charter schools versus the less rich," Newman says. "In this case, the mayor and the less rich lost."

As this book closed in the spring of 2014, the city and Success Academy had reached an agreement that would house the three displaced Success Academy schools in former Catholic schools that the city would lease. Meanwhile, the charter operators who have never received free space and lost out in the budget agreement were scrambling to find ways to get free space or equal building funding for their schools, while once again wishing they could do what they do best—educate students—without having to venture into the political arena.

In a better system, funding would be equal across all types of schools: traditional public schools, "rich" charter schools, and the less rich, independently run, and community-led ones.

Successful charter school models can be replicated.

As the charter movement enters its third decade, numerous networks are running some of the nation's most outstanding charter schools. If they've proved they know how to teach kids in one community, there's no reason to reinvent the wheel for the next community. It's time, many education observers say, to remove the roadblocks that are interfering with expansion in some states and let successful networks replicate as many schools as they can.

Regulatory oversight may be too frequent in some cases.

Charter schools are supposed to benefit from less regulation, not more, but often charter operators and others feel the opposite is true. Sy Fliegel of the Center for Educational Innovation–Public Education Association tells an instructive story: "It has been turned upside down. We have a combined three hundred years of experience in this office, and one day I asked everybody how often they saw a state regulator when they were in traditional public schools. And do you know what the answer was? Once."

Now that the charter movement has matured, some education reformers maintain that it might be worth considering whether charters should be granted for longer periods of time. No one wants to see a struggling school stay open for years. However, many charter schools are now being run by groups with proven track records. If those schools were granted charters for longer than five years, they would still be rigorously monitored, and, if necessary, could be put on probation or shut down for low performance. A ten-year charter would allow them to focus more time on academics and less on the renewal process.

If there's enough interest in charter schools, charter school caps should be lifted.

Finally, if charter schools are working, if parents are clamoring to enroll their kids in them, and if there are plenty of well-qualified organizations to run them, why not allow more? Nationally, hundreds of thousands of students sit on the nation's charter waiting lists, and the battles fought in states like New York to open more charter schools are being repeated over and over.

In 2007, New York's charter school supporters won a hard-fought battle, successfully pushing through legislation that doubled the number of new charter schools to two hundred. But a few years later they were back at it again. Eventually, the charter school cap was raised to 460 schools, but it was a hard-fought victory, coming only after charter supporters were forced to wage another battle they would've preferred not to fight.

The nail-biting scenes depicting charter school lotteries are among the most poignant in *Waiting for Superman* and another education reform movie, *The Lottery.* In real life, similar episodes play out over and over. Such painful scenes are unnecessary, and charter supporters hope that, if families are voting with their feet, politicians will listen.

Perhaps most important, it's time to allow charter schools to innovate and move the needle forward.

One of the next frontiers for schools will be how to best push the envelope with technology, says Dr. Paul E. Peterson, director of the Program on Education Policy and Governance at Harvard University and the author of *Saving Schools: From Horace Mann to Virtual Learning.* Because charter schools are flexible, Peterson believes, they might prove to be better able than traditional public schools to take the lead in developing and figuring out how to best use online blended learning technology to educate students. But charter schools are always under scrutiny and concerned about test scores, Peterson points out, so "a lot of charter school leaders are cautious."

"We need bold figures to take dramatic steps forward, and what we really need is evidence of stunning results (in technology)" says Peterson. He adds that, for the evidence on results to be credible, it needs to be documented by people who don't have a vested interest in producing such programs. "Once we have independent verification that a particular program is producing great results, that will be a tipping point."

But, ultimately, the most important issue to raise is not whether every charter school is better than the school down the street, or who uses technology in the most exciting ways.

While charter schools have introduced many innovations, that's only part of what their contribution should be, says Peterson. "If they group in number so that there is competition between charters and traditional public schools, the impact can be much greater. Indeed, competition might become so intense that both charters and traditional public schools improve side by side. If that happens, charter schools will have made a huge difference in children's lives."

13

A Return to Sisulu-Walker

Back at 125 West 115th Street, as another school year kicked off in the fall of 2013, a tall woman stood outside the doors of the Sisulu-Walker School. Scenes like this one play out every day at schools everywhere: a nurturing educator greeting her students as they begin another school day. But for those who had been around during Sisulu-Walker's early days, this was an especially heartwarming sight: the dynamic young woman was the erstwhile young teacher's assistant from Harlem who had came to Sisulu-Walker in its first year, hoping to hone her budding teaching skills. In what now seemed like a perfect fit, on this day she was *Principal* Michelle Haynes.

After teaching at Sisulu-Walker for a decade, Haynes left in 2009 to work for Victory as an instructional coach and staff developer and then as the acting principal at the high-performing Academy Charter School in Hempstead. Through the years, Haynes never let up on her own educational pursuits, eventually earning double master's degrees. Her heart, though, never left Sisulu-Walker, and like many natural-born teachers, she still longed for the daily, one-on-one contact with students. So by 2012 when an opportunity arose to become Sisulu-Walker's principal, she leapt at the chance to return to the place where her teaching career had begun, there in the neighborhood where she had grown up and had always lived. "It definitely feels like I've come back home," she said.

By the fall of 2013, 230 students in grades K–5 were enrolled in Sisulu-Walker, and about 300 students were on its waiting lists. As always, most of its students qualify for the federal free and reduced-lunch program, and most are African American, including an increasing number of students whose families emigrated from Africa and were drawn, some say, by the Sisulu name.

These days, there are no kindergarten classes squeezed into Embassy Hall. Other than that, things look much the same as they did when a red-haired kindergartener showed up on Sisulu's opening day and sounded a gold school bell, signaling the arrival of New York's charter movement. The hallways sparkle, and students' writings, artwork, and projects fill the corridors. But unlike in the early days, when Klinsky and Marshall Mitchell told Sisulu's parents the school might not immediately be able to offer some programs, like state-of-the-art arts classes, today its staff includes art and music teachers, as well as a full-time nurse and educational specialists.

Much can be learned from how education reform played out at Sisulu-Walker and at so many other charter schools across the country. What universal lessons can be drawn from the story of Sisulu-Walker and of the charter school movement as a whole? Which administrative structures, teaching methods, curriculums, and aspects of individual school culture can apply to other schools? What worked for Sisulu that can work anywhere? And what makes Sisulu or any other school succeed?

There is nothing magical about the charter school structure.

Being set up as a charter school does not, in and of itself, make a school succeed. Each charter school is different from every other charter school, based on the plans and opinions of the school's founders, board, and leaders.

The quality of the school leader sets the quality of the school.

Charter schools, like almost every other school, typically succeed when they have talented principals and fail when they lack that key leadership, sometimes even if the budget, curriculum, and other policies remain unchanged. Sisulu rose to top performance under a series of strong school leaders, later its achievement declined, and it now appears to be rising again with Haynes's leadership. The principal is like the captain of a ship. The school principal, more than anyone, chooses and trains the teachers, works with the parents, and sets the real day-to-day performance expectations. "Michelle Haynes is someone who had a deep mastery of the school," Sisulu-Walker's board chair, Martez Moore, explained. "She's now literally teaching the teachers," he said, "and is a tactical illustration of what great educators can deliver."

With high-quality leadership in place, schools can recruit and train great staffs.

Outstanding teachers follow proven leaders. The quality of the teacher, more than any other factor, determines the success of that classroom.

A successful school principal recruits and retains the right teachers and puts structures for staff training firmly in place. Now at Sisulu-Walker, staff training that takes place two weeks before school starts, along with additional training that takes place after school and on Saturdays, sets the stage for what's to come. During the preservice sessions, teachers learn the content of what they'll be covering. They develop lesson plans and strategies for teaching, and continuously work to improve student achievement.

Schools must create a culture of learning before academic plans can succeed.

"It's important that we all speak the same language, and there have to be clear rules and expectations," Haynes explains. "If a school isn't orderly, nothing is happening, so [at Sisulu] kids are celebrated when they do well. When they don't do what they should, there are consequences."

But, it's not just adherence to the rules and learning facts and figures that create a culture of learning. Students must respect themselves and others, Haynes says. Sisulu-Walker's classrooms have a Virtue Wall, where a different virtue is posted each month, often in Swahili. One month it might be *haki* (fairness), or another month it could be *heshima* (honor). Every Monday morning, a new quote supporting that month's virtue is introduced and discussed at a school-wide town hall meeting. Then students who best represent Sisulu-Walker's virtues are named citizens of the week.

There is no single right curriculum, teaching method, or educational philosophy.

Charter schools, and other schools, have succeeded with a wide range of curriculums and approaches, and schools with identical curriculums have achieved widely varying results. With the right teachers, staff, and culture, a good number of programs can succeed; there is no magic answer. The Sisulu school has continued to evolve its own strategies, while continuing to honor the basic ideas of high expectations and multidisciplinary approaches expressed in its original 1999 application.

Like other schools in New York, Sisulu-Walker's curriculum follows the Common Core, a standards-based curriculum that has now been adopted in forty-five states and Washington, DC. Its teachers, though, are given a good deal of flexibility about how to teach those standards. For math, a specialist develops the school's unit plans, and teachers design their own skill-based worksheets. Students work in small groups, according to which skills they need to be working on, and they play math games to encourage higher-order, problem-solving thinking.

Reading and writing are infused in every aspect of the curriculum, including science and social studies. In addition, Sisulu-Walker devotes 135 minutes a day to language arts, much of it organized around thematic units, such as "Adventure and Survival Stories." For guided reading instruction, students are grouped by ability, and depending on their individual reading levels, they can move to other classrooms, much as they did with the Direct Instruction program.

As for the old Core Knowledge and Direct Instruction debates, Core Knowledge has become more accepted across the country, and the concept is embodied in much of the Common Core itself. Just as Sisulu-Walker's early experiences with the Core Knowledge program showed, DI also continues to produce impressive results at many schools. What's most important, though, is that a school's staff believes in the programs they're using, and has the wherewithal, skills, and enough classroom time to implement them.

Accountability and the ability to rigorously track student progress are critical.

One of the greatest benefits of the charter movement has been that charter schools are forced to prove their merit, or they will be shut down. In the bad old days, too many children in too many communities were sentenced to failing and unaccountable neighborhood schools that never addressed their weaknesses and never changed. Those days are, hopefully, gone forever—at charter schools and traditional schools alike.

Tracking each student's progress is a key ingredient in helping each student succeed. Sisulu-Walker's students are given frequent interim assessments, and teachers can easily analyze those results by inputting them into an Excel spreadsheet. In math, for instance, skills are listed across the top of the chart. The names of students run down the side. A right answer shows up in green; wrong ones appear in red. If a string of red marks appear horizontally across from a student's name, teachers know exactly which skills that student needs to learn. On the other hand, if they see a line of red marks extending vertically under a particular math skill, they can readily see that they need to teach that material again to the entire class.

Victory has developed its own system-wide computerized academic diagnostic testing and tracking systems to keep students at each of its schools from falling through the cracks. Unlike standardized state test scores that arrive late in the school year, the information is constantly updated and readily available. These tools show which students are proficient in specific subject areas, and they identify strengths and weaknesses. If students aren't working on grade level in specific areas, teachers come up with ways to bring them up. With that kind of information, teachers can then organize their classroom lessons more effectively.

Beyond the classroom, Victory's programs also paint a detailed picture of the overall organization of their schools. They track each school's overall proficiency, even showing, for instance, students' progress teacher by teacher.

This kind of information allows teachers to provide individualized attention to every child. Back when Sisulu-Walker took in an influx of students to fill up its two school locations, the technology to quickly pinpoint the specific gaps in students' educations wasn't widely available. It wasn't until the end of the year, when the results of standardized tests came in, that educators could fully quantify what students had learned that year, and by then some of them had moved on. If Sisulu-Walker could have drawn on some of today's technological advances back then, educators would have more quickly known, for instance, not only which first graders were having trouble adding, but also when they caught on. They would have known exactly which students at the PAL building read on a first-grade level, and then could have tracked them as they moved to second-, then third-, and then fourth-grade levels. Today, teachers at technologically advanced schools, like Sisulu-Walker, have that information in their laptops—right at their fingertips.

Efficient state-of-the-art financial systems can also help schools deliver high-quality education and be financially self-sufficient.

Now that some of the glitches facing the early charter schools—particularly some school districts' recalcitrance when it came to passing tax dollars along to charter schools—have been mostly worked out, it's possible for charter schools to survive without an enormous influx of outside funding. Unlike some charter schools, Sisulu-Walker doesn't get free space in city schools, nor does it depend on substantial outside philanthropic funding now. Through the years, it has managed to become financially self-sufficient and, most important, sustainable.

To survive, schools need the same quality of financial reporting and financial management as any other complex enterprise with a multi-million-dollar budget. Today, the board leaders and educators at Sisulu-Walker (using Victory's systems) have access to detailed reports that help them manage the school on a day-to-day basis. The reports allow them to track their grants and budgets and plan for future growth. Perhaps most important, though, the reports don't become yet another mountain of paperwork that's dumped on school officials. Victory's chief financial officer Paul Augello and his team of five staffers meet regularly with principals and the boards of trustees of Sisulu-Walker and Victory's other schools, helping them decipher the numbers and make adjustments, long before the school year ends.

That kind of timely attention to the budget can allow a school to prosper. Empowered by careful budgeting, Sisulu-Walker now offers additional arts opportunities, and throughout the school, students are exposed to technology, including desktop computers and laptops.

Evolution is necessary for success.

In Sisulu-Walker's early years, when it became obvious that expanding to the second building wasn't working, Sisulu-Walker's leaders decided that bigger wasn't necessarily better. In a relatively short time, they were able to shut down the second site and scale back without having to go through layers of bureaucracy. Similarly, when the school decided to change its curriculum in those early days, it could.

In 2012, Sisulu-Walker changed direction again. Faced with declining academic achievement, its board members took deliberate action. Not only did they consider test scores, they also reviewed the school's culture, parental surveys, and teacher input. Once they had collected all the data they needed, they were able to move quickly and make the necessary adjustments, including a leadership change. That approach was in keeping with the government and business experience that some trustees brought to the board, including board chair Moore, who was himself an executive vice president for digital media and head of strategy and business development for BET Networks. Such changes could have been a nearly impossible approach to take at less nimble, traditional public schools.

Flexibility is one of the charter movement's greatest assets, and it's just as important in running schools as it is in business or government. "Every year is critical for a student," Moore says, emphasizing that a lost year in education isn't just one lost year. "There's a multiplier effect," he explains, because it can also have an impact the next year—and in the years after that.

Perhaps most important of all, educators should never stop believing that every child can learn.

Whenever things looked bleak at Sisulu, the founders, trustees, school team, and community never gave up. Instead, they just kept on going. Whenever test scores dropped, the school figured out better ways to teach its students. That's been Sisulu-Walker's mantra since day one, and it's applicable to all schools, whether they're in cities grappling with their own educationally deprived areas, in school districts ravaged by natural disasters, or even in affluent suburbs.

So it's fair to say that what happened at this feisty little school in Harlem truly had been about "tombstone stuff." In the years since Sisulu-Walker opened its doors, hundreds of students have graduated from the school. Many of them went on to attend some of the city's most selective high schools, and many of its earliest graduates are now in college.

But what's sometimes lost with time is just how important the experiences of early charter schools actually were. The first schools out of the block, like Sisulu-Walker, were pioneers that charted a path when no one knew exactly where it might lead. Those that followed built on their successes and learned from their mistakes. Perhaps their greatest legacy is that they survived at all, proving that charter schools can work, even in a hostile environment.

It's hard to believe that the state's charter law is now older than most of the students who filled the former movie palace on that September day in 2009 when Sisulu-Walker celebrated its ten-year anniversary. Most of those students hadn't even been born when their school first opened its doors. But like their future, the future of education reform is a work in progress, just as it was in the early days when no one knew where the budding charter movement was headed.

Could there one day be a charter school for every family wanting to enroll its children in one? Could the best innovations taking place at some of the nation's most successful charter schools be replicated on a larger scale across the traditional schools? Could there even be a day when some new visionary comes up with another bold educational model that makes charter schools obsolete?

Just like the days when a band of idealistic dreamers joined together with the notion that they could start a novel kind of school smack in the middle of one of America's toughest educational zones—and then plunged in headfirst to actually make it succeed—it's still impossible to be certain where education reform, or the next dream, leads. But for anyone doubting that the possibilities are limitless, former New York mayor Michael Bloomberg spoke these words at Sisulu-Walker's ten-year anniversary:

"The future is in our hands," he said. "We have shown that we can make progress. We've shown that all those years when people just sat back and said, 'That's *just* the way it is. There's nothing you can do about it'—that they were wrong."

There's excitement among parents, teachers, and principals, he said, and he concluded, "The kids know that they are, for the first time perhaps, really getting the skill sets that they're going to need to be in control of their own destiny and share in the great American dream." But, in what must have surely resonated with most everyone that fall day, he offered some cautionary words:

"Shame on us if we don't take this to the next level."

Zeyna Diouf

Of all the hundreds of parent conferences that have taken place at Sisulu-Walker, one in particular stands out. It was the day that Rama Diouf* came in with her daughter, Zeyna*, on her first day of kindergarten. It wasn't just that Zeyna didn't know how to count or recognize letters. It wasn't that she spoke very little English. It wasn't even that she had trouble sitting still and paying attention in class. The truly stunning part of their conversation was something Rama Diouf said about herself: as a child, she never went to school.

As a young girl growing up in West Africa, Rama Diouf didn't get an education. She stayed home to help out with the cooking and whatever other household chores needed doing. Rama Diouf barely spoke English. She didn't read. Not surprisingly, she couldn't help Zeyna with her homework like other parents did. On many a night, she struggled to keep from crying.

Diouf had no idea what to expect of Zeyna. She didn't know what to ask of her school. But this was America, and like so many immigrants before her, Rama wanted a better life for her child, one of educational opportunity, one unlike her own. So on that fall day in 2005, speaking in broken English, she talked about her dreams and told her story as best she could. But even as she grasped for the right words, even as she fought

---

*The names of the student and her mom have been changed.

back tears, she was unusually clear about one thing. There was only so much she could do for her child. "The only way Zeyna will succeed is if *you* help her," she said, "because what she learns, she will have to learn from you."

It was a challenge Sisulu-Walker's educators took to heart. Zeyna did too.

As a kindergartner, Zeyna struggled to do her best. A lovely, impeccably groomed child, Zeyna showed up for school with a lively disposition and an infectious smile, but she had few of the early skills that most children bring to kindergarten. Zeyna couldn't understand what anyone was saying. She had no idea what she was supposed to be doing. Before long, she withdrew. She shut down. Her behavior deteriorated. On her bad days, Zeyna would curl up under a table and suck her thumb. On her even worse days, she would cry out in frustration: "I just don't understand what we're doing." Perhaps saddest of all, her smile all but disappeared.

But Zeyna kept trying. Several times a week, she worked with a language specialist, who taught her the most basic of English words. By year's end, she still wasn't ready for first grade, so she repeated kindergarten the following year. But that didn't stop her from feeling her own modest sense of accomplishment at the 2006 kindergarten stepping-up ceremony. When everyone got their diplomas, she got her own diploma cover that looked like everybody else's on the outside, if not the inside. "I want to read," she said, clutching her empty diploma cover that day. "I love school."

As a kindergartner again the next year, Zeyna kept trying. Over the summer, she spoke very little English, and by the time school started up again, her language skills had deteriorated. Still her teachers at Sisulu never gave up on her.

One day, while working with her language teacher, Zeyna moved tenaciously through a group of pictures in an exercise designed to teach her words like *piano, jewelry,* and *table.* Finally, as she was about to leave, it all came together. "What do you wear on your wrist?" her teacher asked. "A bracelet," Zeyna responded. "What do you wear on your waist?" her teacher asked again. "A belt," she said. "And what does 'belt' start with?" was her teacher's final question. "B," Zeyna answered before flashing her huge smile once again. It might have seemed like a tiny accomplishment, but no one at Sisulu-Walker, especially Zeyna, saw it that way. By year's end, she had not only mastered kindergarten-level work. She was working above grade level. She'd be moving up to first grade. She'd get a kindergarten diploma of her own.

As a first grader in the fall of 2007, Zeyna's best was right up there with everybody else's, and she kept reading up a storm. Everyone now called her the "Vocabulary Queen," and she was one of the best writers in the class. In a writing exercise entitled "A Summer Poem," Zeyna wrote eloquently about the wondrous joys of summer, about children going to the beach with their "comrades." Socially, she had blossomed too. She was like a different child. She was poised, friendly, self-confident, and enthusiastic about weighing in during class discussions, and she was eager to help out her classmates as well. She continued to flourish as an inquisitive, successful student.

For Zeyna and her mom, by the time she reached fifth grade, her years at Sisulu-Walker had been the American Dream come true.

"I'm so very, very, very proud, I'm telling you that," Zeyna's mom said. "I'm so happy for her. I didn't want her to have to not go to school. And now she can do her schoolwork all by herself." Zeyna is happy too. "Sisulu-Walker, it's my favorite school in the whole wide world," she said. "I learned to write there. I learned my alphabet. I got clever."

In 2012, Zeyna graduated from Sisulu-Walker, headed to another charter school for middle school. Eventually, she said that day, she wants to become a lawyer.

But that's not the end of her story. While at Sisulu-Walker, Zeyna did a little teaching of her own for her own special student: her mom. "I want her to learn more," Zeyna said of her mom at the time. "I want to teach her to do the stuff I learned at Sisulu-Walker." After all, Zeyna says:

"This is America. Everybody should have a great education here."

NOTES

Introduction

seventy-two children: Program for Sisulu-Walker graduation ceremony for class of 2005.

2.5 million children: National Alliance for Public Charter Schools.

educational "dead zone": Public Education Association, "State of the City Schools, '98," Public Education Association, December 1998, reported in Susan Edelman, "City Schoolkids Fail to Keep Up," *New York Post*, December 23, 1998.

A full 90 percent . . . public schools overall: Victory Schools press release, June 28, 2005.

more than 250 charter schools in the state: New York State Education Department.

about 6,500 charter schools nationwide: National Alliance for Public Charter Schools.

forty-two states and the District of Columbia: National Alliance for Public Charter Schools.

Chapter 1: A Civil Right

Except where noted, most of the material for the first section of this chapter (through the bullets) is from Dr. Wyatt Tee Walker. His quotes are from his interviews with Bounds that took place over several years. Some of the details in the chapter were also provided by his son, Wyatt T. Walker Jr.

Earlier in the service . . . "I want you to take good care of him": The account in this paragraph comes from Wyatt T. Walker Jr. The two quotes in this paragraph are Wyatt T. Walker Jr.'s recollection of what Dr. Martin Luther

King told him, not direct quotes from King. From Wyatt T. Walker Jr.'s, interviews by the author.

"What you ought to do": This story and these words are not King's actual words, but are Dr. Wyatt Tee Walker's interpretation of the message he heard in his head after King was assassinated; from Walker's interviews by the author.

"You're the brilliant science student": This quote is Dr. Wyatt Tee Walker's recollection of what King said to him that day; they are not King's actual words; interview with Walker by the author.

King liked to bring: Walker's interpretation of what King liked to do; interview with Dr. Wyatt Tee Walker by the author.

"Both of us valued education": Walker's interpretation of King's beliefs; interview with Walker by the author.

Ebony *magazine included him: Ebony* magazine, 1993.

New York's public school system had not always: Dr. Margaret "Peg" Harrington and Seymour Fliegel, interviews by the author.

"A Nation at Risk": US Department of Education's National Commission on Excellence in Education, "A Nation at Risk," US Department of Education, April 1983.

Educational "dead zone": Public Education Association, "State of the City Schools, '98," Public Education Association, December 1998. As reported by Edelman, Susan, "City schoolkids fail to keep up," *New York Post*, December 23, 1998.

45 percent . . . 18 percent: Public Education Association, "State of the City Schools, '98." As reported by Archibold, Randal C., "Most New York City Students Will Fail New Graduation Tests, Report Says," *New York Times*, December 23, 1998.

38 percent . . . 57 percent: Ibid.

three hundred thousand students: Public Education Association, "State of the City Schools, '98," as reported by Edelman, "City schoolkids."

ninety thousand kids: Ibid.

bleak futures . . . on welfare or in prison": Public Education Association report as quoted in Edelman, "City schoolkids."

"In reality . . . public school systems": Edelman, "City schoolkids."

When her school ran out of basic school supplies: Sherry, interviews by the author.

Another public educator: Fliegel, interviews by the author; and Fliegel, Seymour, and James MacGuire. *Miracle in East Harlem: The Fight for Choice in Public Education*. New York: Times Books, a division of Random House, Inc. 1993.

Another leading New York City educator: Harrington, interviews by the author.

One of them was a young woman: Haynes, interviews by the author.

Chapter 2: Laying the Groundwork

Clinton had uncharacteristically: Bennet, James, "President, Citing Education as Top Priority of 2d Term, Asks for a 'Call to Action,'" *New York Times,* February 4, 1997.

Clinton's staffers: Dowd, Maureen, "Schism of the Union." *New York Times,* February 6, 1997.

and their coverage . . . on the other?: Goodman, Walter, "Morass of Competing and Colliding Images," *New York Times,* February 5, 1997.

"an unlikely confluence of events": Tom Brokaw quote as reported by: Goodman, Ibid.

automobile accident three months before he was born: Clinton, Bill, *My Life.* New York: Alfred A. Knopf, 2004.

"Now, looking ahead": President William Jefferson Clinton, State of the Union Address, February 4, 1997.

"I challenge every state": President William Jefferson Clinton, State of the Union Address, January 23, 1996.

Now in his hour-long speech: Clinton, State of the Union, February 4, 1997.

seventy times: Bennet, James, "President, Citing Education as Top Priority of 2d Term, Asks for a 'Call to Action,'" *New York Times,* February 5, 1997.

"politics stopped . . . a new nonpartisan commitment": Clinton, State of the Union, January 23, 1996.

"Politics . . . the schoolhouse door": Ibid.

first person to use the word charter: Negri, Gloria, Budde obituary, *Boston Globe,* June 21, 2005.

Wouldn't it be better . . . they promised? Saulny, Susan, "Ray Budde, 82, First to Propose Charter Schools, Dies," *New York Times,* June 21, 2005. Questions are author's interpretation from Budde obituary.

They invited: Seymour Fliegel, interview by the author.

"Fliegel's presentation": Junge, Ember Reichgott. *Zero Chance of Passage: The Pioneering Charter School Story.* Edina, MN: Beaver's Pond Press, Inc., 2012.

Pataki . . . for a charter school law: Material and quotes in these five paragraphs are from former New York governor George Pataki, interview by the author.

"I do think . . . just doesn't make sense": Rudy Crew quotes come from Hartocollis, Anemona, "Crew Speaks Out Against Charter-School Plan," *New York Times,* December 16, 1998.

In 1996, . . . community outreach: "NEA Joins Growing Charters Schools Movement," *Education Daily,* April 18, 1996.

"Frankly, . . . diverse learning needs": Keith Geiger quotes come from Bradley, Ann, "NEA Seeks to Help Start Five Charter Schools," *Education Week,* April 24, 1996.

As part . . . within our public schools": *Education Daily,* Ibid.

But, in what some . . . that same article: Geiger quotes come from *Education Week,* Ibid.

"I am not enthusiastic": Sandra Feldman quotes come from Steinberg, Jacques, "School Leaders Raise Doubt on Pataki's 'Charter' Plan," *New York Times,* January 14, 1997.

In particular . . . for each district: Ibid.

The concerns of many: Material and quotes in these six paragraphs are from Bernstein, Marc F., "Why I'm Wary of Charter Schools," *School Administrator,* August 1999.

he argued that: Bernstein quoting from a letter to the editor he wrote to the *New York Times,* January 1999.

"No teacher . . . educate its remaining students": Ibid.

By then, education reformers: Material and quotes in these two paragraphs are from Seymour Fliegel, interview by the author.

Walker had been inspired: Dr. Wyatt Tee Walker, interview by the author.

"Let me say . . . and across the land": Dr. Wyatt Tee Walker, "Why We Need Charter Schools," Speech given at Norman Thomas High School in New York City, March 27, 1999.

A little noted . . . who had signed the postcards: Marshall Mitchell, interview by the author.

"We were able . . .": Ibid.

As 1998 wound down: Governor George Pataki, interview by the author.

1:30 AM: Levy, Clifford, "Senate Passes Charter Plan for Schools," *New York Times,* December 18, 1998.

$20,000 a year pay raise: Levy, Clifford, with Anemona Hartocollis, "Crew Assails Albany Accord on Opening Charter Schools," *New York Times,* December 19, 1998.

"We always said . . . to the legislators": Marshall Mitchell, interview by the author.

"the single greatest . . . state history": Levy, Clifford, "Senate Passes Charter Plan."

As the years . . . from the state system: Todd Ziebarth, "Measuring Up to the Model: A Ranking of State Charter School Laws," National Alliance for

Public Charter Schools, January 2014; analysis conducted by Ziebarth and Louann Bierlein Palmer.

seventh strongest among the laws of forty-two states and DC: Ibid. When the New York law was first developed, the only national ranking of laws was that of the Center for Education Reform, which put New York's first law in seventh place, according to Jeanne Allen, CER's founder and president emeritus. New York's law has annually moved up and down on the now fifteen-year-old ranking. CER rankings are based on how the law works in practice, whereas that of the NAPCS uses the criteria discussed here in the text.

For example, the New York law: These paragraphs beginning here and continuing through the conclusion of this chapter are an interpretation of the New York charter law and how it would work.

NAPCS gave the New York law a score of just 1: NAPCS, "Measuring Up to the Model."

70 percent of what their home districts spent per student: New York Charter Schools Association.

For example, the 1995–96 summary data: Per Pupil Aid for Charter Schools figures, New York State Education Department.

score of 1 . . . federal categorical funding": NAPCS, "Measuring Up to the Model."

$8,213 per student . . . $5,435 per charter student: Per Pupil Aid for Charter Schools figures.

"The formula in New York City": Seymour Fliegel, interview by the author.

Political and bureaucratic opposition . . . Mikuta asked: Material and quotes in these four paragraphs are from Mikuta, Julie, Memorandum to Tom Freedman, November 3, 1997, Pres. Bill Clinton Presidential Papers.

that reflected . . . education skills: Author's observation.

Chapter 3: A Brother's Legacy

Unless otherwise noted, the material in this chapter about Steve Klinsky's early years, family life, education, business career, observations about the business world, his interpretation of Buber's writings, his motivations for founding the Gary Klinsky Children's Centers, and his accounts of how he founded and designed them was provided by Steve Klinsky in interviews by the author.

The central message of Buber's book: Buber, Martin. *The Way of Man: According to the Teachings of Hasidism.* Chicago: Wilcox & Follett Company, 1951.

"The central folk tale or metaphor": Klinsky interviews by the author.

The program eventually expanded . . . multiple public and private donors: Gary Klinsky Children's Centers and Brooklyn Bureau of Community Service staff, interviews by the author.

and was described by the New York Post: Celona, Larry, "No Slays Yet in Apple's Former Death Precinct—Exclusive," *New York Post*, March 1, 1999.

"No," she responded . . . really love.": quote is based on Klinsky's recollection of the teacher's comments; Klinsky interview by the author.

Chapter 4: Building a Team

and their East Harlem miracle had been substantially undone: Fliegel, interview by the author.

CEI had been active behind the scenes: Fliegel, interview by the author.

By law . . . by a board of trustees: The New York Charter Schools Act of 1998.

The questions and topics included: Ibid.

Consistent with the 501(c)(3) rules: Klinsky about how Victory's schools would be set up, interview by the author.

Klinsky was expecting to lose about $1 million: Klinsky, interview by the author.

They agreed to help him: Fliegel, interview by the author.

"You're one of the good guys": Fliegel, interview by the author.

The American Federation of Teachers (AFT) had recently issued: American Federation of Teachers, "Building on the Best, Learning from What Works. Six Promising Schoolwide Reform Programs." American Federation of Teachers, July 1998.

The first was Core Knowledge: Ibid.

"a gifted curriculum for all kids": Ibid.

A second approach recommended: Ibid.

The major criticism of DI: Interviews with educators by the author.

The standard criticism of Core Knowledge: Interviews with educators by the author.

One morning, at about the same time: From Klinsky's handwritten notes dated April 1, 1999, and interviews with Klinsky by the author. Quotes from the courtroom are not exact quotes, but rather are Klinsky's recollection of them.

Klinsky's starting belief: Klinsky, interview by the author.

The first was Erik Heyer: Heyer, interview by the author.

At about the same time: Lawson, interview by the author.

"Let me get this straight": Lawson and Klinsky, interviews by the author.

The agency's owner knew of a feisty Englishwoman: Bell, interviews by the author.

Soon he hired John Elwell: Elwell, interview by the author.

"Schools need at least a year": Elwell, interview by the author.

had been successfully implementing DI: Feinberg, interviews by the author.

"It was like": The quotes attributed to Klinsky and the late Laurie Brown in these paragraphs are their recollections of what was said and may not be their exact words. Brown and Klinsky, interviews by the author.

Walking on some difficult streets: Klinsky and Mitchell, interviews by the author.

Klinsky also learned: Klinsky and Mitchell, interviews by the author.

Before long, Klinsky realized: Klinsky, interview by the author.

And on days of good luck and success: Klinsky and Mitchell, interviews by the author.

Sitting in one neighborhood kingpin's office: Klinsky, interview by the author.

"But when do I get my money?": This is Klinsky's recollection of the conversation and may not reflect the exact words he or the other person spoke. Klinsky, interview by the author.

Later, on a more somber day: Klinsky, interview by the author.

Marshall Mitchell had an idea: Mitchell, interview by the author.

Chapter 5: Building a Community

apartment building in the Bronx: Cooper, Michael, "Officers in Bronx Fire 41 Shots, And an Unarmed Man Is Killed," *New York Times*, February 5, 1999.

"A hundred sixteenth between Seventh . . . owned it": quotes attributed to Lucas in Jacobson, Mark. *American Gangster and Other Tales of New York*. New York: Grove/Atlantic, 2007.

According to testimony: Jacobson, *American Gangster*.

and he knew Walker's . . . to tell him so: Klinsky, interview by the author.

"maybe," he wrote . . . we'll go far": Klinsky's journal.

But Walker . . . much grander vision: Dr. Wyatt Tee Walker and Wyatt T. Walker Jr., interviews by the author.

"I see a building edifice": Walker's words are as Wyatt Tee Walker and Wyatt T. Walker Jr., recalled them.

When construction crews: Wyatt T. Walker Jr. and Wyatt Tee Walker, interviews by the author.

Walker had his own unique system: Dr. Wyatt Tee Walker, interview with the author.

One day, as Klinsky was wrapping up his work: Klinsky, interview by the author.

his first public appearance took place: Walker, interview by author.

less than 1 percent of Roosevelt's: Numbers compiled by *Newsday* based on figures from New York State Department of Education.

Finally, they came upon: Klinsky, interview by the author.

"The Roosevelt schools . . . we jumped on it": Francis, interview by the author.

$16,000 in rent: Sisulu application.

several hundred thousand dollars in advance: Klinsky, interview by the author.

Sisulu would pay a percentage: Klinsky, interview by the author.

Together, Klinsky and Hasson: Hasson and Klinsky, interviews by the author.

Even so, some political insiders: Klinsky's handwritten notes, April 15, 1999.

"Wrong to tie up": Klinsky's handwritten notes, April 15, 1999.

"Every day that a student": Daniels, interview by the author.

"The legislative background": Cox, interview by the author.

"Klinsky understood organizations": Cox, interview by the author.

"I was determined that": Steffey, interview by the author.

"He put his hands on my shoulders": Steffey, interview by the author.

"I was a bit of a lightning rod figure": Steffey, interview by the author.

"the single greatest improvement": Hartocollis, Anemona, "8 Charter Schools, 4 with Profit Goal, Are Picked by State," *New York Times,* June 16, 1999. *called the arrival of the charter schools "A New Course":* Hildebrand, John, "A New Course," *Newsday,* June 16, 1999.

"A charter school in Roosevelt": "Charter School Will End Status Quo in Roosevelt," *Newsday* editorial, June 17, 1999.

Approving a charter school is the easy part: Newman, interview by the author.

Chapter 6: Building a School

July of 1999 was brutal: Klinsky, interview by the author.

Folding metal chairs were set up: King, interview by the author.

She desperately wanted: Edelman, Susan, "Parents doing their homework on charter school," *New York Post,* July 9, 1999.

"I'm just looking": Ibid.

"It's a new school—a fresh start": Ibid.

In recent weeks, community leaders: Mitchell, interview by the author.

By then, Klinsky: Klinsky, interview by the author.

As Sisulu's fortunes rose: The descriptions of the early days in the rent-by-the-office are from Klinsky, Heyer, and Lawson, interviews by the author.

"Here was Steve": Bell, interview by the author.

"I'm gonna sue you!": These are the words Klinsky recalled the salesman screaming, but may not be his exact words. Klinsky, interview by the author.

"We had to carefully maneuver": Heyer, interview by the author.

A longtime New York City educator: Faustin, interview by the author.

"We all shared the same vision": Faustin, interview by the author.

"It is not the overwhelming demand": Klinsky's handwritten notes.

The group claimed: Hartocollis, Anemona, "Charter Vote Is Assailed as Illegal," *New York Times,* June 20, 1999.

Claiming . . . to happen this fall": Ibid.

if the law were to be followed: Sanders quote, Edelman, Susan, "Legal Threat Hangs Over Harlem Charter Schools," *New York Post,* July 4, 1999.

"Our school will": Klinsky quote, Ibid.

wasn't too late for public comment: Hartocollis, "Charter Vote Is Assailed."

they hadn't violated the law: Hartocollis, Anemona, "Charter Schools Are Approved Again, and Procedures Questioned," *New York Times,* July 14, 1999.

"nothing more than a red herring": Deister quote: Hartocollis, Anemona, "Charter Vote Is Assailed as Illegal," *New York Times,* June 20, 1999.

Years later, Sanders declared: Sanders, Steven, "My Evolution on Charter Schools: Lawmaker Behind 1998 law says the verdict is in, and it's positive," *New York Daily News,* May 13, 2010.

In a 2013 interview for this book: Sanders, interview by the author.

During the summer of 1999: Mitchell, interview by the author.

"Mitch," the political leader said: Mitchell, interview by the author. These are not the exact quotes of the political activist, but are how Mitchell remembered the conversation.

"I liked the idea": Haynes, interview by the author.

Padora Vincent, a Harlem mother: the late Vincent, interview by the author.

Gladys Lamb was another hopeful parent: information in these six paragraphs is from Lamb, interview by the author.

"I don't think this is a good school for you": Lamb's recollection of the teacher's remarks.

As the date for . . . open houses had been held: Mitchell, interview by the author.

Still others, like Vincent: Vincent, interview by the author.

Sisulu's founders had taken great care: Walker, interview by the author.

"When I read the letter": Lamb, interview by the author.

Its owner, the late Sylvia Woods: Woods, Sylvia, and Family. *Sylvia's Family Soul Food Cookbook.* New York: William Morrow and Company, Inc., 1999.

Meeting in a private room: Klinsky, interview by the author.

"I've been praying on this": Klinsky's recollection of the teacher's words.

Chapter 7: Year One

Brown, Victory's curriculum director: Brown, interview by the author.

"When I saw them . . . just how exciting": Brown, interview by the author.

For most, like kindergartner Mylaecha: Lamb, interviews by the author.

Traiquan Payne settled in: Payne and Vincent, interviews by the author.

"She was always . . . what she wanted to do": Vincent, interview by the author.

"I just looked at her": Vincent, interview by the author.

247 children: Sisulu's charter school application.

City buses got lost: Victory Schools staff and Sisulu-Walker educators, interviews by the author.

Because the school: Faustin, interview by the author.

"It was a beautiful building": Faustin, interview by the author.

Klinsky's mother-in-law: Sherry, Haynes, Klinsky, interviews by the author.

Right from the beginning: Sisulu-Walker educators and Victory School staff, interviews by the author.

the regents expressed concerns: Wyatt, Edward, "Charter School's Learning Curve; Operator Faces Challenges in New Educational Venture," *New York Times*, February 23, 2000.

A few weeks later: Klinsky, interview by the author.

Many students: Klinsky and Haynes, interviews by the author.

"My son has really turned around this year": Klinsky's recollections of the father's words, rather than an exact quote.

Some of Sisulu's best-run classrooms: Haynes and Sherry, interviews by the author.

On another day: Klinsky, interview by the author. The reporter's quote is Klinsky's recollection of his words, not the reporter's exact quote.

"And I'm George Walker *Bush":* These are not Bush's exact words, but they are how Walker remembered what was said, Walker interview by the author.

Before Bush's visit: Faustin, interview by the author.

"Principal Faustin . . . teaching these kids!": Faustin's recollection of Bush's words, rather than an exact quote.

Later that day: Bush, George Walker, "A Culture of Achievement," Speech at the Manhattan Institute for Policy Research, October 5, 1999.

So if students had problems: Faustin, interview by the author.

Harrington had started: Harrington, interview by the author.

"She's going from . . . ratio of talent to students": Klinsky, interview by the author.

Harrington knew how to raise: Harrington, interview by the author.

Education reform had settled in: Educators at Sisulu-Walker and Victory, interviews by the author.

An overwhelming 98 percent: Sisulu-Walker parents survey, 2000.

When Erik Heyer was finishing up: Heyer, interview by the author.

But on the financial side: Klinsky, interview by the author.

Klinsky learned a lot: Klinsky, interview by the author.

parents told the New York Post: Carl Campanile, "Kids Make the Grade at First Charter School," *New York Post,* June 22, 2000.

ninety new spaces: Sisulu charter school figures, Victory Schools end-of-the-year report, 2000.

Finally, that summer: Whiteman, interview by the author.

Chapter 8: Battles

121 students in two grades: John A. Reisenbach Charter School Renewal Report, SUNY's Charter Schools Institute, January 2004.

In its second year: Information in these three paragraphs is from the John A. Reisenbach Charter School Renewal Report. Ibid.

Construction woes and heavy rains: "Charter-school experiment taking toll in Albany," *New York Teacher,* October 6, 1999.

housed in temporary modular facilities: Charter Schools Institute, "Third-Year (Second Charter) Visit Report." (Inspection Visit Conducted by School-Works, LLC on behalf of the SUNY CSI.)

some classes spilled out into hallways: Department of Education report as reported by Wyatt, Edward, "Charter School's Problems Yield Cautionary Tale," *New York Times,* August 18, 2000.

accusations of financial mismanagement: Charter Schools Institute, "Third-Year (Second Charter) Visit."

a quarter of its students and two principals had left: Wyatt, "Charter School's Problems."

scores for English language arts were among New York's lowest: Ibid.

many of the school's problems: Charter Schools Institute, State University of New York, "Summary of Renewal Report Findings," Seventh year report; 2005–06.

twenty-three charter schools were up and running: (New York) State Education Department, "Annual Report to the Governor, the Temporary President of the Senate and the Speaker of the Assembly on the Status of Charter Schools in New York State in the 2000–01 School Year. Presented to the Board of Regents," May 22, 2002.

"Can't Wait to Get Going": "Can't Wait to Get Going," *Newsday*, September 3, 2000.

One of them, Reginald Brinson: Brinson, interview by the author.

Kathleen Sherry, who had left Sisulu: Sherry, interview by the author.

Educators, including principal Dr. Terry Tchaconas: Tchaconas, interview by the author.

"I had started out working": Tchaconas, interview by the author.

Meanwhile, educators, like Catherine Jackvony: Jackvony, interview by the author.

"It's going to be a lot harder": Jackvony, interview by the author.

claiming it was unconstitutional: Swirsky, Joan, "Roosevelt's Tug of War Over Its Charter School; The New Academy Moves Into Its Permanent Quarters, but the Public School District Drags Its Heels Over Payments," *New York Times*, November 19, 2000.

If that lawsuit prevailed: Klinsky and other Victory officials, interviews by the author.

Simultaneously, thorny real estate issues surfaced: Klinsky and other Victory officials, interviews by the author.

In the summer of 2000: Klinsky, interview by the author.

"We want you to pull the Roosevelt application": This is how Klinsky remembers the conversation.

So, ever open to improvisation: Dr. Margaret "Peg" Harringon, interview by the author.

When Catherine Jackvony: Jackvony, interview by the author.

more than $600,000: numbers provided by Victory Schools.

needed to confirm RCA's enrollment figures: Swirsky, "Roosevelt's Tug of War."

This was a blatant violation: Charter proponents, interviews by the author.

"This wasn't a business issue": Klinsky, interview by the author.

Klinsky, through Victory: Klinsky, interview by the author.

principal Terry Tchaconas: Tchaconas, interview by the author.

would be a lasting one: Brinson, interview by the author.

it was legally owed: Klinsky, interview by the author.

every one of them: Roosevelt Children Academy parents survey.

142 students had applied for 48 openings: Numbers as reported by Victory Schools in its report "Victory Schools 2000–01 Results."

academic expectations among teachers: Charter Schools Institute, "Third-Year (Second Charter) Visit."

including Tchaconas's closet-sized office: Tchaconas, interview by the author.

13 percent of them scored: ITBS scores as reported by Victory Schools in its report, "Victory Schools 2000–01 Results."

55 percent did: Ibid.

second and third respectively: Victory Schools press release, June 26, 2003.

ranked sixth . . . on the same test: New York ELA scores and Victory Schools press release, July 13, 2004.

87 percent . . . 70 percent: New York ELA scores and Victory Schools press release, July 25, 2005.

92 percent . . . 72 percent: New York Math scores and Victory Schools press release, August 21, 2006.

The Roosevelt school began: Victory officials.

As for Brinson's daughter, Regine: Brinson, interview by the author.

"Our teachers did everything": Regine Brinson, interview by the author.

"She enjoyed school": Brinson, interview by the author.

"I loved the school": Regine Brinson, interview by the author.

Chapter 9: In the Valley

Victory's goal was to blend: Klinsky, interview by the author.

save more than forty union jobs: Letter from the Baltimore Teachers Union's President Sharon Y. Blake, April 3, 2001.

"With Victory's assistance, the BTU (Baltimore Teachers Union) and the City of Baltimore were able to avert a pending State takeover and retain local control for Baltimore's public schools. Victory's actions helped to prevent the loss of over 40 union jobs that would have occurred in this instance. Moreover, Victory's involvement facilitated an 11 percent pay increase for these members.

"The BTU chose to partner with Victory in this agreement based on the long and successful track record of collaborating with and involving the teachers unions that Victory's staff has clearly demonstrated. We have found our experience working with Victory to be no different and we look forward to creating a truly successful partnership with them in the City of Baltimore."

This work was favorably featured: Winters, Rebecca, "Grading the Philadelphia Experiment," *TIME*, June 23, 2003.

and researchers from the Harvard Kennedy School: Victory Schools press release, April 21, 2010.

The increase in the school's rental costs: Klinsky, interview by the author.

But all of: Sisulu and Victory educators and staff members, interviews by the author.

during his occasional visits: Klinsky, interview by the author.

"but you're *the ones reading to* me": Cox, interview by the author.

The professional development: Haynes, interview by the author.

There were bright spots among the children: Interviews with parents by the author.

Now, Traiquan was one of Haynes's students: Payne and Vincent, interviews by the author.

"She kept telling me how talented I am": Payne and Vincent, interview by the author.

And perhaps most encouraging: Whiteman, interview by the author.

Faustin had returned: Faustin, interview by the author.

24 percent of them: New York State English Language Arts exam.

After hearing about the weak scores: Klinsky, interview by the author.

Despite all of these efforts: Sisulu and Victory educators and staff members and Klinsky interviews by the author.

some DI critics thought: Interviews with educators by the author.

"Why is Sisulu using DI . . .": Not direct quotes, but how Sisulu and Victory educators and staff members and Klinsky recall these comments in interviews by the author.

96 percent of its parents: Sisulu-Walker parent survey.

Some trustees had harbored doubts: These sentences are from interviews with educators, staff members, and Sisulu and Victory officials; quotes are not the exact words, but they are how they are recalled in interviews by the author.

He received reports: Klinsky, interview by the author.

Klinsky felt more and more isolated: Klinsky, interview by the author.

Walker had been felled by a series of strokes: Walker, interview by the author.

It was the worst of all worlds: Klinsky, interviews by the author.

Chapter 10: A Light Shines

his mind was already made up: Stovall, Harrington, Heyer, Klinsky interviews by the author.

"This," he said, "is tombstone stuff": Klinsky, Stovall, Harrington, and Heyer interviews by the author.

"and I left there fired up": Stovall, interview by the author.

had given approximately $3 million: Klinsky, interview by the author.

"The first seven years": Letter written by the parent of a Sisulu student to the Charter Schools Institute at SUNY, August 4, 2003.

"I beam with delight": Letter written by the parent of a Sisulu student to the Charter Schools Institute at SUNY, July 23, 2003.

"I have witnessed the failure": Letter written by the grandmother of a Sisulu student to the Charter Schools Institute at SUNY, July 26, 2003.

Sisulu ranked as the highest-performing: New York State fourth-grade English Language Arts exam scores for the 2003–04 academic year, as reported in a Victory Schools press release, "Victory Schools Ranks #1 in Academic Quality on 4th Grade State Exams," July 13, 2004.

"This year's fourth-grade is": Allen, Victory Schools press release, July 14, 2004.

"When Sisulu began in 1999": Fields, Victory Schools press release, July 14, 2004.

Sisulu's students had also learned much more: Haynes, interview by the author.

And there was Traiquan Payne: Payne, Vincent, and Haynes, interviews by the author.

"Every time a child learns": "Victory Schools Targets Public/Private Partnerships for Student Success," US Department of Education, *The Education Innovator,* April 19, 2004.

It cited . . . Baltimore's Westport Academy: Ibid.

Time *magazine ranked Victory:* Winters, Rebecca, "Grading the Philadelphia Experiment," *Time,* June 23, 2003.

"We have found . . . in our community to be": US Department of Education, *The Education Innovator,* 2004.

In May 2004, Pearson Scott Foresman: Victory Schools press release, May 6, 2004.

And that same month, the Maryland State Education Department: Victory Schools press release, May 11, 2004.

"When you applaud Dr. Walker's role in civil rights": Text of Klinsky's speech provided to author by Klinsky.

Across the room: Klinsky, interview by the author.

A full 90 percent of them: New York City ELA and math exams, 2004–05 academic year and Victory Schools press release, June 28, 2005.

One of her students, Tori Saldivia: Saldivia and Whiteman, interviews by the author.

Another of her students, Traiquan Payne: Payne and Vincent, interviews by the author.

Many of Sisulu-Walker's graduates: Haynes, interview by the author.

As for Tori Saldivia: Whiteman and Saldivia, interviews by the author.

Traiquan Payne had also landed on his feet: Payne, interview by the author.

Just as everyone had expected, Mylaecha: Lamb, interview by the author.

"The Sisulu-Walker Charter School of Harlem": Song written by Mylaecha Aska and Tori Saldivia, Aska, Saldivia, Lamb, Whiteman, interviews by the author.

Mylaecha and Tori worked hard: Lamb, interview by the author.

"It was going to be a big transition": Lamb, interview by the author.

"My decision to put Tori": Whiteman, interview by the author.

But when a small group of singers: Lamb, interview by the author.

"Thank you so much for allowing me to address you": Text of Klinsky speech, June 22, 2005, provided to the author by Klinsky.

Chapter 11: Evolution: Coming of Age

"When I was first elected: Bloomberg at Sisulu-Walker's ten-year anniversary celebration, September 30, 2009.

seventeen nascent charter schools: Ibid.

ninety-nine: New York City Charter School Center, "New York City Charter Schools are Growing," 2013–14 report, www.nyccharterschools.org.

thirty thousand: Ibid.

about forty thousand more children: Bloomberg at Sisulu-Walker's anniversary celebration.

"I strongly support": Ibid.

183 charter schools: New York City Charter School Center.

more than fifty thousand students: Ibid.

The New York French American Charter School: Edith Boncompain, interview by the author, and report on www.nyfacs.net.

The New York Center for Autism Charter School: Julie Fisher, interview by the author, and report on www.nycacharterschool.org.

Meanwhile, the Equity Project Charter School: www.tepcharter.org.

Still other charter schools: Ann Powell, interview by the author, and report on www.successacademies.org.

Perhaps New York City's . . . Waiting for Superman: Marty Lipp, interview by the author, and report on www.hcz.org.

and in early 2014 . . . housing and public safety: White House press release, January 8, 2014.

The Knowledge Is Power Program: Steve Mancini, interview by the author, and report on www.kipp.org.

Still other networks: Gabriel Sanchez, interview by the author, and report on www.greendot.org.

Achievement First is: Amanda Pinto, interview by the author, and report on www.achievementfirst.org.

90 percent proficiency rate: New York State ELA and math exams

$100 million . . . matching grant program: Harlem Children's Zone press release, June 6, 2013.

$7 million in one evening's gala: Gordon, Amanda, "Scene Last Night: Loeb, Christie, Tepper, Singer, Bommer," *Bloomberg Businessweek*, May 23, 2013.

$21,000: Sisulu-Walker figures provided by Victory Education Partners.

$500,000 a year in rent: Sisulu-Walker figures provided by Victory Education Partners.

In 2013, CSEE's students: Test scores in these two paragraphs are from the New York State ELA and math exams, 2013.

eleventh highest out of the seventy-three: New York City Charter School Center rankings, 2013.

At eighth grade . . . CSEE continued: New York State ELA and math exams, 2013.

former automobile showroom: Donna Douglas, interview by the author.

In 2013 . . . for Hempstead overall: New York State ELA and math exams, 2013.

One mile due north: Celia Domenech, interview by the author.

outscored the traditional schools: New York State ELA and math exams, 2013.

In a 2010 article: Olster, Scott, "Forget Superman, charter schools are waiting for Oprah," *Fortune*, September 30, 2010.

As of 2013: Numbers in these three paragraphs are from Victory Education Partners.

This performance record: "KIPP: 2012 Report Card," 2012, www.kipp.org /reportcard.

"So that has been . . . dreams come true": Martez Moore, speech at Sisulu-Walker's ten-year anniversary celebration.

Chapter Twelve: What Have We Learned?

"To me, the charter school movement": Klinsky, interview by the author.

The gold standard of charter school research: Hoxby, Caroline M., Sonali Murarka, and Jenny Kang, "How New York City's Charter Schools Affect Achievement, August 2009 Report." New York City Charter Schools Evaluation Project, Cambridge, MA: September 2009.

By 2013, 79 percent: "A Growing Movement: America's Largest Charter School Communities," Eighth Annual Edition, National Alliance for Public Charter Schools, December 2013.

In a six-year study by Stanford University's Center for Research: "Charter School Performance in Louisiana," Stanford University's Center for Research on Education Outcomes. August 8, 2013. Additionally, according to the study the results were "dramatic" in New Orleans. About half of the city's charter schools significantly outperformed their local traditional public schools in reading; 62 percent of the charters significantly outperformed those same schools in math. At the same time, when compared to traditional public schools, only 6 percent of the city's charter schools significantly underperformed those schools in reading, and 4 percent did so in math.

Marcus A. Winters, senior fellow of the Manhattan Institute for Policy: Winters, Marcus A., "Everyone Wins: How Charter Schools Benefit All New York City Public School Students," Manhattan Institute for Policy Research, October 2009.

Total charter enrollment: New York City Charter School Center.

$500,000 in rent: Sisulu-Walker figures provided by Victory Education Partners.

had been at odds: Baker, Al, and Javier C. Hernandez, "De Blasio and Operator of Charter School Empire Do Battle," *New York Times*, March 4, 2014.

help "save": Baker and Hernandez, "De Blasio and Operator."

"Charter schools need affordable housing, too": Umansky, David, *New York Post*, March 11, 2014.

$2,350 per student: New York City Charter School Center.

The new budget . . . "less rich lost": Harvey Newman, interview by the author.

were scrambling to find ways: Ibid.

"It has been turned upside down": Fliegel, interview by the author.

One of the next frontiers: Quotes in these four paragraphs are from Peterson taken from interviews by the author.

Chapter 13: A Return to Sisulu-Walker

"It definitely feels": Haynes, interview by the author.

By the fall of 2013: Haynes, interview by the author.

"Michelle Haynes is . . . : Martez Moore, interview by the author.

Now at Sisulu-Walker: Haynes, interview by the author.

"It's important that we all speak": Haynes, interview by the author.

Students must respect themselves: Haynes, interview by the author.

forty-five states and Washington, DC: www.corestandards.org.

Its teachers, though, are given a good deal: Haynes, interview by the author.

As for the old Core Knowledge: Haynes and other educators, interviews by the author.

Tracking each student's progress: Haynes, interview by the author.

This kind of information: Staff members at Victory Education Partners.

Perhaps most important, though: Paul Augello, interview by the author.

Not only did they consider: Martez Moore, interview by the author.

"The future is in our hands": Mayor Michael Bloomberg at Sisulu-Walker's ten-year anniversary, September 9, 2009.

Chapter 14: Zeyna Diouf

*The names of the student and her mom have been changed to protect their identities. Unless otherwise noted, the information in this chapter is from interviews with them and Sisulu-Walker's educators over a six-year period.

"The only way Zeyna will succeed": This is not an exact quote but rather the words the mother and a Sisulu-Walker staff member recall her saying.

As a kindergartner: Observations by Zeyna's mother and teachers.

"I want to read": Zeyna Diouf, interview by the author.

One day, while working: Observations by the author.

"I'm so very, very, very proud": Rama Diouf, interview by the author.

"Sisulu-Walker, it's my favorite school": Zeyna Diouf, interview by the author.

"I want her to learn more": Zeyna Diouf, interview by the author.

BIBLIOGRAPHY

Books

Buber, Martin. *The Way of Man: According to the Teachings of Hasidism*. Chicago: Wilcox & Follett Company, 1951.

Clinton, Bill. *My Life*. New York: Alfred A. Knopf, 2004.

Fliegel, Seymour, and James MacGuire. *Miracle in East Harlem: The Fight for Choice in Public Education*. New York: Times Books, 1993.

Jacobson, Mark. *American Gangster and Other Tales of New York*. New York: Grove/Atlantic, Inc., 2007.

Junge, Ember Reichgott. *Zero Chance of Passage: The Pioneering Charter School Story*. Edina, MN: Beaver's Pond Press, Inc., 2012.

Peterson, Paul E. *Saving Schools: From Horace Mann to Virtual Learning*. Cambridge, MA: Belknap Press, 2010.

Woods, Sylvia, and Family. *Sylvia's Family Soul Food Cookbook*. New York: William Morrow and Company, Inc., 1999.

Articles

Archibold, Randal C., "Most New York City Students Will Fail New Graduation Tests, Report Says," *New York Times*, December 23, 1998.

Baker, Al and Javier C. Hernandez, "De Blasio and Operator of Charter School Empire Do Battle," *New York Times*, March 4, 2014.

Beekman, Daniel, "Federal Suit Filed in Feud over Harlem Charter School," *New York Daily News*, March 18, 2014.

Bennet, James. "President, Citing Education as Top Priority of 2d Term, Asks for a 'Call to Action.'" *New York Times*, February 4, 1997.

Bernstein, Marc F. "Why I'm Wary of Charter Schools." *School Administrator*, August 1999.

Bradley, Ann. "NEA Seeks to Help Start Five Charter Schools." *Education Week*, April 24, 1996.

Campanile, Carl. "Kids Make the Grade at First Charter School." *New York Post*, June 22, 2000.

Celona, Larry. "No Slays Yet in Apple's Former Death Precinct—Exclusive." *New York Post*, March 1, 1999.

Cooper, Michael. "Officers in Bronx Fire 41 shots, And an Unarmed Man Is Killed." *New York Times*, February 5, 1999.

Dowd, Maureen. "Schism of the Union." *New York Times*, February 6, 1997.

Edelman, Susan. "City Schoolkids Fail to Keep Up." *New York Post*, December 23, 1998.

Edelman, Susan. "Parents Doing Their Homework on Charter School." *New York Post*, July 9, 1999.

Edelman, Susan. "Legal Threat Hangs Over Harlem Charter Schools." *New York Post*, July 4, 1999.

Education Daily, "NEA Joins Growing Charter Schools Movement," April 18, 1996.

The Education Innovator, "Victory Schools Targets Public/Private Partnerships for Student Success." US Department of Education, April 19, 2004.

Goodman, Walter. "Morass of Competing and Colliding Images." *New York Times*, February 5, 1997.

Gordon, Amanda. "Scene Last Night: Loeb, Christie, Tepper, Singer, Bommer." *Bloomberg Businessweek*, May 23, 2013.

Hartocollis, Anemona. "Crew Speaks Out Against Charter-School Plan." *New York Times*, December 16, 1998.

Hartocollis, Anemona. "8 Charter Schools, 4 with Profit Goal, Are Picked by State." *New York Times*, June 16, 1999.

Hartocollis, Anemona. "Charter Vote Is Assailed as Illegal." *New York Times*, June 20, 1999.

Hartocollis, Anemona. "Charter Schools Are Approved Again, and Procedures Questioned." *New York Times*, July 14, 1999.

Hildebrand, John. "A New Course." *Newsday*, June 16, 1999.

Lestch, Corinne, "Mayor de Blasio Changes Tone on Charter Schools, Says He Will Find 'Great' Place for Success Academy Students." *New York Daily News*, March 23, 2014.

Levy, Clifford. "Senate Passes Charter Plan for Schools." *New York Times*, December 18, 1998.

Levy, Clifford, with Anemona Hartocollis. "Crew Assails Albany Accord on Opening Charter Schools." *New York Times*, December 19, 1998.

Negri, Gloria, Budde obituary, *Boston Globe*, June 21, 2005.

New York Teacher. "Charter-school experiment taking toll in Albany." *New York Teacher*, October 6, 1999.

Newsday editorial. "Charter School Will End Status Quo in Roosevelt," June 17, 1999.

Newsday. "Can't Wait to Get Going." September 3, 2000.

Olster, Scott. "Forget Superman, Charter Schools Are Waiting for Oprah." *Fortune*, September 30, 2010.

Sanders, Steven. "My Evolution on Charter Schools: Lawmaker Behind 1998 Law Says the Verdict Is in, and It's Positive." *New York Daily News*, May 13, 2010.

Saulny, Susan, "Ray Budde, 82, First to Propose Charter Schools, Dies." *New York Times*, June 21, 2005.

Steinberg, Jacques. "School Leaders Raise Doubt on Pataki's 'Charter' Plan." *New York Times*, January 14, 1997.

Swirsky, Joan. "Roosevelt's Tug of War Over Its Charter School; The New Academy Moves into Its Permanent Quarters, but the Public School District Drags Its Heels over Payments." *New York Times*, November 19, 2000.

Umansky, David. "Charter Schools Need Affordable Housing, Too." *New York Post*, March 11, 2014.

Winters, Rebecca. "Grading the Philadelphia Experiment." *Time*, June 23, 2003.

Wyatt, Edward. "Charter School's Problems Yield Cautionary Tale." *New York Times*, August 18, 2000.

Wyatt, Edward, "Charter School's Learning Curve; Operator Faces Challenges in New Educational Venture." *New York Times*, February 23, 2000.

Documents and Memorandums

Mikuta, Julie. Memorandum to Tom Freedman, November 3, 1997. Pres. Bill Clinton presidential papers.

"Sisulu Victory Academy. Harlem Charter Public School Application." 1999.

State University of New York's Charter Schools Institute. John A. Reisenbach Third-Year Charter School Renewal Report. January 2004.

Third-Year (Second Charter) Visit Report. Charter Schools Institute (Inspection Visit Conducted by SchoolWorks, LLC on behalf of the SUNY CSI.)

"Summary of Renewal Report Findings," Charter Schools Institute, State University of New York, Seventh year report; 2005–06.

Studies and Reports

American Federation of Teachers. "Building on the Best, Learning from What Works. Six Promising Schoolwide Reform Programs." American Federation of Teachers, July 1998.

Hoxby, Caroline M., Sonali Murarka, and Jenny Kang. "How New York City's Charter Schools Affect Achievement, August 2009 Report." Second report in series. Cambridge, MA: New York City Charter Schools Evaluation Project, September 2009.

New York State Education Department. "Annual Report to the Governor, the Temporary President of the Senate and the Speaker of the Assembly on the Status of Charter Schools in New York State in the 2000–01 School Year. Presented to the Board of Regents." New York State Education Department, May 22, 2002.

Public Education Association. "State of the City Schools, '98." Public Education Association, December, 1998.

Stanford University's Center for Research on Education Outcomes. "Charter School Performance in Louisiana." Stanford University, August 8, 2013.

SUNY Charter Schools Institute. "Summary of Renewal Report Findings."

US Department of Education. "A Nation at Risk." US Department of Education National Commission on Excellence in Education, April 1983.

Ziebarth, Todd. "Measuring Up to the Model: A Ranking of State Charter School Laws, Fifth Edition." National Alliance for Public Charter Schools, January 2014.

Winters, Marcus A. "Everyone Wins: How Charter Schools Benefit All New York City Public School Students." Manhattan Institute for Policy Research, October 2009.

Speeches

Bush, President George W. "A Culture of Achievement." Speech given at the Manhattan Institute, October 5, 1999.

Clinton, President William Jefferson. State of the Union Address, January 23, 1996.

Clinton, President William Jefferson. State of the Union Address, February 4, 1997.

Klinsky, Steve. Speech honoring Dr. Walker at the Alhambra Ballroom, October 22, 2004.

Klinsky, Steve. Speech at Sisulu-Walker's graduation ceremony, June 2005.

Walker, Dr. Wyatt Tee Walker. "Why We Need Charter Schools." Speech given at Norman Thomas High School, New York City, March 27, 1999.

Interviews

Allen, William. Interviews by the author.

Aska, Mylaecha. Interviews by the author.

Augello, Paul. Interviews by the author.

Bell, Cheryl. Interviews by the author.

Boncompain, Edith. Interview by the author.

Brinson, Reginald. Interviews by the author.

Brinson, Regine. Interviews by the author.

Brown, the late Laurie. Interviews by the author.

Domenech, Celia. Interview by the author.

Cordero, Mary Ranero. Interviews by the author.

Couvillion, Jacques, Interviews by the author.

Cox, Edward. Interviews by the author.

Cruz, Sobeida. Interview by the author.

Daniels, Randy. Interviews by the author.

Douglas, Donna. Interview by the author.

Elwell, John. Interviews by the author.

Faso, John. Interview by the author.

Faustin, Berthe. Interview by the author.

Feinberg, Jane. Interview by the author.

Fisher, July, Interview by the author.

Fliegel, Seymour. Interviews by the author.

Francis, Robert. Interviews by the author.

Handy, Phil. Interview by the author.

Harrington, Dr. Margaret. Interviews by the author.

Hasson, Seamus. Interview by the author.

Haynes, Michelle. Interviews by the author.

Heyer, Erik. Interviews by the author.

Jackvony, Catherine. Interviews by the author.

Jones, Karen, Interviews by the author.

Jones, Philip. Interviews by the author.

King, Rebecca. Interview by the author.

Klinsky, Steve. Interviews by the author.

Lamb, Gladys. Interviews by the author.

Lawson, Emily. Interviews by the author.

Lipp, Marty. Interview by the author.

Mancini, Steve. Interview by the author.

Mitchell, Marshall. Interviews by the author.

Moore, Martez. Interviews by the author.

Murphy, Peter. Interviews by the author.

Newman, Harvey. Interviews by the author.

Pataki, George. Interviews by the author.

Payne, Traiquan. Interviews by the author.

Peterson, Paul. Interviews by the author.

Pinto, Amanda. Interview by the author.

Powell, Ann. Interview by the author.

Price, Judith. Interviews by the author.

Rees, Nina. Interview by the author.

Saldivia, Tori. Interviews by the author.

Sanchez, Gabriel. Interview by the author.

Sanders, Steven. Interviews by the author.

Sherry, Kathleen. Interviews by the author.

Solomon, Josh. Interviews by the author.

Stovall, James, Interviews by the author.

Steffey, Scott. Interviews by the author.

Tchaconas, Terry. Interviews by the author.

Vincent, Padora. Interviews by the author.

Walker, Dr. Wyatt Tee. Interviews by the author.

Walker, Wyatt T., Jr. Interviews by the author.

Whiteman, Gail. Interviews by the author.

Ziebarth, Todd. Interviews by the author.

Index